Consolidation

Core Science

Bryan Milner, Jean Martin and Peter Evans

T0382378

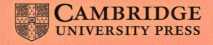

CAMBRIDGE
UNIVERSITY PRESS

Series editor	Bryan Milner
Biology editor	Jean Martin
Chemistry editor	Peter Evans
Physics editor	Bryan Milner
Authors	Jenifer Burden
	Paul Butler
	Zoë Crompton
	Sam Ellis
	Peter Evans
	Jean Martin
	Bryan Milner
Consultants	Kate Chaytor
	Nigel Heslop
	Matryn Keeley

CAMBRIDGE
UNIVERSITY PRESS

University Printing House, Cambridge CB2 8BS, United Kingdom

Published in the United States of America by Cambridge University Press, New York

Cambridge University Press is part of the University of Cambridge.

It furthers the University's mission by disseminating knowledge in the pursuit of education, learning and research at the highest international levels of excellence.

www.cambridge.org
Information on this title: www.cambridge.org/9780521588492

© Cambridge University Press 1998

First published 1998
8th printing 2008

A catalogue record for this publication is available from the British Library

ISBN 978-0-521-58849-2 Paperback

Designed and produced by Gecko Ltd, Bicester, Oxon

Cover photo: Bungee jumper / Telegraph Colour Library

....

Contents

CHEMISTRY

Matter

Chemical reactions

Earth science

PHYSICS

Light and sound

Forces

Energy and electricity

v

■ Acknowledgements

We are grateful to the following for permission to reproduce photographs.

Page 2, 4c, Andrew Syred/Microscopix; 3t, 3c, 3l, Biophoto Associates; 4t, John Lawrence/Power Stock Photo Library; 14t, 17tl, 17tc, 17bl, 24tr, 50t, 64tl, Dr Alan Beaumont; 14cl, Dr David Patterson/Science Photo Library; 14cr, NIBSC/Science Photo Library; 16tl, 24tl, 64cl, Nigel Cattlin/Holt Studios International; 16tr, P. Morris; 17tr, P. Morris/Ardea; 17br, Dennis Green/Windrush; 18t, 30c, CEPHAS/Stockfood; 18b, 30b, 31lower tr, 31b, 44, 127, 158tl, 158tr, 158br, 159t, 159c, Trevor Clifford Photography; 24b, John Clegg/Ardea; 26, James Stevenson/ Science Photo Library; 28t, 28c, Matt Meadows, Peter Arnold Inc./Science Photo Library; 30t, Anthony Blake Photo Library; 31tl, E & D Boyard/Still Pictures; 31tr, Mark Edwards/ Still Pictures; 36, Mike Hewitt/Action Plus Photographic; 38, John Watney/Science Photo Library; 39t, Richard Francis/Action Plus Photographic; 39cl, Terje Rakke/ Image Bank; 39cm, 46t, Steven Behr/Stockfile; 39cr, Steve Dunwell/ Image Bank; 40tl, Chris Barry/Action Plus Photographic; 40tr, Geoff Waugh/Action Plus Photographic; 46b, Chris Wilkinson/ProSport; 49, John Walmsley; 50tc, © 1997 Lior Rubin/Natural Science Photos; 50b, A P Barnes/Natural Science Photos; 54, Horticultural Research International; 58 Martin Bond/Science Photo Library; 62, Jon Beer; 64tr, Eric Dragesco/Ardea; 64cr, Jack A. Bailey/Ardea; 66, Alexis Duclos/Frank Spooner Pictures; 69bl, Jim Hudson/Environmental Images; 69br, Greg Glendell/Environmental Picture Library; 75c, 126t, Michael Holford; 75b, Alfred Pasieka/Science Photo Library; 76, Crown copyright is reproduced with the permission of the Controller of Her Majesty's Stationary Office; 78, Alan Smith/ Getty Images; 84, John Wright/Hutchison Library; 86tl, Mark Wagner/Aviation Images; 86tc, 136, GSF Picture Library; 86tr, Ron Dahlquist/Getty Images; 86cl, Christine Osborne Pictures; 86cr, BOC Gases; 98, 103tl, 103tr, 120, 121t, 121c, 124b, 125, 129, 133c, Andrew Lambert; 112, Steve Barsky; 121bl, 124t, NHM Picture Library; 123, 133t, 140, B & C Alexander; 124c, Anglo-American Corporation of South Africa Limited; 126c, 126b, Neill Bruce; 132t, John Mason/ Ardea; 132c, Jack Dykinga/Getty Images; 133b, Jeremy Hoare/Garden and Wildlife Matters; 134, Popperfoto; 135t, Hulton Getty Images; 135c, James Nelson/Getty Images; 141, 215, Chris Howes FRPS; 143t, Colin Newson/ Wildlife Matters; 143c, William Cross/Skyscan; 148, Nicholas Judd; 158bl, David Redferns; 164, Aviation Picture Library; 166, Lockheed Aircraft Corporation/Aviation Picture Library; 186, Frank Zullo/Science Photo Library; 195t, David Hoffman/Still Pictures; 195c, Gilbert Gilkes & Gordon Ltd; 195b, Gilbert Gilkes & Gordon, Kendal, Cumbria, LA9 7BZ; 210, Bryan Milner.

Picture research: Maureen Cowdroy

Core Science

1.1 Cells

Every living thing is made up of small units called **cells**.

Look at the photograph of plant root cells.
It has been magnified many times so that you can see the cells.

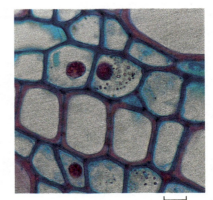

Plant root cells.   0.01 mm

1 Copy and complete the sentences.

The plant root is made of small _____.
Each cell is about _____ of a millimetre across.

■ Animal and plant cells

Animals and plants are made from cells.

Animal and plant cells are the same in some ways.
We say that they have some of the same <u>features</u>.

Animal and plant cells are also different in some ways.

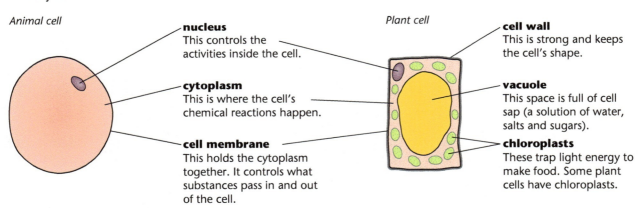

Animal cell

nucleus
This controls the activities inside the cell.

cytoplasm
This is where the cell's chemical reactions happen.

cell membrane
This holds the cytoplasm together. It controls what substances pass in and out of the cell.

Plant cell

cell wall
This is strong and keeps the cell's shape.

vacuole
This space is full of cell sap (a solution of water, salts and sugars).

chloroplasts
These trap light energy to make food. Some plant cells have chloroplasts.

2 What job do these parts of a cell do?

(a) the nucleus

(b) the cytoplasm

(c) the cell membrane

3 Copy the table. Then complete it to show differences between animal and plant cells.

Feature	Animal cell	Plant cell
Does it have a nucleus?	yes	
Does it have a cell membrane?		
Does it have cytoplasm?		
Does it have a cell wall?		
Does it have a vacuole?	no	
Does it have chloroplasts?		some plant cells do

Living things with only one cell

Some very simple living things are made of only one cell. We say they are **unicellular**.

Some unicellular organisms are like animals, but others are more like plants.

4 Look at the photographs.

   (a) Which cell, A, B or C, is most like a plant?

   (b) Write down <u>two</u> reasons for your answer.

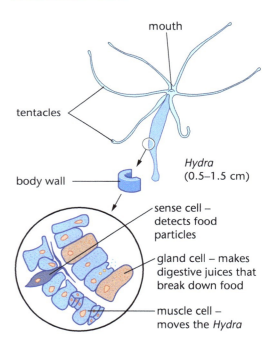

A — This cell has no fixed shape.

B — flexible coat, chloroplast

C — rigid cell wall, chloroplast

Living things with many cells

When a living organism is made up of many cells, we say it is **multicellular**.

Hydra is a simple multicellular animal. Its cells are not all the same. The *Hydra* needs different types of cell to do different jobs.

5 Write down <u>one</u> difference between unicellular and multicellular organisms.

6 Describe <u>two</u> different jobs done by two different types of cell in a *Hydra*.

mouth

tentacles

body wall

Hydra (0.5–1.5 cm)

sense cell – detects food particles

gland cell – makes digestive juices that break down food

muscle cell – moves the *Hydra*

WHAT YOU NEED TO REMEMBER (Copy and complete using the **key words**)

Cells

Living things are made up of _____.

Some living things have only one cell; they are _____.
Living things with many cells are _____.

Both animal and plant cells have a _____, _____ and _____ _____.

Only plant cells have a _____ _____ and _____, and some plant cells have _____.

More about cells: C+ 1.10

1.2 Working together

Your body is made of millions of cells.

Each cell has its own special **job** to do, but it doesn't work on its own.

▪ Cells work together

Cells that do the same job are often grouped together. A group of similar cells is called a **tissue**. For example, muscle tissue is made up of lots of muscle cells.

1 Look at the description of a factory. Then copy and complete the sentences describing the human body.

A human body has millions of living _____ working in it. Each _____ has its own _____ to do. Cells of the same type join together to make a _____.

▪ Tissues work together

Different tissues join together to make **organs**, such as bones and muscles. For example, your biceps muscle is an organ. It pulls on bones to bend your arm.

2 Copy and complete the sentences.

My biceps is an _____, formed from several tissues joined together. Tissues in the biceps include _____, _____ and _____ tissue.

3 Copy and complete the table.

Tissue in the biceps (an organ)	What it does
	pulls lower part of arm upwards
epithelium tissue	
	connects muscle to bone

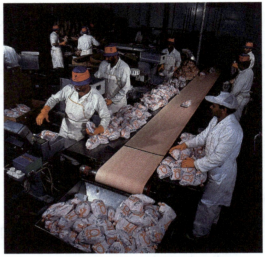

A large factory has many people working in it. The people work in <u>teams</u> to get things done. Each team has a particular <u>job</u> to do.

This is what the fibres in muscle tissue look like under a microscope.

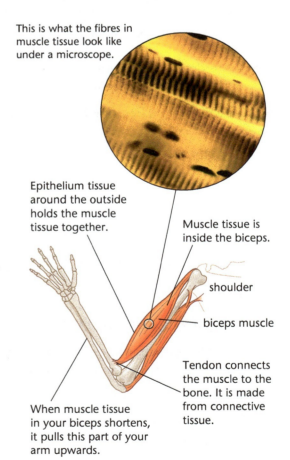

Epithelium tissue around the outside holds the muscle tissue together.

Muscle tissue is inside the biceps.

shoulder

biceps muscle

Tendon connects the muscle to the bone. It is made from connective tissue.

When muscle tissue in your biceps shortens, it pulls this part of your arm upwards.

■ Plants have tissues and organs too

<u>Xylem</u> is a type of tissue found in plants. Xylem cells join to form long tubes inside the plant. Each cell is tiny, but the tubes they make are very long. These tubes carry water to all parts of the plant.

4 Why must xylem cells join together to form vessels or long tubes to do their job properly?

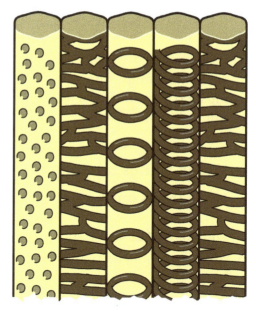

These xylem vessels go from the roots to the rest of the plant.

The picture shows where the xylem is in a root. A root is an organ, so it has other tissues too.

5 Copy and complete the table.

Tissue in a plant's root	What it does
xylem	
phloem	

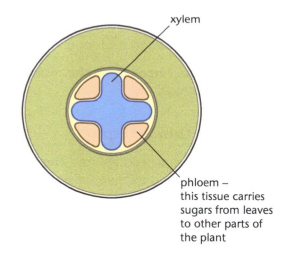

xylem

phloem – this tissue carries sugars from leaves to other parts of the plant

A slice through a root.

WHAT YOU NEED TO REMEMBER (Copy and complete using the **key words**)

Working together

We call groups of similar cells a _____.
Different tissues are grouped together into _____.

Cells, tissues and organs are all suited to the _____ they do.

More about tissues and organs: C+ 1.11

1.3 Life processes

All living things, from the smallest to the biggest, must do certain things to stay alive. We call these things <u>life processes</u>.

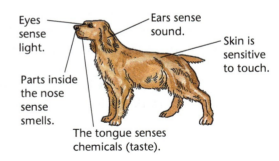

Eyes sense light.

Ears sense sound.

Skin is sensitive to touch.

Parts inside the nose sense smells.

The tongue senses chemicals (taste).

■ Living things are sensitive

Living things can **sense** changes around them.

> 1 Write down <u>five</u> things that a dog can sense.
>
> 2 Write down <u>two</u> things that plants are sensitive to.

Shoots grow towards light.

Roots grow towards water.

DID YOU KNOW?

Your skin is sensitive to a change in temperature of only 0.5°C.

■ Living things move

Animals **move** to find food.

Plants don't need to do this. Some <u>parts</u> of plants move though.

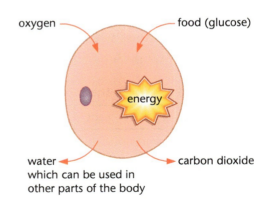

oxygen

food (glucose)

energy

water which can be used in other parts of the body

carbon dioxide

Respiration happens in cells.

■ Living things respire

Living things need energy. They all get this energy from food and oxygen by respiration.

Animals and plants both **respire**.

> 3 Where in plants and animals does respiration happen?
>
> 4 What waste product is made when cells respire?

■ Living things reproduce and grow

Living things eventually die. So they need to produce young. We say that they **reproduce**.

Young plants and animals then **grow** until they are old enough to reproduce themselves.

> 5 How many years do boys usually grow for?

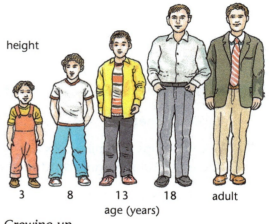

height

| 3 | 8 | 13 | 18 | adult |

age (years)

Growing up.

■ Living things need nutrition

All living things must have **nutrition** (food). It gives them the energy and materials they need to move and to make new cells. They make new cells all the time so they can grow, reproduce, and repair damage to the body.

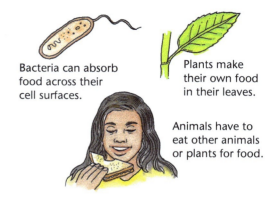

Bacteria can absorb food across their cell surfaces.

Plants make their own food in their leaves.

Animals have to eat other animals or plants for food.

6 Copy and complete the table.

Living things	How they get their food
bacteria	
plants	
animals	

■ Living things excrete

All living things make waste materials. These wastes are poisonous. You must get rid of them from your cells and your blood. Getting rid of waste is called <u>excretion</u>.

7 List <u>three</u> things you excrete from your body.

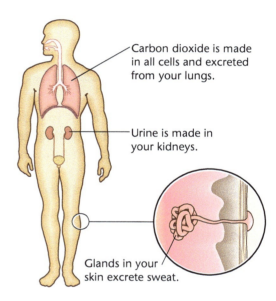

Carbon dioxide is made in all cells and excreted from your lungs.

Urine is made in your kidneys.

Glands in your skin excrete sweat.

*Humans **excrete** sweat, urine and carbon dioxide.*

■ What is special about living things?

Some non-living things move and can use oxygen to release energy from fuel. But non-living things cannot make new materials for their bodies. This means that they <u>cannot</u> **grow** or **reproduce**. Producing young that grow is something only living things can do.

DID YOU KNOW?

You <u>don't</u> excrete faeces. Undigested food never really gets inside your body. It just goes through a very long tube between your mouth and your anus.

WHAT YOU NEED TO REMEMBER (Copy and complete using the **key words**)

Life processes

Living things can s_____, m_____, r_____, g_____, r_____, e_____, and they need n_____.

Non-living things cannot _____ or _____.

1.4 Cycles of life

All living things grow and change during their lives.

Flowering plants and many animals, including humans, start life as two special cells. These special cells are called <u>sex cells</u> or **gametes**.

1 Copy and complete the table.

	Female sex cell	Male sex cell
humans	_____	_____
flowering plants	inside _____	inside _____

For a new human or plant to grow, the male and female sex cells must join together. The diagram shows what happens in a human.

2 Copy and complete the sentences.

A male gamete and a female gamete join together to make a single _____.
This process is called _____.

■ Getting plant sex cells together

Flowers produce sex cells. Male sex cells must meet up with female sex cells. To make sure this happens, each part of a flower has a different job to do.

3 Copy and complete the table.

Flower part	What it does
anther	
filament	
stigma	
style	
ovary	
petal	
nectary	

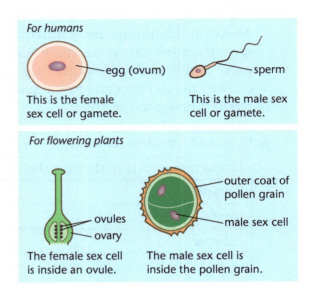

For humans

egg (ovum)

This is the female sex cell or gamete.

sperm

This is the male sex cell or gamete.

For flowering plants

ovules
ovary

The female sex cell is inside an ovule.

outer coat of pollen grain

male sex cell

The male sex cell is inside the pollen grain.

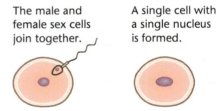

The male and female sex cells join together.

A single cell with a single nucleus is formed.

This process is called **fertilisation**.

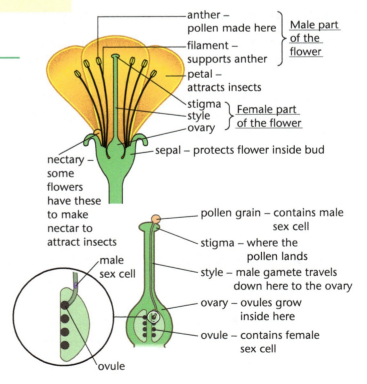

anther – pollen made here ⎫ Male part
filament – ⎬ of the
supports anther ⎭ flower

petal – attracts insects

stigma ⎫ Female part
style ⎬ of the flower
ovary ⎭

sepal – protects flower inside bud

nectary – some flowers have these to make nectar to attract insects

male sex cell

ovule

pollen grain – contains male sex cell

stigma – where the pollen lands

style – male gamete travels down here to the ovary

ovary – ovules grow inside here

ovule – contains female sex cell

■ Sexual intercourse in humans

A new human develops inside a woman's body.

Sperm have to be placed inside her body so that one of them can reach the egg and fertilise it. This happens during sexual intercourse.

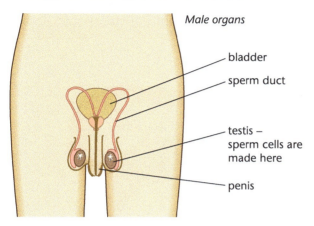

Male organs

- bladder
- sperm duct
- testis – sperm cells are made here
- penis

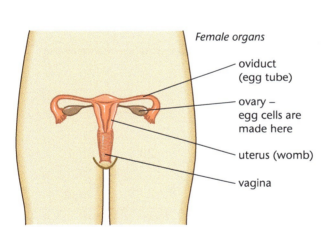

Female organs

- oviduct (egg tube)
- ovary – egg cells are made here
- uterus (womb)
- vagina

The sperm cells travel from the testes through to the penis. They are pushed into the vagina during sexual intercourse.

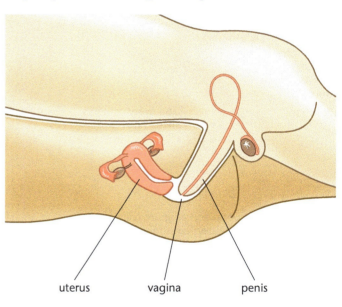

uterus   vagina   penis

4 Where are human female sex cells made?

5 Where are human male sex cells made?

6 Copy and complete the sentences.

During sexual intercourse, sperm from a man's _____ travel through his _____.
They go into the woman's body through her _____.

WHAT YOU NEED TO REMEMBER (Copy and complete using the **key words**)

Cycles of life

The sexual reproductive systems of plants and animals make special sex cells or _____.

Gametes join together in a process we call _____.

1.5 The start of pregnancy

Eggs are made in the ovaries. A woman releases an egg (ovum) from one of her ovaries once a month. The egg travels down the **oviduct** (egg tube). If the egg meets a sperm, they may join together. We call this **fertilisation**. From this moment the woman's pregnancy begins.

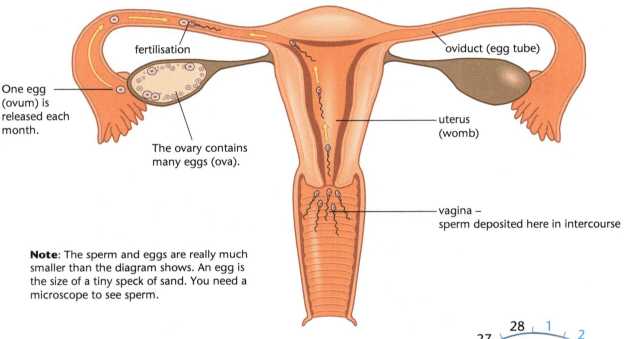

fertilisation

oviduct (egg tube)

One egg (ovum) is released each month.

uterus (womb)

The ovary contains many eggs (ova).

vagina – sperm deposited here in intercourse

Note: The sperm and eggs are really much smaller than the diagram shows. An egg is the size of a tiny speck of sand. You need a microscope to see sperm.

1 Where inside a woman are sperm deposited?

2 How do sperm reach the egg?

3 Where inside a woman do the sperm and egg meet?

The inside of the **uterus** has a thick lining ready to receive a fertilised egg. If the egg released each month does not meet a sperm, the lining is changed for a new one. The old lining breaks down and leaves the woman's body through her vagina. This is her monthly **period**.

4 Why do women have periods?

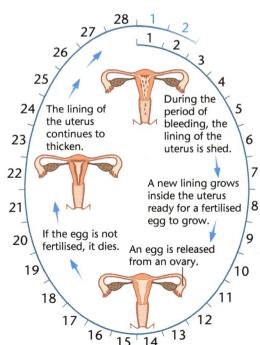

During the period of bleeding, the lining of the uterus is shed.

The lining of the uterus continues to thicken.

A new lining grows inside the uterus ready for a fertilised egg to grow.

If the egg is not fertilised, it dies.

An egg is released from an ovary.

■ What happens to a fertilised egg?

As the fertilised egg travels down the oviduct to the uterus, it begins to grow. The first cell splits into two to form two cells. Then each of these cells splits, to make four cells altogether. This process continues, forming a ball of cells.

Inside the uterus, the ball of cells sinks into the thick, soft lining. We call this **implantation**.

The ball of cells changes shape as it grows, and forms a head, body, arms and legs. It is then called an <u>embryo</u>.

As the weeks go by and the embryo grows, it starts to look more and more human. We then call it a <u>fetus</u>.

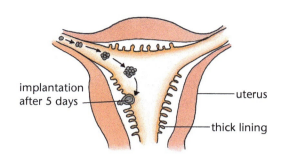

implantation after 5 days — uterus — thick lining

Time since fertilisation

4 weeks — embryo (1 cm) actual size

8 weeks — fetus (3 cm) $\frac{1}{2}$ size

12 weeks — fetus (12 cm) $\frac{1}{5}$ size

28 weeks — fetus (34 cm) $\frac{1}{10}$ size

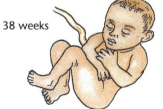
38 weeks — baby (52 cm) $\frac{1}{12}$ size

5 Put these sentences into the right order. The first one is in the correct place.

- The fertilised egg grows into a ball of cells.
- The ball of cells grows into an embryo.
- The embryo grows into a fetus.
- The ball of cells attaches to the uterus.

6 Copy and complete the table.

Weeks since fertilisation	Size (cm)	What we call it
4		
8		
12		
38		

WHAT YOU NEED TO REMEMBER (Copy and complete using the **key words**)

The start of pregnancy

The _____ and egg (ovum) join in an _____. We call this _____.

The fertilised egg divides as it travels down the oviduct to the uterus.
The ball of cells sinks into the lining of the _____. We call this _____.

If an egg is not fertilised, the lining of the uterus breaks down and causes the bleeding called a monthly _____.

More about pregnancy and periods: C+ 1.12, 1.13

1.6 New plants

For a flowering plant to reproduce, a female sex cell in the plant must join with a male sex cell from another plant.

The male sex cell is in a pollen grain. Pollen from an **anther** of one flower must be moved to the **stigma** of another flower. We call this **pollination**. In some plants wind carries the pollen. In other plants the pollen is carried by insects or other small animals.

1 Copy and complete the sentences.

The pollen from one plant travels from its anther to the _____ of another plant.
This transfer of pollen is called _____.

■ After pollination, what next?

When pollen has landed on a stigma, the male sex cell must travel to the female sex cell in an ovule. The diagram shows how this happens.

2 Put the sentences into the correct order to describe how the male sex cell reaches the ovule. The first sentence is in the correct place.

Pollen grain lands on the stigma.

■ The male sex cell moves down the pollen tube into the ovule.

■ The pollen tube grows down to an ovule.

■ The pollen tube reaches the ovary.

■ A pollen tube grows down through the style.

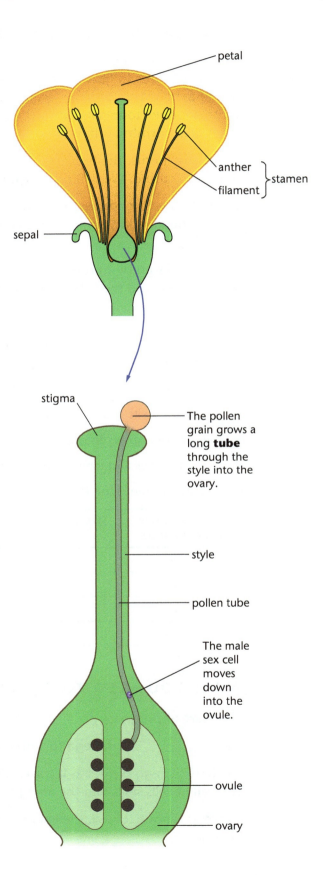

petal

anther
filament } stamen

sepal

stigma

The pollen grain grows a long **tube** through the style into the ovary.

style

pollen tube

The male sex cell moves down into the ovule.

ovule

ovary

■ Inside the ovule

The male sex cell travels down the **pollen** tube into the ovule.

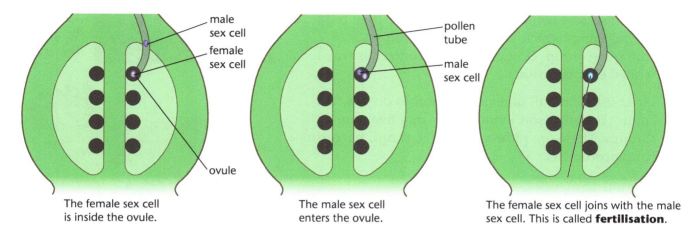

The female sex cell is inside the ovule.

The male sex cell enters the ovule.

The female sex cell joins with the male sex cell. This is called **fertilisation**.

---

3 What happens when the male sex cell enters the ovule?

4 What do we call this process?

■ Wrong flower, wrong pollen

Pollen will not always land on another flower of the same type.

Some scientists did an experiment to find out whether pollen could fertilise ovules of a different type of plant. The diagram shows what happened.

5 (a) What did the scientists do?

(b) What did they find out?

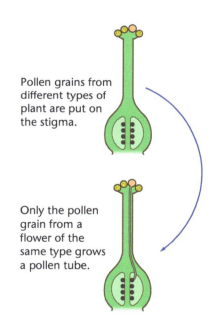

Pollen grains from different types of plant are put on the stigma.

Only the pollen grain from a flower of the same type grows a pollen tube.

WHAT YOU NEED TO REMEMBER (Copy and complete using the **key words**)

New plants

There are three steps to make a new plant.

1 Pollen is transferred from an _____ of one flower to the _____ of another flower of the same type. We call this _____.

2 A pollen _____ grows down through the style. The male sex cell uses this to reach the female sex cell.

3 The two sex cells join together. The female sex cell and the male sex cell join to make one cell. We call this _____.

1.7 Classification

Scientists sort living things into groups. They put living things which have the same features into the same group. Grouping living things this way is called **classification**.

Scientists don't all agree about how to do this, but many scientists sort living things into five main groups. These are **plants**, **animals**, **fungi**, **bacteria** and **protoctists**.

1 What is classification?

These groups contain living things which can look very different. For example, mushrooms have caps, stalks and lots of underground threads, but yeast cells are microscopic. Scientists classify both of them as fungi because they have important features which are the same. Their cells have walls but they don't contain chloroplasts. So they cannot make their own food.

2 Copy and complete the table.

Group	Features	Examples
plants		
animals		
fungi		
bacteria		
protoctists		

Sometimes scientists group living things in a different way. For example, it can be useful to group together the living things which can only be seen with a microscope. Scientists call these micro-organisms or **microbes**.

3 Write down the names of three groups that have microbes in them.

Plants make their own food.

Animals must eat other living things.

Yeast (a unicellular fungus)

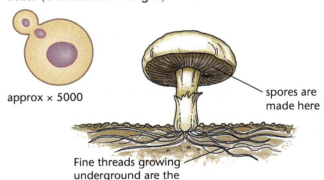

approx × 5000

spores are made here

Fine threads growing underground are the biggest part of the fungus.

Mushroom (a multicellular fungus)

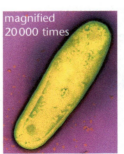

magnified 20 000 times

Bacteria are unicellular and microscopic. They don't have a proper nucleus.

Most protoctists are unicellular and microscopic. Some have features of animals. Others are more like plants.

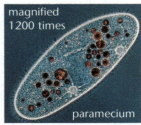

magnified 1200 times

paramecium

■ Classifying plants

There are lots of different kinds of plants, so it's useful to sort them into smaller groups. The key shows the four main groups.

A bracken

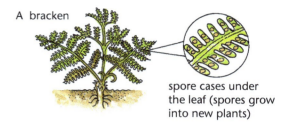

spore cases under the leaf (spores grow into new plants)

Key

1 Plant makes seeds.   Go to 2.

   Plant makes spores.   Go to 3.

2 Seeds are made in cones. **conifers**

   Seeds are made in flowers. **flowering plants**

3 Plant has no proper roots. **mosses and liverworts**

   Plant has leaves, stems
   and roots.   **ferns**

B poppy

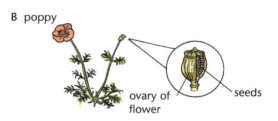

ovary of flower   seeds

4 Copy the table. Use the key to find out which groups plants A, B, C and D belong to. Then complete your table.

Plant	Group
A bracken	
B poppy	
C *Pellia*	
D Scots pine	

C *Pellia*

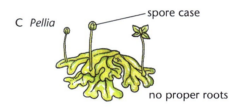

spore case

no proper roots

D Scots pine

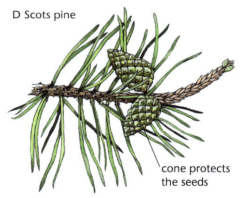

cone protects the seeds

More about classification: C+ 1.14

1.8 Groups of animals

All animals are alike in some ways. For example, they all get their food by eating something else.

But there are still plenty of differences between animals. This is why we split the different animals into smaller groups.

First we split them into two groups.

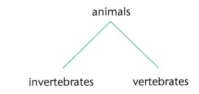

animals

invertebrates   vertebrates

This animal has a soft body.

backbone

1   Copy and complete the sentences.

Animals are split into _____ main groups.
Animals without a backbone are called _____.
If they have a backbone they are _____.

■ Invertebrates

Most kinds of animals do not have a backbone. They are <u>invertebrates</u>.

Invertebrates are usually fairly small, except for a few types that live in the sea.

The table below shows the five main groups of invertebrates. It also tells you the main features of each group.

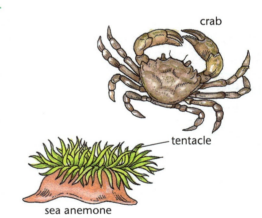

crab

tentacle

sea anemone

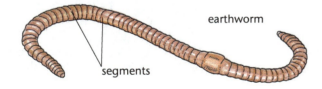

earthworm

segments

liver fluke

shell

snail

2   Copy the table and add the name of <u>one</u> example for each group.

Invertebrate group	Main features	Example
coelenterates	have tentacles and a bag-shaped body	
flatworms	have thin flat bodies	
annelid worms	have soft segmented bodies	
molluscs	have soft bodies with a hard shell	
arthropods	have a hard outer skeleton and jointed limbs	

■ Vertebrates

We can also put vertebrates into different groups.
These photographs show one example from each
group of vertebrates.

3 Copy the following diagram. Then use the information from the photographs to complete it.

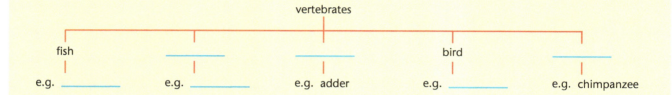

vertebrates

fish _____ _____ bird _____

e.g. _____ e.g. _____ e.g. adder e.g. _____ e.g. chimpanzee

*Frogs have moist skin with no
scales. They are amphibians.*

*The adder is a reptile. It has
a dry scaly skin and its eggs
have tough shells.*

*Goldfish have scales and
fins.*

*Chimpanzees are mammals.
They have hair and feed their
young on milk.*

*The golden plover has feathers
and lays eggs with hard shells.*

WHAT YOU NEED TO REMEMBER

Groups of animals

*You need to be able to classify animals into their main groups, just as you have done in the questions
on this spread.*

1.9 Variation

Different species of plants and animals look different. Even members of the same species are different in some ways. We say that they **vary**.

> 1 Look at the pictures. Write down <u>three</u> ways that tomatoes can be different from each other.

To grow yellow tomatoes, you need to plant seeds from other yellow tomatoes. This is because tomato colour is passed on from one generation to the next. We say it is **inherited**.

> 2 **(a)** Tomato T is from a plant bred from two yellow-fruited plants. If you plant seeds from this tomato, what colour tomatoes will you get?
>
> **(b)** Use the picture to help you to explain your answer.

■ **Does inheritance cause all differences?**

> 3 Look at the bunch of tomatoes in the diagram. Write down <u>one</u> reason why:
>
> **(a)** on August 4th, tomato A is bigger than tomato B;
>
> **(b)** when they are fully grown, A and B are the same size.

The two plum tomatoes in the photograph are both fully grown. They are different from each other because they grew in different conditions. We say that the **environment** caused the difference.

> 4 Write down <u>two</u> differences in the environment which could have made one tomato grow bigger than the other.

Tomatoes vary.

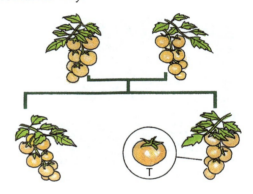

tomatoes on August 4th

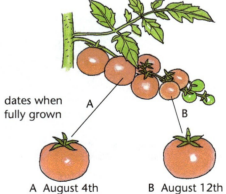

dates when fully grown

A August 4th   B August 12th

Plum tomatoes.

■ Inheritance or environment?

Sandy grew some plants using the seeds from one lupin plant. She measured their heights. They were all different. She put them into groups in a table.

Height of plants (cm)	Tally	Total
41–50	I	1
51–60	III	3
61–70	NI I	6
71–80	IIII	4
81–90	II	2

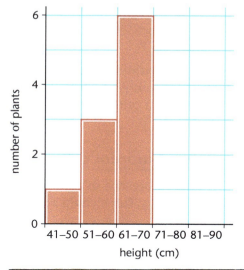

5 Copy and complete the bar chart of Sandy's results.

6 Look at the flowers. Sandy collected one from each plant. Copy and complete the table.

Colour	Tally	Total
blue	NI IIII	9

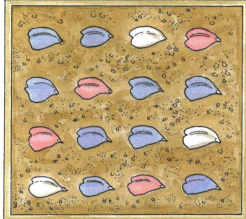

Differences between plants or animals of the same species can be caused by:

- inheritance;
- the environment;
- a **mixture** of inheritance and environment.

7 Read the information in the box. Then explain, as fully as you can, why Sandy's plants differed in:

(a) size;

(b) flower colour.

DID YOU KNOW?

The embryo plant in a lupin seed is made from two sex cells. The colour of a lupin, and how big it <u>can</u> grow, are both inherited from the parent plants. How big a lupin <u>actually</u> grows also depends on its environment.

WHAT YOU NEED TO REMEMBER (Copy and complete using the **key words**)

Variation

Members of a species _____. Some of the differences between them are passed on from their parents. We say that these differences are _____.

The _____ also causes differences. These differences are not passed on.

A _____ of inheritance and environment causes other differences.

More about inheritance and environment: C+ 1.15, 2.16

1.10 Specialised cells

Your body has many different types of cell. Each of them has the right features to do a particular job. We say that each cell is <u>specialised</u> to do its job.

■ **Different animal cells**

The air you breathe in contains tiny particles of dust and microbes. These could damage your lungs.

1 (a) Which cells in your nose help your body to overcome this problem?

(b) Explain how these cells do their job.

At the start of reproduction, sperm and egg cells (ova) join together to develop into a new animal. Male animals make sperm cells. These must reach the female egg cells if they are to **fertilise** them.

2 Describe how sperm cells and egg cells are adapted to make reproduction successful.

■ **Different plant cells**

Palisade cells are found inside the leaves of plants.

The diagram shows the special structures that these cells have.

3 (a) What special structures do plant palisade cells have?

(b) How do these help them to do their job?

Plants also need water to live. Their roots take in water from the soil.

4 Explain in as much detail as you can how root hair cells are adapted to do their job.

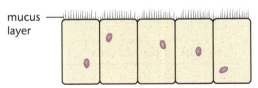

These hairs (cilia) move particles to the back of the throat. The particles are swallowed and then destroyed by stomach acid.

mucus layer

Ciliated epithelium cells line your nose.

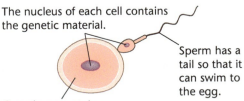

The nucleus of each cell contains the genetic material.

Sperm has a tail so that it can swim to the egg.

Cytoplasm contains food for the embryo so that it can start to grow.

Sperm and egg cells.

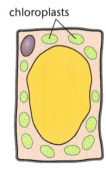

chloroplasts

Palisade cells have green discs called chloroplasts which trap light energy. The cell uses light to make food.

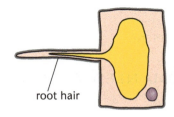

root hair

Root cells have tiny hairs to increase the root's surface area. This helps the root take in water.

WHAT YOU NEED TO REMEMBER

Specialised cells

You will need to be able to recognise specialised animal and plant cells like those on this page, and explain how each cell is specialised to do its job.

1.11 Organ systems

■ Your **organs** carry out the processes of life. For example, a woman's vagina, ovaries, oviducts and uterus are all involved in reproduction. These four organs share the work so that reproduction can happen. They are an **organ system**.

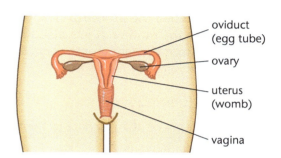

oviduct (egg tube)

ovary

uterus (womb)

vagina

1 The female reproductive system in plants has the same job as in animals but it has a different design. Copy and complete the table.

Job	Animal organ	Plant organ
makes the egg	ovary	
sperm or pollen is put here	vagina	
sperm or male sex cell travels along here to meet the egg	oviduct	
fertilised egg develops here	uterus	

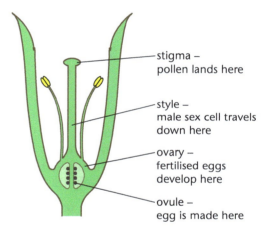

stigma – pollen lands here

style – male sex cell travels down here

ovary – fertilised eggs develop here

ovule – egg is made here

■ The cells in your body produce waste substances. These waste substances are poisonous so your body has to get rid of them. We say that they have to be <u>excreted</u>.

One of these waste products is <u>urea</u>. Several organs work together to get rid of urea. The diagram shows the organs that make up this system.

2 Use the information from the diagram to complete a flow chart that shows what happens to urea in your body. The first line is done for you.

> Liver cells make urea and pass it into the blood.

↓

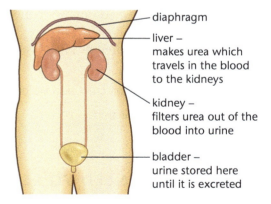

diaphragm

liver – makes urea which travels in the blood to the kidneys

kidney – filters urea out of the blood into urine

bladder – urine stored here until it is excreted

WHAT YOU NEED TO REMEMBER (Copy and complete using the **key words**)

Organ systems

Groups of similar cells are called _____. These join together to form _____.

Organs work together as _____ _____. They enable life processes to take place.

1.12 Pregnancy and birth

Feeding the fetus

As a fetus grows inside the uterus, so does a special organ called the **placenta**. The placenta joins the baby to the mother. It lets blood from the mother and blood from the fetus come very close to each other without actually mixing.

1 Where is the placenta?

2 What connects the placenta to the fetus?

3 (a) What <u>two</u> substances pass from the mother to the fetus across the placenta?

   (b) What <u>two</u> substances pass from the fetus to the mother?

Birth

When the baby is ready to be born, the uterus muscles start to **contract**. This is called <u>labour</u>. Gradually the contractions get stronger, more often and more painful. The mother also contracts her abdomen muscles to help push the baby out.

Finally the baby is born, usually head first, through the vagina. The umbilical cord is tied and cut. About 15 minutes later the placenta peels away from the uterus and is pushed out. We call this the <u>afterbirth</u>.

4 Write down <u>two</u> different sets of muscles that contract to push the baby out.

5 Why is the umbilical cord tied before it is cut?

6 What is the afterbirth?

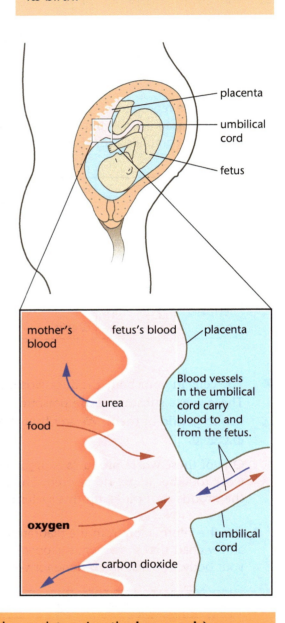

placenta

umbilical cord

fetus

mother's blood

fetus's blood

placenta

urea

food

Blood vessels in the umbilical cord carry blood to and from the fetus.

oxygen

umbilical cord

carbon dioxide

WHAT YOU NEED TO REMEMBER (Copy and complete using the **key words**)

Pregnancy and birth

When an embryo embeds itself in the uterus lining, a special organ called the _____ forms.
Nutrients and _____ pass from the mother to the fetus.
Waste from the _____ passes into the mother's blood.

After about 38 weeks, the uterus muscles _____ to push the baby out.
The placenta is no longer needed so it is also pushed out.

1.13 The menstrual cycle

A woman can release hundreds of ova (eggs) during her life. Most of these are never fertilised.

About once a month, an **ovary** releases an ovum. Each month the **uterus** lining thickens so it is ready for an embryo to grow.

If the ovum is not fertilised, the lining is not needed. It breaks down and passes out of the body with a little blood. A new lining then starts to grow and the cycle starts over again. We call this the menstrual cycle.

1 Why does the uterus lining thicken?

2 What day in the cycle is an ovum released?

3 How long does a period usually last?

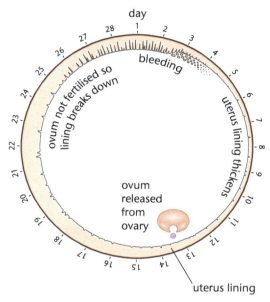

The menstrual cycle. Days are numbered from the first day of bleeding.

The cycle is controlled by **hormones**. These hormones are chemicals made by the ovaries under the control of the brain. The ovaries make two hormones: oestrogen and progesterone. These hormones also affect how a woman feels at different times in the cycle.

4 Which hormone makes an ovary release an ovum?

5 Many women feel tense just before their period. What might cause this?

Changes in the amounts of two hormones during the menstrual cycle.

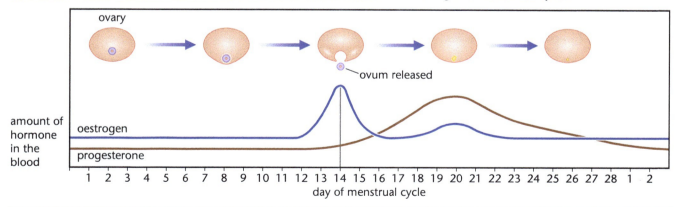

WHAT YOU NEED TO REMEMBER (Copy and complete using the **key words**)

The menstrual cycle

The menstrual cycle is a way of making sure that the lining of the _____ is ready for the implantation of an embryo each time an _____ releases an ovum (egg). The menstrual cycle is controlled by _____ .

1.14 Changing classifications

People have not always **classified** things in the same way.

A very famous Greek scientist called Aristotle lived from 384–322 BC. He wrote down ideas of grouping living things into two sets of plants and animals.

1 What features did Aristotle use to separate plants from animals?

2 How did he split the animal group up into smaller groups?

An Italian doctor called Andrea Cesalpino (1519–1603) used differences in reproductive parts to split plants into smaller groups. We still classify plants like this today.

3 How do we use plant reproduction to help us classify plants?

The Swedish botanist Linnaeus (1707–1778) used differences inside their bodies to help split up animals into smaller groups.

4 What is the major difference between the circulatory systems inside fish and mammals?

The **microscope** was invented at the beginning of the 16th century. Scientists saw microbes for the first time.

These organisms could not be grouped as plants or animals, because some had features of both groups! In 1861 John Hogg classified microbes as the third main group of living things.

5 Why can *Euglena* not be classified using Aristotle's system?

The famous English scientist Charles Darwin (1809–1882) studied how living things have developed over millions of years from earlier simple organisms. This is called **evolution**. He used fossils to help identify which living things had common ancestors. Knowing how different plants or animals are related to each other is very helpful when we are trying to classify them.

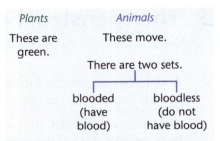

Plants — These are green.
Animals — These move. There are two sets.
— blooded (have blood)
— bloodless (do not have blood)

Aristotle's system of classification.

Ferns, mosses and liverworts produce spores.

Conifers and flowering plants produce seeds.

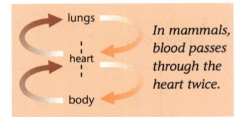

In fish, blood passes through the heart once for every circulation through the body.
heart — body — gills

lungs — heart — body
In mammals, blood passes through the heart twice.

Euglena is green <u>and</u> it moves.

WHAT YOU NEED TO REMEMBER (Copy and complete using the **key words**)

Changing classifications

Living things have not always been _____ in the same way.
Scientists have gathered new information using scientific instruments like the _____.
They have also had new ideas like the theory of _____.

1.15 Champion leeks

Edward grew these leeks from one packet of seeds.

1 (a) Write down <u>two</u> ways that the leeks vary.

(b) Write down <u>two</u> possible reasons why they vary.

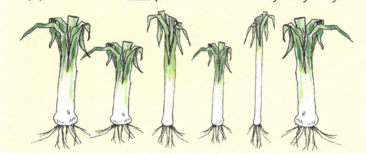

REMEMBER

How living things develop depends partly on what they inherit from their parents and partly on their environment.

Sarah and Ben give the leeks fertiliser and water. They take out the weeds to give the leeks space and light.

■ Growing better leeks

Sarah and Ben enter their leeks in shows every year. They keep trying to grow the biggest and best leeks.

The environment affects how well leeks grow, so Sarah and Ben make sure they give the plants all that they need.

2 Look at the pictures. Write a list of the things Sarah and Ben do to make the plants grow well.

Even though they give all the leeks all the things they need, the plants still vary.

Sarah and Ben don't buy new packets of seeds every year. They **choose** their biggest and best plants and **breed** from them.

3 Look at the pictures. Describe how Sarah and Ben get their seeds.

We breed plants and animals with the characteristics we want. We call this **selective breeding**.

Sarah and Ben let these flower and pollinate each other.

They eat these.

They collect the seeds.

They grow next year's plants from these seeds.

WHAT YOU NEED TO REMEMBER (Copy and complete using the **key words**)

Champion leeks

We can _____ the plants and animals which best suit our needs.
We can _____ from them so they pass on their useful characteristics.
We call this _____ _____.

2.1 Illness and health

Good health means feeling well in body and mind. There are many reasons for illness.

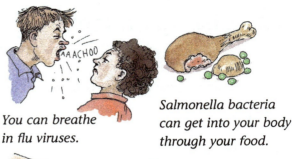

You can breathe in flu viruses.

Salmonella bacteria can get into your body through your food.

■ Microbes cause some diseases

Microbes are very small living things. You need a microscope to see them. Viruses, bacteria and some fungi are microbes. Some microbes can get inside your body and give you a disease. You can catch these diseases from other people.

1 Write down <u>three</u> ways that microbes can get into your body.

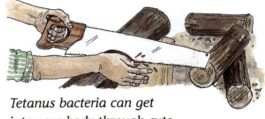

Tetanus bacteria can get into your body through cuts.

■ You can be born with some diseases

Some diseases are **inherited** from your parents. You don't <u>catch</u> these diseases, you are <u>born</u> with them. Nobody else can catch inherited diseases from you. But you can pass them on to your own children.

2 (a) What is sickle-cell anaemia?

(b) Can you catch sickle-cell anaemia from someone who has it? Give a reason for your answer.

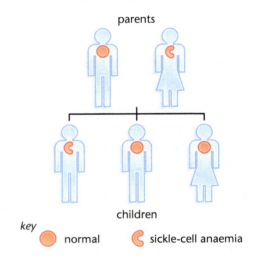

Sickle-cell anaemia is an illness that people can inherit from their parents. Their red blood cells are the wrong shape and do not carry oxygen very well.

■ Cells can go wrong

Your body makes new cells all the time. New cells are made when a cell divides in two. If cells divide too quickly, they go out of control and a tumour grows. We call this <u>cancer</u>. Ultraviolet rays and tar in cigarettes can cause cancer.

3 Why is it important that sun cream has UV (ultraviolet) protection?

4 Could someone with skin cancer pass it on to you?

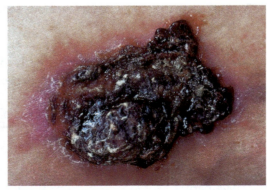

Ultraviolet rays from the Sun can cause skin cancer.

■ A poor diet can make you ill

It is important to eat the right sorts of foods in the right amounts to stay healthy. Too much food can make you overweight and put a strain on your heart. Just one mineral or **vitamin** missing from your diet can make you ill.

5 Copy and complete this table.

Illness	Cause of illness
heart disease	
	not enough iron
	too much sugar
weak bones	
poor sight in dim light	

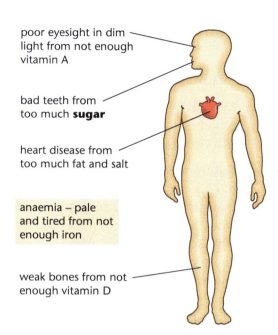

poor eyesight in dim light from not enough vitamin A

bad teeth from too much **sugar**

heart disease from too much fat and salt

anaemia – pale and tired from not enough iron

weak bones from not enough vitamin D

Some examples of problems caused by a poor diet.

■ Stress

Even if you eat the right foods and don't catch or inherit a disease, you can still be ill. Your mind needs to feel well too, but for many people the pressures and tensions of their lives cause stress. Stress can give you headaches, stomach ulcers and high blood pressure. You can help reduce stress by taking more time to exercise, relax and sleep.

6 Some doctors say that keeping a pet can reduce stress. Why do you think this is?

WHAT YOU NEED TO REMEMBER (Copy and complete using the **key words**)

Illness and health

You need to look after your body.

Some _____, such as viruses, fungi and bacteria, can make you ill.

Lack of just one mineral or _____ in your diet can cause a disease.
Too much fat, salt or _____ can harm you.

Some illnesses are passed on from parents to their children; we say that they are _____.

More about microbes: C+ 2.9

2.2 Some chemicals can damage your body

■ Smoking

The job of your lungs is to get oxygen into your blood and carbon dioxide out of your body. We call this <u>gas exchange</u>.

Cigarette smoke contains carbon monoxide. Some of this carbon monoxide is carried in your blood instead of oxygen. So your heart and lungs have to work harder to get the oxygen you need. This is why smokers get out of breath easily. The chemicals in cigarette smoke can also cause lung cancer and heart disease.

1 Most athletes don't smoke. Why is this?

2 How does a smoker's lung look different from a non-smoker's lung?

■ Alcohol

Alcohol is a poison. When you drink alcohol, your liver works hard to get rid of it. Your liver breaks the alcohol down into carbon dioxide and water. Too much alcohol damages your liver.

Alcohol also slows your brain down. People who have been drinking are clumsy and slow to react.

3 Which organ removes alcohol from your body?

4 (a) Look at the table. Jordan had two pints of beer. How long did it take his body to get rid of all the alcohol?

(b) How much does the amount of alcohol in Jordan's blood go down each hour?

(c) If Jordan drank only one pint of beer, how long would it take his body to remove the alcohol?

REMEMBER

All the cells in your body need oxygen. They get this from your blood.

Non-smoker's lung.

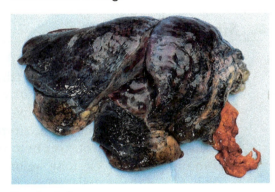

Smoker's lung.

This table shows the amount of alcohol in Jordan's blood after he drank two pints of beer.

Time (hours)	Amount of alcohol in the blood (grams per litre)
0	8
1	6
2	4
3	2
4	0
5	0

■ Medicines

Medicines are drugs you take when you are ill to help you feel better. For example, you take drugs like aspirin or paracetamol for a headache.

5 Why is it dangerous to take more aspirin or paracetamol than you should?

Antibiotics are drugs that kill bacteria. You can take antibiotics for a sore throat. It is important to take all of the antibiotics the doctor gives you.

6 What happens if you stop taking antibiotics too early?

WARNING

Never take a bigger dose of a medicine than it says on the packet. Too much aspirin can damage your stomach. Too much paracetamol can damage your liver. An overdose of these drugs can kill you.

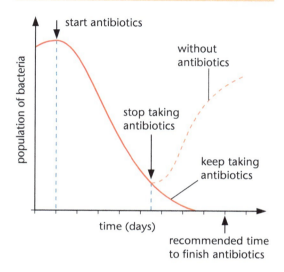

■ Illegal drugs

Some people take drugs like ecstasy, LSD and cannabis or sniff solvents to feel different. All these drugs **damage** your body and when the effects wear off you can feel worse than you did before.

Some people who are training to be athletes may be offered illegal drugs called steroids which help them build muscle quickly. Steroids have side effects such as mood changes and heart damage.

7 (a) Write down two different reasons why people might want to take illegal drugs.

(b) In each case, write down two reasons why taking illegal drugs isn't a good idea.

Athletes caught taking steroids to improve their performance are banned from competitions.

WHAT YOU NEED TO REMEMBER (Copy and complete using the **key words**)

Some chemicals can damage your body

Drugs that can help your body if you use them properly are called _____.

Smoking, alcohol, solvents and other drugs _____ your body.

More about antibiotics: C+ 2.9   More about smoking: C+ 2.10

2.3 Healthy eating

To stay **healthy** you need to eat the right sorts of foods in the right amounts. We call this a balanced diet.

■ Dishes of the world

People around the world can get a healthy diet from all sorts of different foods.

What you need	Foods you can get them from
carbohydrates	rice, potatoes, noodles, chapatis, bread, maize, pasta
fats	oil, dairy foods, meat
proteins	fish, prawns, lentils, peas, meat
fibre	lentils, vegetables

1 **(a)** Write down <u>one</u> food which is a good source of protein in the West Indian dish.

   (b) Write down <u>one</u> food which is a good source of fibre in the Indian dish.

   (c) Write down <u>one</u> food which is a good source of carbohydrate in the Chinese dish.

■ Staple foods

Staple foods contain a lot of carbohydrate or starch. They make up a large part of people's diets. In Britain the staple foods are wheat (bread) and potato, in India one of the staple foods is rice and in parts of Africa it is maize.

2 Copy and complete the sentences.

   Staple foods contain mainly _____.
   You need this in your diet for _____.

DO YOU REMEMBER?
from *Core Science 1*

The food you eat must contain:
- **carbohydrates** and **fats** for energy;
- **proteins** for growth;
- **fibre** to stop you getting constipated;
- small amounts of **vitamins** and **minerals**.

You must also drink plenty of water.

West Indian dish: fish and rice.

Indian dish: dahl (made from lentils) and chapatis.

Chinese dish: prawn stir-fry and noodles.

■ A problem with maize

Children need more than just staple foods to be healthy.

Maya lives in Africa. She is weak and ill. Her skin cracks easily and her liver is damaged. She has an illness called kwashiorkor and she will probably die before she is five years old. Maya's family is poor, so she eats maize for most of her meals.

3 Write down <u>two</u> reasons why a diet of just maize is unhealthy.

4 Why do children need to eat protein?

5 Look at the picture of Maya and write down <u>two</u> things you can see wrong with her.

Maya's baby brother is healthy. He feeds on his mother's breast milk. Milk contains all the protein and vitamins that a young child needs.

6 If Maya can get the right food, she will get better within a month. Write down <u>one</u> food she could eat to give her more protein.

■ Other diets can also be a problem

Many people get enough to eat but they eat too much of some things and not enough of others. We say their diets are not balanced. A lot of people in Britain have bad teeth from eating too much sugar. A few people have an illness called scurvy from not eating enough fresh fruit.

7 Look at the picture. If you eat meals like this all the time you will not be very healthy. Write down <u>two</u> reasons why.

Maize is often called corn-on-the-cob. Where maize is the staple food, many children don't get all the protein and vitamins they need.

Maya has kwashiorkor

after one month's treatment

WHAT YOU NEED TO REMEMBER (Copy and complete using the **key words**)

Healthy eating

You need to eat a variety of food to stay _____. The important things in your diet are
c_____, f_____, p_____, f_____, v_____, m_____ and water.

More about vitamins: C+ 2.11

2.4 Digesting your food

DO YOU REMEMBER? from *Core Science 1*

Only small **soluble** molecules can pass into your blood to be carried to your cells. This means that the food you eat has to be broken down.

Your teeth grind up your food.

Saliva makes food soft and slippery so that you can swallow it easily. Then muscles push the food along the oesophagus (gullet) to your stomach.

Glands add digestive juices to the food. These contain **enzymes** that break down large food molecules into smaller ones. This is **digestion**.

Digested food passes from your small **intestine** into your blood. This is absorption.

1 Your friends think that chewing food makes it small enough to be absorbed into your blood. Explain why this is not true.

2 Copy and complete the sentences.

Even small pieces of food contain large _____. Digestive juices contain _____ which break these down.

■ Different kinds of enzymes

A balanced meal contains different types of foods. Different enzymes digest each different type of food.

3 Copy the table. Use the diagram to help you to complete the table.

Gland	What its enzymes digest
salivary glands	_____
stomach lining	_____
_____	no enzymes, but juice splits fats into tiny drops
pancreas	_____, _____, _____
small intestine lining	_____, _____, _____

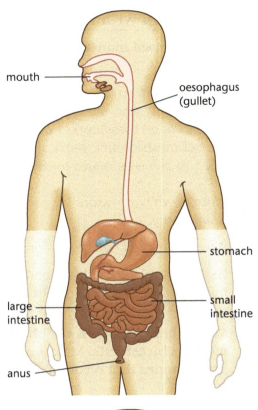

mouth

oesophagus (gullet)

stomach

large intestine

small intestine

anus

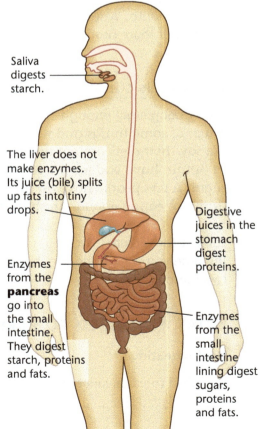

Saliva digests starch.

The liver does not make enzymes. Its juice (bile) splits up fats into tiny drops.

Enzymes from the **pancreas** go into the small intestine. They digest starch, proteins and fats.

Digestive juices in the stomach digest proteins.

Enzymes from the small intestine lining digest sugars, proteins and fats.

■ What are different foods digested into?

The food you eat is a mixture of large molecules. The diagram shows what these molecules are. It also shows the smaller molecules that are produced when the large molecules are digested.

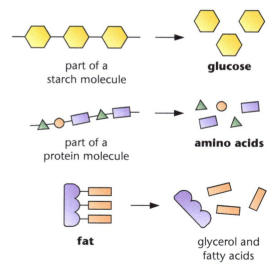

part of a
starch molecule

glucose

part of a
protein molecule

amino acids

fat

glycerol and
fatty acids

4 Copy and complete a table, using the headings shown, to show what happens to starch, protein and fats.

Large molecules ...	... are digested into these small molecules

■ What happens where?

Different parts of the digestive system have different jobs.

5 Put these sentences into the correct order. Use the diagram on page 32 to help you do this. You don't need to write out the sentences, just use the letters A to F.

A   Muscles in the stomach wall churn up food. The lining makes digestive juices.

B   Solid waste called faeces leaves the anus. Most of this waste is fibre that we cannot digest. It helps to keep the intestine healthy because it gives muscles in the intestine wall something to push on to move the food along.

C   Muscles in the gullet wall squeeze food along. There are muscles like these all the way through the digestive system.

D   In the mouth, teeth grind the food into small pieces. Salivary glands make saliva. This wets the food so it can be easily swallowed. Saliva also starts to digest some of the food.

E   Glands in the small intestine lining add digestive juices to the food. Small digested food molecules pass into the blood.

F   Water is absorbed from the large intestines.

WHAT YOU NEED TO REMEMBER (Copy and complete using the **key words**)

Digesting your food

Large food molecules are broken down by ___._____ in digestive juices. We call this _____.

Digestive juices are made in your salivary _____, stomach lining, _____ and small intestine lining.

You absorb these small, _____ molecules in your small _____.

More about enzymes: C+ 2.12

2.5 Using your food

■ Food to make new cells

Like all living things, you are made of cells. To stay healthy, you need to make new cells all the time.

Young people need new cells to grow. Even adults need new cells.

> 1 Look at the picture. Write down <u>two</u> reasons why adults need to produce new cells.
>
> 2 Where do you get the proteins and other materials you need to make new cells?

■ Cells need energy too

Cells get the energy they need from food. Food that is used by your cells for energy is your body's fuel.

> 3 Look at the diagram, then copy and complete the sentences.
>
> The energy which cells need comes from a fuel called _____. Cells need _____ to make the glucose give up its energy.

When cells release energy from glucose, we say they **respire**.

■ How your cells get glucose

You don't eat much glucose. Your digestive system digests substances such as starch to produce the glucose that your cells need.

Enzymes break starch down into small glucose molecules in your digestive system.

You absorb the small glucose molecules into your blood system.

Your **blood** transports them around your body.

They pass into your **cells** so that your cells can use them.

DO YOU REMEMBER?
from *Core Science 1*

Food gives you **energy** for moving, growing and keeping warm.

Food also gives you **materials** for making new cells.

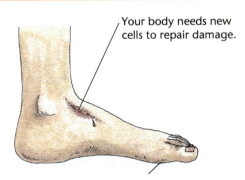

Your body needs new cells to repair damage.

Skin cells have to be replaced as they get worn away.

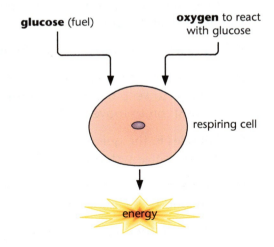

glucose (fuel)   oxygen to react with glucose

respiring cell

energy

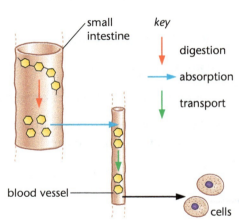

small intestine

key

digestion

absorption

transport

blood vessel

cells

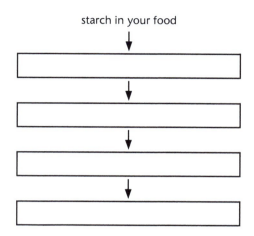

starch in your food

4 Copy and complete the flow chart by writing the following ideas in the correct order.

- used by your cells to provide energy

- absorbed into your blood

- digested by enzymes into glucose

- transported to your body cells

Cells make waste

Cells release waste when they respire.

5 Look at the diagram on the right, and the one in the middle of the opposite page. Then copy and complete this table.

Respiring cells	
take in	**release**

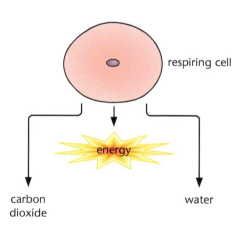

respiring cell

energy

carbon dioxide

water

Carbon dioxide waste is poisonous. To stay healthy, you have to get rid of it. You breathe it out. We say that your lungs <u>excrete</u> it.

WHAT YOU NEED TO REMEMBER (Copy and complete using the **key words**)

Using your food

Molecules of glucose from digested food travel in your _____ to all the _____ in your body. Cells break down the _____ to release _____.
We say they _____. They need _____ to do this.

Your food also supplies cells with the _____ they need to make new cells and to repair or replace damaged ones.

More about respiration: C+ 3.11

2.6 What happens when you exercise?

When you **exercise**, your muscles work harder. Your muscle cells need to release more energy so they respire faster. Some of the energy released by respiration makes you warmer. So your body becomes hotter when you exercise.

REMEMBER

The cells of your muscles need oxygen and glucose to produce energy. Cells make carbon dioxide and other waste which the blood carries away.

You sweat. This evaporates and helps to cool you down.

Your heart beats faster and moves blood more quickly round your body.

You breathe faster and more deeply to take in more oxygen.

Some of the energy released by your muscle cells makes you hotter.

1 When you exercise:

   (a) how do you get more oxygen into your body?

   (b) how does the oxygen reach cells more quickly?

2 **(a)** Why do you feel hot when you exercise?

   (b) What does your body do to help cool you down when you exercise?

How do you get the energy to exercise?

3 Copy and complete the sentences. Use the diagram to help you.

In muscles, _____ and glucose pass out of the blood and into the cells. The cells break down glucose using oxygen to release _____.
We call this _____.

A waste product called _____ _____ is produced. Blood carries this to the _____ where it is breathed out.

You **breathe** air in and out.

Cells in your muscles use oxygen and glucose to get energy. This process is called **respiration**.
Carbon dioxide is a waste product

Your blood **transports** oxygen and glucose to your muscles and carries carbon dioxide away

Gases go into and out of your body in your lungs. Oxygen goes into the blood and carbon dioxide goes into the air. We say that your lungs **exchange** gases.

WHAT YOU NEED TO REMEMBER (Copy and complete using the **key words**)

What happens when you exercise?

These are the things that must happen so your muscle cells can release energy when you exercise:

- You _____ air in and out of your lungs.

- In your lungs, oxygen goes into the blood and carbon dioxide goes out. We call this gas _____.

- Your blood _____ glucose and oxygen to your muscle cells.

- Cells break down glucose to release energy. This is _____.

All these things go on more quickly when you _____.

More about exercise: C+ 2.13

2.7 Keeping fit

Exercise helps you feel good in mind and body. It helps you control your weight, and strengthens your muscles, heart and bones. It can be good fun too.

1 Write down <u>four</u> good reasons why everyone needs to exercise.

■ Improving your circulation

The flow of blood around your body is called your <u>circulation</u>. Your heart gets stronger and your blood circulation improves as you train.

2 Use the diagram to help you put these sentences about circulation into the right order. The first sentence is in the correct place.

Your heart pumps blood to your body cells.

- Blood collects oxygen and gets rid of carbon dioxide.

- Blood from body cells returns to the right side of your heart.

- Blood leaves your lungs in veins to go back to the left side of your heart.

- Your heart pumps blood to your lungs.

- Body cells take oxygen from the blood and put carbon dioxide in.

3 In one circuit round the body, how many times does blood go through your heart?

Capillaries are the smallest blood vessels in your body. They carry the blood between arteries and veins. There are millions of tiny capillaries all over your body bringing blood close to every cell.

4 Why do you need capillaries?

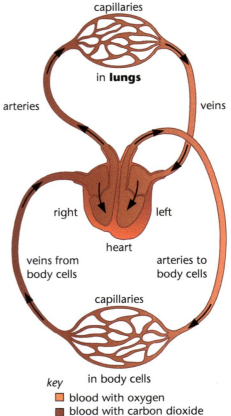

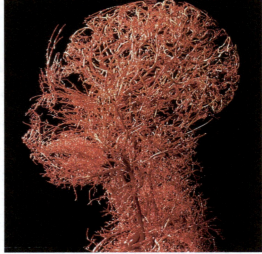

Capillary walls are thin. **Oxygen** *and* **glucose** *pass from the blood to the cells.* **Carbon dioxide** *passes into the blood.*

■ Getting started with exercise

If you are not very active now, you must build up slowly. Aim to exercise for at least 30 minutes three times a week. The more you exercise, the fitter you will become. Different types of exercise use different muscles so try to do more than one type of exercise.

5 Why is swimming good for you?

6 Why do rugby players get a lot of joint injuries?

7 What advantages does aerobics have over cycling as a form of exercise?

Team games, such as rugby and hockey, are good for stamina and strength. Sudden stops and turns may damage ankles and knees.

Swimming is a great way to get fit, especially if you are overweight. There is less stress on your joints because the water supports you.

Cycling is good for leg strength and stamina (being able to keep going). Always wear a cycle helmet.

Exercise classes (dance and aerobics) give you an all-over workout.

WHAT YOU NEED TO REMEMBER (Copy and complete using the **key words**)

Keeping fit

Your _____ pumps blood around your body.

Blood carries _____ and _____ to cells and takes away _____ _____ and other waste.

You need to be able to label a diagram of your circulation.

capillaries in _____

arteries ⟍ ⟋ veins

veins ⟋ heart ⟍ arteries

_____ in body tissues

More about gas exchange: C+ 2.14   More about capillaries: C+ 2.15

2.8 Take care when you exercise

Look at the pictures. These athletes are doing warm-up exercises in which they are gently stretching their muscles. If they do this, they are less likely to strain a muscle.

1 Why should you warm up before you play a sport?

But even when you have warmed up, you can sometimes injure muscles and joints.

Athletes do warm-up exercises before a race.

■ Sprains

Omar has twisted his ankle playing football. He has injured one of the **joints** between the bones; we call this a <u>sprain</u>. The ligament that holds his ankle joint in place has been over-stretched. It hurts and Omar can't stand on that foot. Luckily his friend Baljeet has learnt first aid.

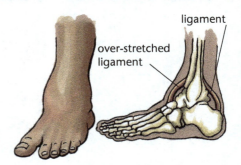

Omar's twisted ankle has started to swell up and bruise.

2 What is a sprain?

3 Why did Baljeet put a wet cold towel on Omar's ankle?

Later, Baljeet bandaged the ankle firmly.

Baljeet raised Omar's leg and put a wet cold towel on it to reduce swelling.

4 Why do you think it is important not to tie the bandage too tight?

Omar needs to rest his ankle for a few days and not run until the ankle stops hurting.

A firm bandage supports Omar's ankle but doesn't stop blood flowing to his toes.

■ **Strains**

Jenny has strained her thigh playing hockey. A <u>strain</u> is an injury to a muscle. Strains are common sports injuries caused by sudden or awkward movements (like stopping and turning). Jenny needs similar first aid to Omar.

5 Is a 'pulled muscle' a sprain or a strain?

6 Write down <u>three</u> things Jenny should do to help her strained thigh get better.

■ **Muscle teamwork**

Muscles make your body move by pulling on bones that are held to other bones at joints.

You need to be able to bend and straighten your arm at your elbow. For this you have two muscles, your biceps and triceps.

Most joints are worked by **pairs** of muscles, one to bend it and one to straighten it. This is because muscles can only make your body move when they shorten or **contract**.

The diagram shows how these muscles work.

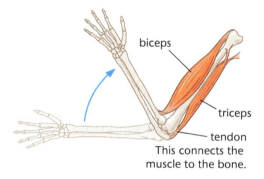

*Your biceps contracts to bend your arm. Your triceps **relaxes** to let this happen.*

7 What connects muscles to bones?

8 Copy and complete the sentences.

To bend your arm, your biceps _____ and your triceps _____. To straighten your arm, your _____ contracts and your _____ relaxes.

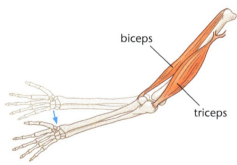

Your triceps contracts to straighten your arm. Your biceps relaxes to let this happen.

WHAT YOU NEED TO REMEMBER (Copy and complete using the **key words**)

Take care when you exercise

Your bones _____ and _____ parts of your body.

The _____ between bones let you move.
Muscles cause movement when they _____.
Muscles are in _____.
When one muscle of a pair contracts, the other _____.

More about muscles: C+ 2.16

2.9 Self-defence

Your body defends itself against microbes such as bacteria and viruses all the time, even in your sleep.

White blood cells destroy the microbes that cause disease. Some white blood cells **digest** the microbes. Others make **antibodies** which destroy them in other ways. Usually after a few days of being ill, the white blood cells kill enough microbes for you to start feeling better.

> 1 How do white blood cells 'eat' microbes?

■ Immunisation

Once you have had a disease, you don't normally catch it again. We say that you are <u>immune</u> to the disease.

You can become immune to a disease without actually having the disease at all. For example, most children in Britain have an injection (or 'jab') to stop them catching tuberculosis (TB). We call this <u>immunisation</u>. The diagram shows how a TB jab works.

> 2 (a) Why do we have jabs?
>
>   (b) How does a TB jab work?

■ Antibiotics

If you don't have a TB jab and you catch TB, your body finds it difficult to kill the bacteria. Medicines called **antibiotics** can help. Antibiotics can kill **bacteria** but they can't kill viruses such as those that cause flu (influenza).

> 3 Why can antibiotics help to cure TB but not flu?

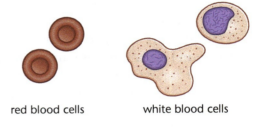

red blood cells   white blood cells

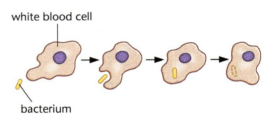

white blood cell

bacterium

A white blood cell surrounds and digests a bacterium.

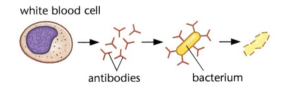

white blood cell

antibodies   bacterium

A white blood cell makes antibodies to destroy a bacterium.

A TB jab contains a weak version of TB bacteria.

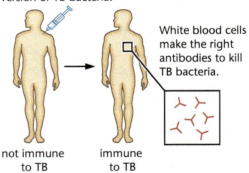

White blood cells make the right antibodies to kill TB bacteria.

not immune to TB   immune to TB

WHAT YOU NEED TO REMEMBER (Copy and complete using the **key words**)

Self-defence

Some of your white blood cells make _____ to destroy microbes, others _____ microbes. Your white blood cells make new kinds of antibodies when you are infected by, or immunised against, a new disease. _____ are drugs which kill _____ in your body.

2.10 Smoking and health

People who smoke tobacco breathe a mixture of chemicals into their **lungs**. These chemicals harm them in many different ways.

■ Nicotine

Nicotine causes addiction to cigarette smoking. It increases the smoker's heart rate and blood pressure which can lead to heart disease.

Cilia are tiny hairs that clean dirt and microbes from the lungs. Nicotine paralyses cilia and stops them from working. This makes smokers cough.

Coughing damages the **air sacs** in smokers' lungs so that they can't absorb oxygen so well.

■ Carbon monoxide

Carbon monoxide is a poison that is carried instead of oxygen in the red blood cells. Smokers carry less oxygen in their blood and this can cause damage to their heart.

■ Tar

Tar contains chemicals that cause cancer. 90% of deaths from lung cancer are due to smoking.

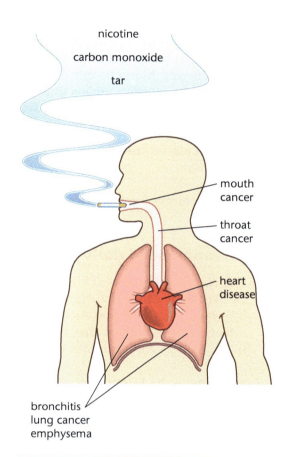

nicotine

carbon monoxide

tar

mouth cancer

throat cancer

heart disease

bronchitis
lung cancer
emphysema

1 Why do smokers cough?

2 Which <u>two</u> chemicals in cigarette smoke cause heart disease?

3 What substance in cigarette smoke causes cancer?

4 Write down <u>two</u> reasons why smokers have less oxygen in their blood.

5 (a) Write down <u>two</u> things that can cause bronchitis.

   (b) Why are smokers more likely to get bronchitis?

DID YOU KNOW?

<u>Bronchitis</u> affects your lungs and bronchial tubes. They make too much mucus because of dirt or microbes in your lungs. Smokers are 50 times more likely to get bronchitis than non-smokers.

<u>Emphysema</u> makes you short of breath. This happens when smoke or dust damages the air sacs in your lungs.

WHAT YOU NEED TO REMEMBER (Copy and complete using the **key words**)

Smoking and health

Coughing damages the _____ _____ in your lungs. Nicotine paralyses the _____ which normally help to keep dirt and microbes out of your _____.
These things mean your lungs do not work as well if you smoke.

2.11 Vitamin tablets

You need **vitamins** and **minerals** to stay healthy. If you eat a **balanced** diet, you get enough vitamins and minerals. Many people don't eat a healthy diet so they take vitamin tablets (but you can get too much of a good thing). You can actually **poison** yourself by taking too many.

Arctic explorers used to eat polar bear liver. Some of them died.

1 What could the explorers have died from?

■ Recommended daily allowance

The correct amount of a vitamin to eat in one day to be healthy is called your <u>recommended daily allowance</u> (RDA). If you decide to take vitamin tablets, watch out that they do not add up to more than the RDA for vitamin A and D.

2 (a) What is the RDA for vitamin A?

 (b) What is the RDA for vitamin D?

Too much vitamin D over a period of months can damage your kidneys and blood vessels.

Too much vitamin A causes weight loss, irritability, cracked skin and weakened bones.

Ben takes a cod-liver oil capsule and a multi-vitamin tablet every day.

3 (a) What is Ben's total daily intake of vitamin A in addition to what he gets from his food?

 (b) What is his total daily intake of vitamin D in addition to what he gets from his food?

 (c) What advice would you give Ben?

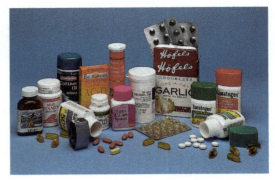

There are many different vitamin and mineral tablets.

Doctors found out that arctic explorers were poisoned by the large amount of vitamin D in the polar bear liver they had eaten.

multi-vitamin and iron tablets

In each tablet:		RDA
Vitamin A	800 µg	100%
Vitamin B$_{12}$	1 µg	100%
Vitamin C	60 mg	100%
Vitamin D	5 µg	100%
Vitamin E	10 mg	100%
Iron	14 mg	100%

In each capsule		RDA
Vitamin A	800 µg	100%
Vitamin D	5 µg	100%

mg (milligram) = $\frac{1}{1000}$ of a gram

µg (microgram) = $\frac{1}{1000}$ of a milligram

cod-liver oil

WHAT YOU NEED TO REMEMBER (Copy and complete using the **key words**)

Vitamin tablets

To stay healthy you need _____ and _____.
Some people who don't eat a _____ diet take vitamin tablets.
Too much vitamin A or D can _____ you.

2.12 More about enzymes

Enzymes **speed up** chemical reactions but do not get used up. We say that they are **catalysts**.

Cells in your body make many different kinds of enzyme. Each enzyme speeds up a **different** chemical reaction in your body.

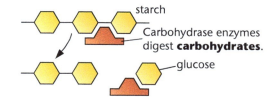

starch

Carbohydrase enzymes digest **carbohydrates**.

glucose

■ Digestive enzymes

A different type of enzyme breaks down each type of food. For example, protease enzymes break down proteins.

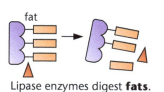

fat

Lipase enzymes digest **fats**.

1 An enzyme in saliva called amylase digests starch. Is amylase a carbohydrase, a protease or a lipase?

2 Which type of enzyme breaks down fats?

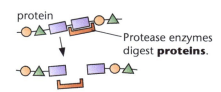

protein

Protease enzymes digest **proteins**.

■ Enzymes can work at different speeds

Certain things affect how fast an enzyme works (its **rate**). One of these is **temperature**.

Carla set up an experiment using the enzyme amylase to digest starch. The table shows Carla's results.

3 What broke down the starch?

4 What effect does increasing the temperature from 15°C to 30°C have on the rate at which the enzyme works?

5 What effect does boiling have on the enzyme?

6 Why did Carla set up a tube with starch and water only?

Time (minutes)	0	5	10	15
Starch and water at 15 °C	✓	✓	✓	✓
Starch and amylase at 15 °C	✓	✓	✓	✗
Starch and amylase at 30 °C	✓	✗	✗	✗
Starch and boiled amylase at 30 °C	✓	✓	✓	✓

✓ = starch still in tube (so it hasn't been digested)
✗ = no starch left in tube (so it has been digested)

WHAT YOU NEED TO REMEMBER (Copy and complete using the **key words**)

More about enzymes

Enzymes are _____. They _____ _____ chemical reactions.

Different enzymes speed up _____ reactions.

Carbohydrases digest _____. Proteases digest _____. Lipases digest _____.

The _____ at which an enzyme work depends on certain conditions, for example _____.

45

2.13 Born athletes

Top athletes are born with an ability to take in and use oxygen at a much faster rate than most other people. We say that they inherit this ability.

There is a limit to how much any athlete can improve by training.

1 Write down three parts of her body that an athlete improves when she trains.

2 Even if they train, some athletes will never become top athletes. Why is this?

When cells respire, they use **oxygen** and produce carbon dioxide.

3 Copy and complete the word equation for respiration.

glucose + _____ → _____ _____ + water + energy

The sports scientist in the picture is trying to find out if the young athlete could become a top athlete. She is measuring the amount of a gas that the athlete's lungs put into the air he breathes out.

4 Write down the name of the gas in the air she is measuring.

5 She will know from her measurements how fast the athlete's body is taking in and using oxygen. Explain this as fully as you can.

6 How will she know whether he could become a top athlete or not?

This athlete's heart, lungs and muscles work better since she started training.

DID YOU KNOW?

The air we breathe in contains hardly any carbon dioxide.

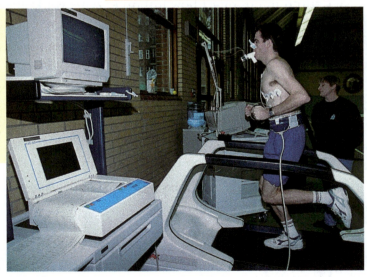

WHAT YOU NEED TO REMEMBER (Copy and complete using the **key words**)

Born athletes

The word equation for the respiration of glucose is:

_____ + _____ → carbon dioxide + _____ + _____

2.14 How to get a good exchange rate

Some substances are constantly going into your blood and into your body cells. Other substances are constantly coming out. We say that **exchanges** are happening in your body all the time.

■ Exchanges in your lungs

Your **lungs** are organs that carry out gas exchange.

1 What gas moves from the air in your lungs into your blood?

2 What gas moves from the blood to the air in your lungs?

Your lungs are made of tiny air sacs. There are thousands of air sacs so gas exchange can occur over a large area. (The total **surface area** inside your lungs is about the size of a tennis court.) Air sacs are covered by many capillaries carrying blood to make sure that lots of oxygen goes into the blood.

3 Write down <u>two</u> reasons why your lungs are good at taking in oxygen.

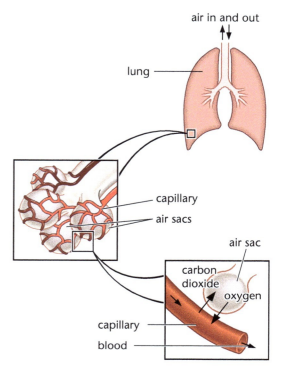

■ Exchanges in your small intestine

Your **small intestine** is part of your digestive system. It is here that you absorb digested food into your blood. The food has to pass through the lining of your intestine. So the greater the surface area of your intestines, the more food you can absorb.

4 Why does your small intestine have villi?

5 Why do the villi have lots of capillaries inside them?

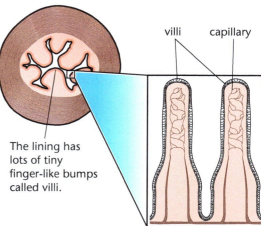

The lining has lots of tiny finger-like bumps called villi.

Cross-section of the small intestine.

WHAT YOU NEED TO REMEMBER (Copy and complete using the **key words**)

How to get a good exchange rate

Organs where _____ take place have a good blood supply and a large

_____ _____.

Examples are your _____ and _____ _____.

2.15 Capillaries in action

Capillaries are very small and thin. The walls are only **one cell** thick so that substances move easily in and out.

Glucose and oxygen leave the blood from capillaries, and waste like carbon dioxide goes in. A waste product called urea is made in liver cells. So, this also goes into the blood in the liver. Each substance moves from where there is a lot of it (high concentration) to where there is only a little (low concentration).

We say that the substances **diffuse** from where there is a high concentration to where there is a low concentration.

1 What is the job of capillaries?

2 What two substances do the cells need that the capillaries carry?

3 What two waste substances do the capillaries carry away?

Oxygen and glucose don't go straight from capillaries to cells. First, they diffuse into the tissue fluid that surrounds the cells. Then they diffuse into the cells.

4 Copy and complete the sentence.

Carbon dioxide diffuses from cells into _____ _____ and then into _____.

5 Copy the table. Then complete it using these words:

low, medium, high.

	Concentration of substance	
	carbon dioxide	oxygen
in cells		
in tissue fluid		
in capillaries		

REMEMBER

Capillaries are the smallest blood vessels in your body. The blood in capillaries brings substances to cells and takes away waste.

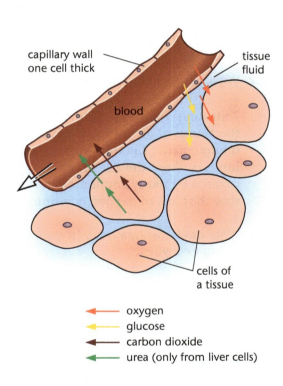

capillary wall one cell thick

tissue fluid

blood

cells of a tissue

→ oxygen
→ glucose
→ carbon dioxide
→ urea (only from liver cells)

REMEMBER

A <u>tissue</u> is a group of similar cells.

WHAT YOU NEED TO REMEMBER (Copy and complete using the **key words**)

Capillaries in action

Substances pass between the blood and the tissues through capillary walls.
They _____ in and out easily because capillary walls are only _____ _____ thick.

2.16 Different athletes for different events

Everyone looks different. This is partly due to <u>inheritance</u> and partly due to <u>environment</u>.

■ Inheritance

Part of how you look comes from your parents, for example, your eye colour or the shape of your nose. We say that these features are <u>inherited</u>.

1 Write down two things about how you look that you could have inherited.

Your muscles have a mixture of fast and slow twitch fibres in them. The mixture you have is inherited. Fast twitch muscles work quickly for a short time and slow twitch muscles work more slowly but can work for a lot longer.

Nathan and Yasir are in the school athletics team. Yasir runs the 100 m sprint. Nathan runs the 5000 m long distance race.

2 What sort of muscle fibres do you think Nathan has inherited most of to be good at long distance running?

3 Could Nathan ever be a good sprinter?

■ Environment

You can change part of how you look. For example, you can change your weight by what you eat or your hair by cutting or dyeing it.

To be a good athlete, you need to train regularly to improve your speed, strength and stamina.

4 Nathan sometimes avoids training. He says he is a born long distance runner so he doesn't need to train. Do you agree?

Example of inherited features.

Yasir

Nathan

100 m sprinter

5000 m long distance runner

mother

daughter

An example of the environmental effect. The daughter did not inherit big muscles. She got them through training.

WHAT YOU NEED TO REMEMBER

Different athletes for different events

You need to know examples of variation due to inheritance and variation due to environment.

3.1 Daily and seasonal change

The **temperature** and the amount of **light** vary according to the time of day and the **season** of the year.

We see different animals at different times of the day.

We see different animals and plants at different times of the year (seasons).

The animals and plants on these pages were all seen in Sandra's garden. But they were not all seen at the same time.

■ Animals of the night

Look at the pictures.

1 (a) Write down the name of <u>one</u> animal seen at night.

(b) Describe and explain <u>one</u> way this animal is adapted for hunting in dim light.

2 What do we call animals which are active at night?

■ Animals in winter

Food is harder to find in winter. So animals eat more than they need during the summer and store it in their bodies as fat.

3 (a) Copy and complete the table.

Animal	Why it needs to store food
rabbit	
hedgehog	
willow warbler	

(b) Which of these animals won't Sandra see moving around in her garden in the winter?
Give reasons for your answers.

Butterflies feed during the day.

Owls see well in dim light. They feed at night, so we say that they are <u>nocturnal</u>.

It can be hard to find food in winter.

During hibernation, hedgehogs use up the fat stored in their bodies.

Willow warblers need to store fat. This provides the energy they need to migrate to warmer countries.

Plants in winter

In winter it is cold. There can be frost and snow. The days are short and it is rarely bright or sunny. But plants with green leaves can still make some food.

Plants must be able to survive the changing seasons. We say they are **adapted** to do this.

Different plants are adapted to the changing seasons in different ways.

The picture shows Sandra's garden. Only one kind of plant in her garden can make food in winter.

4 (a) Write down the name of this plant.

(b) Explain why you chose it.

The other plants must use stored food to stay alive. They also use this food to grow new leaves in the spring.

5 Look again at the picture of Sandra's garden. Then copy and complete the table.

Plant	What it is like in winter
	bulb under the ground
	its twigs have no leaves
	only the seeds are alive
	it has green leaves

6 Copy and complete the sentence.

Most plants use _____ food to survive the _____ and to grow new _____ in the spring.

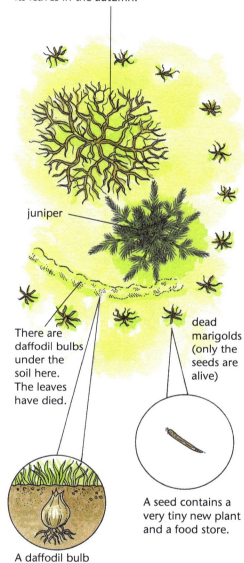

Sandra's garden – a birds-eye view.

A cherry tree is deciduous. This means that it loses its leaves in the autumn.

juniper

There are daffodil bulbs under the soil here. The leaves have died.

dead marigolds (only the seeds are alive)

A seed contains a very tiny new plant and a food store.

A daffodil bulb contains stored food.

WHAT YOU NEED TO REMEMBER (Copy and complete using the **key words**)

Daily and seasonal change

The _____ and the amount of _____ vary according to the time of day and the _____ of the year. Plants and animals are _____ to survive these changes.

More about birds and the seasons: C+ 3.8

3.2 Photosynthesis: a scientific detective story

All living things need **food** to grow.

Plants make their own food. Leaves take in all the things they need to make this food. The process the leaves use to make food is called **photosynthesis**.

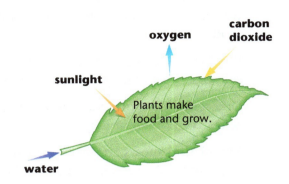

1 Look at the diagram. Write down <u>three</u> things a plant needs for making food.

It took scientists a long time to find out all this. They found out a little bit at a time.

■ **Substances which plants take in**

About 350 years ago, a Dutch scientist called Van Helmont planted a young tree in a pot. For the next five years all that he put into the soil was water.

The diagrams show what happened.

90 kg of dry soil + 1 kg young tree + water

5 years

89.95 kg of dry soil (only 50 g less) + 100 kg tree (99 kg more)

2 Van Helmont thought that the tree needed only water to grow. Why did he think this?

A tree does need water to grow, but it needs other things too.

Scientists now know that a tree needs lots of another substance to grow.

3 Look at the box on the right.

  (a) How do scientists know that trees need another substance as well as water to grow?

  (b) What is the substance called?

  (c) Where must this substance come from?

DO YOU REMEMBER?
from *Core Science 1*

■ Trees and other plants contain a lot of carbon.

■ There is no carbon in water.

■ Plants cannot use the carbon in soil.

■ There is carbon in the carbon dioxide in the air.

A substance that plants give out

More than 200 years ago, a scientist called Joseph Priestley made an important discovery. The diagrams show what he found out.

4 (a) What happens to a burning candle in an enclosed space?

(b) How did Priestley 'restore' the air so the candle would burn again?

A French scientist called Lavoisier called the part of the air that lets a candle burn <u>oxygen</u>.

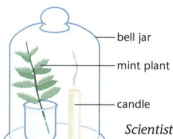

bell jar
mint plant
candle

Scientists already knew that a candle in a jar burns for a short time then goes out.

Priestley found that after a few days, the candle would burn again.

Later, other scientists realised that this only happened in sunlight.

Fitting the pieces together

Scientists are like detectives. They fit bits of evidence together to tell a story. In 1845 a man called Mayer put all the bits together and worked out how plants make food from water, carbon dioxide and light. He worked out the story of photosynthesis.

5 Copy and complete the following.

In sunlight:

- plants put a gas called _____ into the air;

- plants take a gas called _____ _____ out of the air.

6 Why do we call the process 'photosynthesis'?

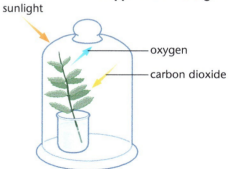

sunlight
oxygen
carbon dioxide

DID YOU KNOW?

'Photo' means 'light', and 'synthesis' means 'making'.

So 'photosynthesis' means 'making with **light**'.

WHAT YOU NEED TO REMEMBER (Copy and complete using the **key words**)

Photosynthesis: a scientific detective story

Green plants make their own _____ using the energy from _____. This process is called _____.

Plants make food and grow.

More about photosynthesis: C+ 3.9

53

3.3 Growing tomato plants without soil

Plants have roots for two reasons:

- roots **anchor** plants in soil;

- roots take in **water** and **minerals**.

The tomato plants in the photograph are growing in water, not soil.

1 Normally, roots anchor plants in the soil. Why haven't the plants in the photograph fallen over?

This way of growing plants is called <u>hydroponics</u>.

■ How do plants get all the things they need?

Plants are mainly made from three chemical elements: carbon, hydrogen and oxygen. They get these elements from carbon dioxide and water.

Plants also need small amounts of other elements to grow. They get these elements from minerals in the soil.

Plants need lots of …

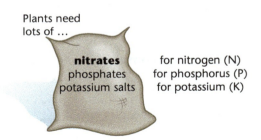

nitrates   for nitrogen (N)
phosphates   for phosphorus (P)
potassium salts   for potassium (K)

2 Look at the diagrams, then copy and complete the table.

Element	Minerals it is present in
nitrogen	
	phosphates
potassium	
magnesium	
	sulphates

Plants need some …

magnesium salts   sulphates

for magnesium   for sulphur
(Mg)   (S)

3 Where does a plant usually get minerals from?

4 Write down <u>one</u> way that you could give minerals to tomato plants grown in water rather than soil.

Some of the chemical elements that plants need.

■ What do tomato plants use minerals for?

Some parts of a plant need more of some minerals than other parts do.

5 Look at the drawing, then copy and complete the table.

Mineral	What it is important for
	growing leaves
phosphates	
potassium	
magnesium	

6 Explain, as fully as you can, why plants need chlorophyll to grow.

When a plant grows from a seed, it makes roots, stems and leaves first. Then it flowers and makes its fruit. This means that the amount of each mineral a plant needs changes as it grows.

The table on the right shows the amounts of some minerals in fertilisers specially made for young plants and for older plants.

7 (a) Write down the names of the two minerals which young plants need most.

(b) Explain your answer as fully as you can.

8 (a) As the plant gets older, it needs more of a particular mineral. Write down the name of this mineral.

(b) Which parts of the plant start to grow at this time?

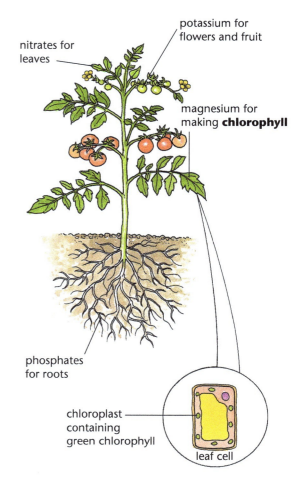

potassium for flowers and fruit

nitrates for leaves

magnesium for making **chlorophyll**

phosphates for roots

chloroplast containing green chlorophyll

leaf cell

Chlorophyll traps the light needed by a plant to make food in **photosynthesis**.

Mineral	Relative amount of minerals needed	
	by a young plant	by an older plant
nitrates	7	7
phosphates	7	7
potassium	5	7

WHAT YOU NEED TO REMEMBER (Copy and complete using the **key words**)

Growing tomato plants without soil

A plant has roots to _____ it in soil and for taking in _____ and _____.

The main minerals a plant needs are _____, phosphates and potassium.
A small amount of magnesium is important for making _____.
A plant needs chlorophyll for _____.

More about minerals needed by plants: C+ 3.10

3.4 Feed the world

The energy chain

The picture shows what happens to the energy stored in plants when an animal eats them.

1 Copy and complete the table to show what happens to the energy stored in each 3000 kJ of grass when a bullock eats it.

Energy (kJ)	What happens to it
1000	
2000	

So only one-third of the energy in the grass is useful to the animal for its life processes.

2 Some of this useful energy is stored in new cells in the animal as it grows. Write down how much energy this is.

3 Look at the diagram, then explain:

(a) why an animal that only eats other animals still depends on green plants for food;

(b) why all animals, including humans, depend on the Sun for food.

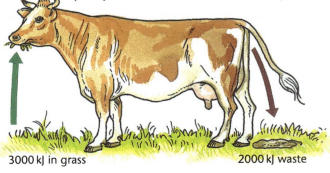

1000 kJ used for life processes:
- keeping warm;
- moving about;
- growing new cells (100 kJ is in the materials of the new cells).

3000 kJ in grass   2000 kJ waste

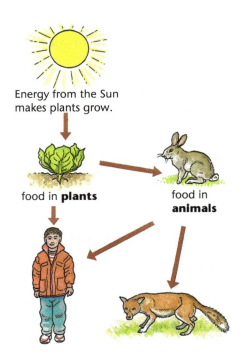

Energy from the Sun makes plants grow.

food in **plants**   food in **animals**

56

■ Getting enough energy

Experts think that a person needs at least 8400 kJ of energy from food every day.

Some of this energy is for keeping **warm**. People who live in cool countries need more than 8400 kJ because they use more energy for keeping warm.

4 Why can people in hot countries survive on less food than people in cold countries?

5 Look at the map of Africa. In how many countries does the average person get less than 8400 kJ per day?

In China, most people get enough to eat. However, people are changing their eating habits. People who can afford it are eating more meat and less rice than they used to. This change in diet means that China will soon not be able to grow enough food for everyone.

6 Look at the picture. Use it to help you to explain why meat for some will mean less food for others in China.

Not all the energy stored in plants can be used. A lot of energy is wasted every time food is eaten. This is why an area of land feeds more vegetarians than meat-eaters.

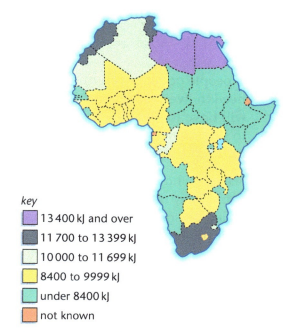

key

- 13 400 kJ and over
- 11 700 to 13 399 kJ
- 10 000 to 11 699 kJ
- 8400 to 9999 kJ
- under 8400 kJ
- not known

Energy value of food eaten (per person) per day in African countries.

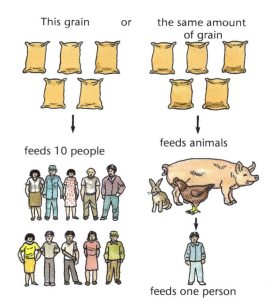

This grain   or   the same amount of grain

feeds 10 people   feeds animals

feeds one person

WHAT YOU NEED TO REMEMBER (Copy and complete using the **key words**)

Feed the world

Only green plants can make food.

We get our food from _____, or from _____ which ate plants.

Our food gives us the _____ and _____ we need to move, grow and keep _____.

More about food and energy: C+ 3.11

3.5 Food in Biosphere 2

If people go to live on another planet, they will need to live in a space station. The station will have to provide everything they need to stay alive. The only thing that they will get from outside is energy from the Sun.

Scientists have been testing how this might work. They did this in a special building called Biosphere 2 in the Arizona desert. Four men and four women were sealed inside the building for two years.

Biosphere 2.

To survive the scientists needed:

- food;
- oxygen;
- water;
- a way of getting rid of waste;
- energy for cooking etc.

1 The glass and steel building was like a greenhouse, so it let in lots of light. Explain, as fully as you can, why having a lot of light was important.

Over 4000 different plants and animals were also sealed inside. The animals and plants in each separate area of Biosphere 2 depend on their environment and on each other to survive. We say they form an <u>ecosystem</u>.

2 Look at the plan. Write a list of the ecosystems in Biosphere 2. Start your list with the rain forest.

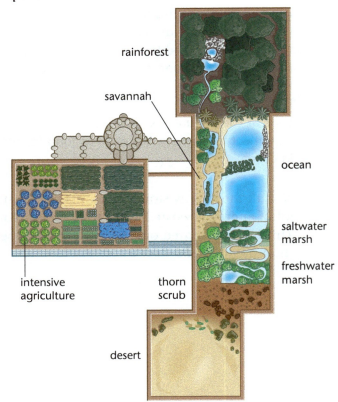

Biosphere 2 is a little bigger than two football pitches.

■ Food chains

A food **chain** shows how the food made by **plants** passes from one living thing to another. The diagram shows a few of the food chains in Biosphere 2.

3 What do they all start with?

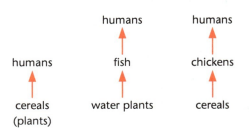

■ Food webs

Most plants and animals belong to more than one food chain. We can join food chains together to make a food **web**.

4 Copy any one of the food chains from the bottom of the opposite page. Then add the other chains to it to make a single diagram. You should write down the name of any plant or animal once only. Finally, write down the name of this diagram.

■ What happened to waste in Biosphere 2?

People and animals produce waste. In Biosphere 2, they had to do something with this waste and with the unwanted bits of plants. All these wastes contain water and minerals that plants need to grow. So these wastes were recycled.

5 Look at the diagram, then copy and complete the sentences.

Microbes break down _____ to carbon dioxide, water and minerals. Plants use waste carbon _____ for photosynthesis. Minerals are plant nutrients. So all the waste is used again. We say it is _____.

■ How did the humans get enough oxygen?

Green plants make oxygen at the same time as they make food.

6 Write down the name of the process in which plants make food and oxygen.

Unfortunately, the people and animals in Biosphere 2 didn't get enough oxygen or food. You can read more about this on C+ 3.12.

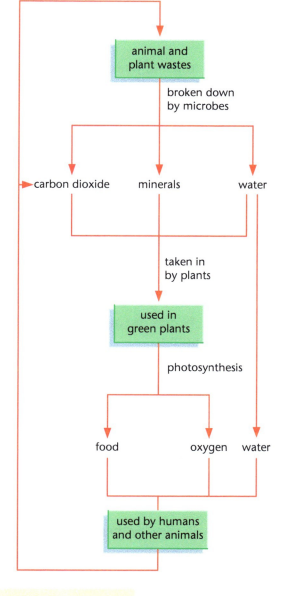

WHAT YOU NEED TO REMEMBER (Copy and complete using the **key words**)

Food in Biosphere 2

Food chains show how food made by _____ passes from one living thing to another. In a habitat, most plants and animals belong to more than one food _____, so we combine food chains to form a food _____.

More about Biosphere 2: C+ 3.12

3.6 Can great crested newts survive?

The picture shows a great crested newt. These animals are struggling to survive in Britain. To understand why, you need to know how they live.

Newts can live in water and on land. They are adapted for life on land and for life in ponds.

> **1** Look at the picture. Write down:
>
> **(a)** <u>two</u> ways newts are adapted to life on land;
>
> **(b)** <u>one</u> way newts are adapted to life in water.

■ The newt's year

Newts' bodies are at the same temperature as their surroundings.

Newts cannot keep their bodies warm enough to move about when the weather is cold. So, in winter, they find a sheltered, damp place to hibernate.

The chart shows what newts do at different times of the year.

> **2** During which months do newts hibernate?
>
> **3** When do they lay their eggs?

Newts' eggs have no shells. Like frogs' eggs, they hatch into tadpoles which can only live in water. Adult newts spend most of the year on land.

> **4** Copy and complete the following.
>
> A newt's habitat must provide:
>
> ■ a pond for the eggs to hatch into _____;
>
> ■ _____ and _____ places on land so it doesn't lose too much water from its skin;
>
> ■ small _____ to eat;
>
> ■ a safe place to _____ in the winter.

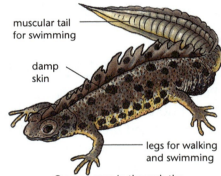

muscular tail for swimming
damp skin
legs for walking and swimming
Oxygen goes in through the newt's lungs and damp skin.

Great crested newt.

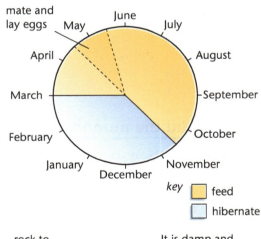

mate and lay eggs — May, June, July, August, September, October, November, December, January, February, March, April

key: feed / hibernate

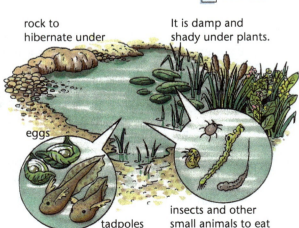

rock to hibernate under
It is damp and shady under plants.
eggs
tadpoles
insects and other small animals to eat

60

■ The first year of a newt's life

Tadpoles are adapted to get the oxygen they need from water. Adult newts are adapted to get oxygen from the air.

5 Copy and complete the table.

Stage of life	Takes oxygen from	Uses
tadpole	water	gills
adult		

■ Suitable habitats for newts

Newts need large ponds with plenty of plants around them.

Fifty years ago there were many large ponds. Most farms and villages had them.

Most of these ponds have now gone. The pictures show why.

6 Write down <u>two</u> reasons why there are now fewer ponds in the countryside than there were.

7 Adult newts can live on land. So how does having fewer ponds affect them?

Ponds are now more common in towns than in the country. Quite a lot of gardens have ponds, but they are usually too small for newts.

8 Write down <u>two</u> ways we can make new ponds suitable for newts.

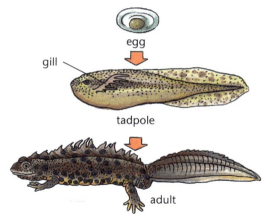

egg

gill

tadpole

adult

The front legs grow first, then the back legs. The gills then disappear. The newt now breathes air through its skin and lungs.

*This pond has gradually filled up with mud, a **natural** change.*

*Changes caused by **humans**, for example building houses or making fields bigger, also cause ponds to disappear.*

WHAT YOU NEED TO REMEMBER (Copy and complete using the **key words**)

Can great crested newts survive?

A habitat must provide the right _____ for an animal or plant to _____.

Animals and plants are adapted to their habitats, so changes may affect them. Some changes are _____, but _____ cause others.

More about disappearing species and survival: C+ 3.13 to 3.15

3.7 The American crayfish invasion

Crayfish live in rivers. Many people like to eat them. So people started crayfish farms. They kept the crayfish in large tanks of fresh water.

Fish-farmers in Britain didn't use the native British crayfish. Instead, they brought the American crayfish over here in 1976.

1 Look at the pictures. Write down one way the American crayfish differs from the native British crayfish.

■ Escaping American crayfish

Many American crayfish escaped from fish-farms and got into nearby rivers. They can survive out of water and move over land. So they soon reached more rivers.

The map shows how far they spread in only four years.

2 Explain, as fully as you can, how American crayfish were able to spread so quickly.

3 (a) No American crayfish reached Ireland. Write down one possible reason for this.

   (b) Describe one way they might reach Ireland in future.

■ How do American crayfish affect native crayfish?

American crayfish compete with each other and with the native crayfish for **food** and **space**.

4 Write down <u>one</u> way that American crayfish are better adapted to compete for these things than native crayfish.

5 (a) What do you think happens to the population of native crayfish when American crayfish reach a river?

   (b) Explain your answer.

American crayfish   native British crayfish

These crayfish belong to two different species. Both live in fresh water. They can't survive in sea water.

• before 1980
• 1980 onwards

Ireland

Distribution of American crayfish.

Why are American crayfish so successful?

American crayfish are bigger than native crayfish so they can kill and eat larger animals. They have more choice of food. If one kind of food runs out, they can eat something else.

Animals which kill and eat other animals are called **predators**. The animals they eat are their **prey**.

6 Look at the food web. Write down the names of <u>three</u> animals that American crayfish prey upon.

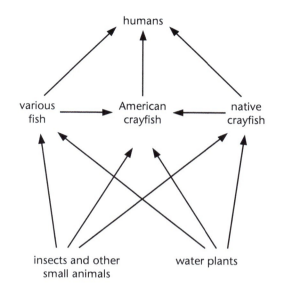

Simplified food web.

The number of each different kind of animal in a habitat is called its **population**. As the population of a predator increases, the population of its prey goes down.

American crayfish are now more common in some rivers than proper fish. This is because the American crayfish have eaten many fish and fish eggs. Only humans eat the crayfish.

As well as preying on fish and native crayfish, American crayfish carry a disease which kills native crayfish.

7 Write down <u>three</u> reasons why some scientists think that the native crayfish may die out (become extinct).

8 Explain why people interested in conservation of wildlife might agree with the message on the poster.

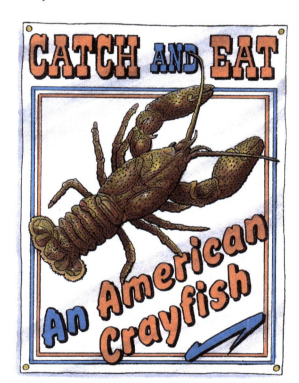

WHAT YOU NEED TO REMEMBER (Copy and complete using the **key words**)

The American crayfish invasion

Animals compete for _____ and _____. This affects the sizes of populations.

Predation also affects _____ size.
A big population of _____ decreases the population of _____.

More about disappearing species and survival: C+ 3.13 to 3.15

3.8 Stay-at-homes and migrants

Ptarmigans need to be camouflaged against different backgrounds.

Many birds live in one place all the year round. Some grow different-coloured feathers in winter and summer. One example is the ptarmigan (say 'tarmigan'; the 'p' is silent).

1 (a) Write down <u>one</u> difference between the ptarmigan's feathers in winter and in summer.

(b) Explain <u>one</u> advantage of the change.

Robins live in Britain all year round too. They also have winter and summer feathers, but they are the same colour.

Robin.

Redstart.

■ Greek robins migrate

Robins and redstarts are two different birds but Aristotle, in ancient Greece, thought that they were the same. He thought that they changed with the **seasons**. The photographs show what he observed.

2 In what <u>two</u> ways are robins and redstarts alike?

3 Why did Aristotle think robins changed?

4 Write down <u>one</u> feature which might make you think that they were different kinds or species of birds.

We know now that robins and redstarts are two different kinds of bird. Both **migrate** to find conditions which suit them.

5 Look at the map. Why do you think:

(a) robins leave Russia for the winter?

(b) redstarts leave Africa for the summer?

Aristotle was well-known for his careful observations, but even he made a mistake. This shows how important it is to observe accurately.

Why Aristotle was confused.

WHAT YOU NEED TO REMEMBER (Copy and complete using the **key words**)

Stay-at-homes and migrants

Some animals change with the _____.

Others _____ to places where conditions are suitable.

CORE +
Follows on from: 3.2

3.9 More discoveries about photosynthesis

In 1880 a biologist called Engelmann wanted to find out more about photosynthesis. He knew that it happened inside some plant cells, but he wanted to know exactly where in the cell it happened.

He knew two other things:

- plants make oxygen during photosynthesis;
- bacteria always move towards oxygen.

1 Look at the diagram that shows Engelmann's results. Which part of the cell:

(a) did the bacteria move to?

(b) must be giving out oxygen?

(c) must be carrying out photosynthesis?

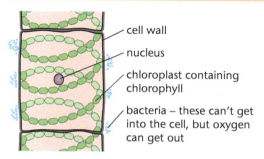

REMEMBER

sunlight   carbon dioxide

Plants make food and grow.

water   oxygen

The **chlorophyll** in the chloroplasts traps the light energy needed for photosynthesis.

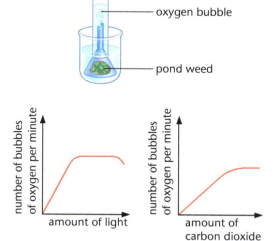

cell wall

nucleus

chloroplast containing chlorophyll

bacteria – these can't get into the cell, but oxygen can get out

Engelmann saw that bacteria collected near the chloroplasts.

oxygen bubble

pond weed

■ Measuring the rate of photosynthesis

A plant makes food faster at some times than others. If a plant makes food more quickly, it will also give off oxygen more quickly. So we can measure the rate of photosynthesis of pond weed by counting the bubbles of oxygen that it gives off each minute.

2 The graphs show some results. Write down what happens to the rate of photosynthesis when:

(a) the amount of light increases;

(b) the carbon dioxide concentration increases.

number of bubbles of oxygen per minute

amount of light

number of bubbles of oxygen per minute

amount of carbon dioxide

WHAT YOU NEED TO REMEMBER (Copy and complete using the **key words**)

More discoveries about photosynthesis

The word equation for photosynthesis is:

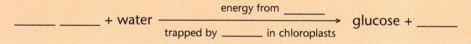

_____ _____ + water $\xrightarrow[\text{trapped by \_\_\_\_\_ in chloroplasts}]{\text{energy from \_\_\_\_\_}}$ glucose + _____

3.10 Growing enough food

If people have no money to buy food, they only eat what they can grow. If the amount of a crop they harvest is smaller than it should be, we say that the **yield** is poor.

1 The children in the photograph don't get enough to eat. Write down at least <u>two</u> effects of too little food on these children.

Sometimes the yield of a crop is poor because the plants didn't get enough water. At other times it is poor because there weren't enough **minerals** in the soil the plants grew in.

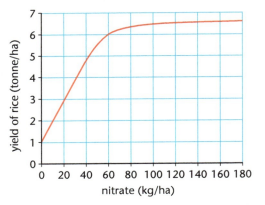

2 What do we mean when we say the yield of a crop is poor?

3 Write down <u>two</u> things which affect the yield of a crop.

4 Look at the graph. Then describe, as fully as you can, the effect of nitrate on the yield of rice.

5 (a) What is the yield at 60 kg/ha of nitrate?

(b) A farmer decided to use no more than 60 kg/ha of fertiliser. Explain why this is a sensible decision.

Artificial **fertilisers** like ammonium nitrate are made in factories. **Natural** fertilisers come from animals or plants. Natural fertilisers also contain nitrates.

6 Why do farmers and gardeners add fertilisers to soil?

7 Write down:

(a) <u>two</u> differences between natural and artificial fertilisers;

(b) the names of <u>three</u> natural fertilisers.

artificial fertilisers   natural fertilisers

manure

compost   seaweed

We know exactly how much of each mineral artificial fertilisers contain.

Natural fertilisers contain variable amounts of various minerals.

WHAT YOU NEED TO REMEMBER (Copy and complete using the **key words**)

Growing enough food

The amount of water and minerals a crop receives affects its _____.
When we add fertilisers to soil, we add _____.
Some _____ are artificial, others are _____.

3.11 Plants and animals respire

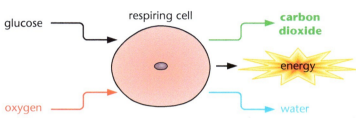

Respiration.

Baljit and Craig did experiments to find out if living plants and animals make carbon dioxide.

1 Baljit said that they needed to keep the plant in the dark. Explain why she was correct.

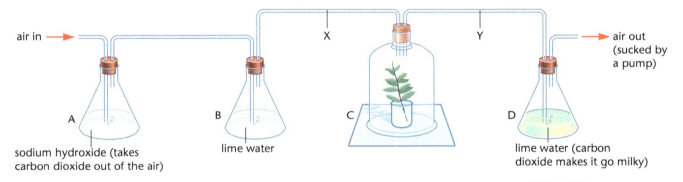

They covered the bell jar (C) with black plastic and turned on the pump. The table shows what happened.

2 (a) How do you know that the air at X contains no carbon dioxide?

(b) How do you know that the air at Y contains carbon dioxide?

(c) Where must the carbon dioxide at Y have come from?

After this experiment, Craig took the plant out of bell jar C and put a mouse inside instead.

3 Copy the table of results and complete it for the mouse experiment.

	Lime water after 10 minutes	
Experiment	Flask B	Flask D
1 Plant in the dark	clear	milky
2 Mouse		

WHAT YOU NEED TO REMEMBER (Copy and complete using the **key words**)

Plants and animals respire

The breakdown of food to release energy is called _____.
Respiration which uses _____ is called aerobic respiration.

glucose + oxygen ⟶ _____ _____ + water + energy

3.12 Problems of Biosphere 2

Plants produce food and oxygen. Scientists thought that the plants in Biosphere 2 would produce all the food and oxygen that the animals, including the humans, needed.

The humans were at the top of all the food chains in Biosphere 2. They ate lots of different foods, but the diagram shows just one of the food chains.

As you go along this food chain, the **number** of plants or animals gets smaller at each stage. We can show this in a different diagram. It is pyramid-shaped, so we call it a **pyramid** of numbers.

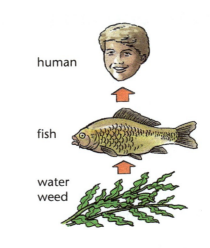

1 Look at the food chain and pyramid of numbers that start with water weed.

In your own words describe the pyramid to compare the number of each organism in each level.

2 Draw a pyramid of numbers for the food chain:

grass → rabbits → humans

3 Look at the two pyramids which start with wheat. Which one feeds most people?

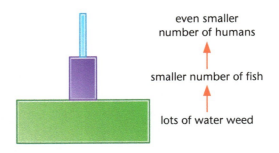

Sadly, the plants in Biosphere 2 didn't produce enough food or oxygen. The people were hungry and scientists had to pump extra oxygen in.

4 One scientist thinks that they should send only six people into Biosphere 2 next time.
Another thinks that the people in Biosphere 2 should eat more plants and less meat.
Explain why each of these ideas could work.

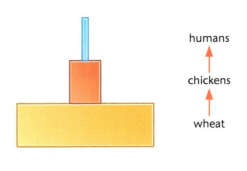

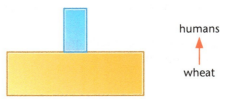

WHAT YOU NEED TO REMEMBER (Copy and complete using the **key words**)

Problems of Biosphere 2

We can show the _____ of plants and animals at each level in a food chain as a _____ of numbers.

3.13 Disappearing species

Each species of plant or animal is adapted to survive in its habitat. If we **pollute** or destroy a habitat, plants and animals can no longer live there.

Hedges provide shelter and food, so they are habitats for many plants and animals. When a farmer **destroyed** the hedges to make this big field, birds and other animals had to **move out**.

1 Write down <u>two</u> reasons why fewer birds lived in this field after the hedges were taken out.

The United Nations Environment Programme (UNEP) reports that thousands of species will die out (become extinct) in the next few years because humans have destroyed their habitats.

2 Look at the chart and table, then write down:

  (a) the percentage of species of birds likely to die out in the next few years;

  (b) the number of species of all kinds of animals in immediate danger of extinction;

  (c) the total number of species of animals and plants which could die out soon if we don't take more care with their habitats.

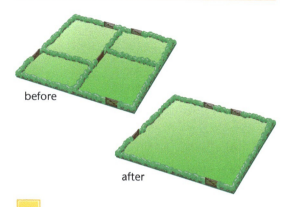
before

after

species in danger of extinction *now*

	Number of species in serious danger now	Number of species likely to be in danger soon
vertebrates	602	2719
invertebrates	582	2647
plants	3632	26 106

3 Look at the photographs. Write a few sentences about what you think happened.

This is what happens when we pollute the environment with crude oil.

3.14 Survival

Only a few of the eggs in this frogspawn will survive long enough to grow into frogs. So only a few survive long enough to breed themselves.

400 eggs → 300 tadpoles → 20 young frogs → 1 or 2 adult frogs

1 (a) About how many eggs does a frog lay each spring?

(b) About how many grow into adult frogs?

2 Write down <u>two</u> reasons why most tadpoles die.

Rules for tadpole survival

(1) Make sure you get plenty of food. You will have to compete for it with other tadpoles.

•

(2) Don't let a predator catch and eat you. You have to watch out for them and be able to hide or escape.

•

Tadpoles aren't all the same. They vary in certain ways. The diagrams show some of the characteristics that can vary.

3 (a) Draw a tadpole. Label it with <u>three</u> characteristics which help it to survive.

(b) Choose <u>one</u> characteristic and explain <u>two</u> ways it helps the tadpole to survive.

Some characteristics are passed on to the tadpole in the **genes** from the parent frogs. We say they are **inherited**. If this tadpole is better **suited** to its environment than other tadpoles, it is more likely to survive and **breed**. It will pass on its genes and its characteristics to its young.

4 What will happen to a tadpole's genes if it is not as well suited to its environment as other tadpoles?

Some tadpoles grow faster than others.

Some tadpoles have stronger tails and can swim faster.

Some tadpoles have better eyesight than others.

WHAT YOU NEED TO REMEMBER (Copy and complete using the **key words**)

Survival

Animals and plants vary. Some variation is _____.
Animals and plants which inherit characteristics most _____ to their environments are more likely than others to survive, _____ and pass on their _____.

3.15 A problem with pesticides

Pests are unwanted animals and plants. We use pesticides to kill them.

Pesticides are poisonous. We say they are **toxic**.

Pesticides get everywhere, even to the Antarctic. Some break down quickly. Others last for many years in cells and in the environment. The ones which last longest, like DDT, are now banned in most countries.

1 Use the information on the bar chart to help you to complete the following.

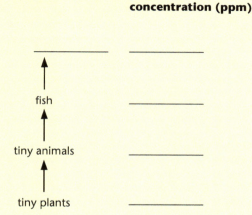

food chain	pesticide concentration (ppm)
_____	_____
fish	_____
tiny animals	_____
tiny plants	_____

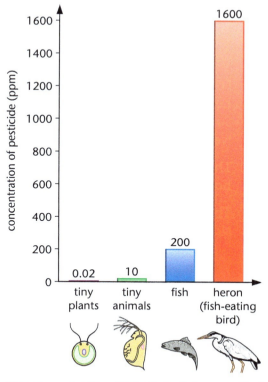

*The amount of pesticide there is in a particular amount of a plant or animal is called the **concentration**. We measure the concentration of pesticides in parts per million (ppm).*

2 Copy and complete the sentences.

The higher an animal is in a food _____, the _____ pesticides it contains.

The pesticide concentration is _____ times greater in the fish than in the tiny animals, and _____ times greater in the herons than the fish.

3 The drawing shows why fish can have such a high concentration of pesticides in their bodies. Draw a similar diagram to show why fish-eating birds can have even more pesticides in their bodies.

Thousands of tiny animals. Each one has a dose of pesticide.

are eaten by

One fish gets thousands of doses of pesticide every day.

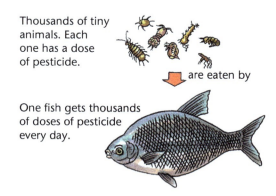

WHAT YOU NEED TO REMEMBER (Copy and complete using the **key words**)

A problem with pesticides

We use pesticides to kill _____. Pesticides are poisonous or _____.

Pesticides build up in food chains. So animals which are near the top of a food chain contain a higher _____ of pesticides than those nearer the bottom of a chain.

1.1 Using everyday materials

Before we make anything, we should think about what it has to do.

For example, the roof of a house should not be too heavy and should keep out the wind and the rain. So we must cover it with a material that is light in weight, fairly strong and waterproof.

These are the **properties** that the material must have.

The roof of the house in the picture is covered with slates.

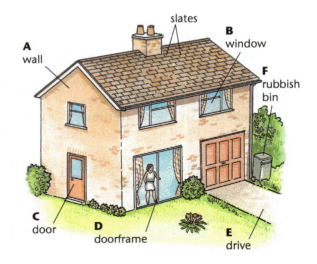

1 What properties do you think slate has?

Other materials used to build a house

Different **materials** have different properties. So we can use them for different **jobs**.

We have to match the properties of the material with the job it has to do.

2 Match each labelled part of the house with a material you could make it from.

Choose from the materials in the table. In some cases there is more than one material you could use. Set out your answers like this:

A wall – brick

3 Now write <u>one</u> sentence saying why you chose each material for each part of the house. Write your sentences like this:

'We can make walls from <u>bricks</u> because <u>they are hard</u>, <u>strong and weatherproof</u>.'

Material	Properties
wood	strong but easily cut into shape
glass	transparent
brick	hard, strong and weatherproof
concrete	can be mixed and poured but sets hard
aluminium	easily cut into shape, does not corrode or rot
plastic	light, strong, tough, and waterproof, does not rot

■ Different materials for different situations

A car is made from many different materials. Each material has the right properties for the job it has to do.

4 (a) Write down the materials that are used to make the parts of the car that are labelled on the picture. Choose from:

steel   plastic   rubber   glass

(b) In each case, write down one property of the material that makes it suitable for its job.

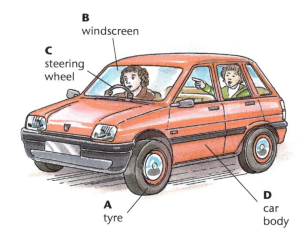

B windscreen
C steering wheel
A tyre
D car body

■ Comparing cars and houses

Cars and houses must let in light and also keep out the rain. But cars must be able to move about and we want houses to last a very long time.

5 Copy and complete these sentences using the properties in the box.

The windows of a house and the windscreen of a car must be _____ and _____.
But the windscreen of a car must also be _____.

The walls of a house and the body of a car must both be _____ and _____. But the body of the car must not be too _____.

Some properties of materials
heavy
transparent
weatherproof
strong
shatter-resistant

WHAT YOU NEED TO REMEMBER (Copy and complete using the **key words**)

Using everyday materials

We make things from _____.

We use different materials to do different _____.
This is because they have different _____.

More about materials: C+ 1.9, 1.10

1.2 Metals and non-metals

There are more different metallic elements than non-metallic elements. But the Earth's crust is made mainly of elements that are non-metals. Look at the pie chart.

1 **(a)** Which are the two most common elements in the Earth's crust?

(b) Are these two elements metals or non-metals?

(c) What fraction of the Earth's crust is made up of metallic elements? Is it $\frac{1}{4}$, $\frac{1}{3}$, $\frac{1}{2}$ or $\frac{3}{4}$?

■ Metal or non-metal?

We can decide whether an element is a metal or a non-metal by looking at its properties.

DO YOU REMEMBER? from *Core Science 1*

Metals are usually:
■ solid at ordinary temperatures;
■ shiny;
■ hard;
■ heavy;
■ strong;
■ tough;
■ easily shaped;
■ conductors of thermal energy;
■ conductors of **electricity**.

Non-metals:
■ may be solid, liquid or gas at ordinary temperatures;
■ do not **conduct** heat (thermal energy);
■ do not usually conduct electricity.
Non-metal solids are brittle.

2 For each of the three elements in the drawings say whether the element is a metal or a non-metal. Give a reason for your choice.

(a) chlorine   **(b)** gold   **(c)** iodine

DO YOU REMEMBER?
from *Core Science 1*

Elements are simple substances. All other substances are made from elements joined together in different ways. In nature, there are about 90 different elements.

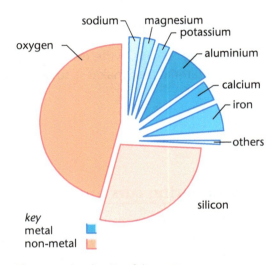

Elements in the Earth's crust.

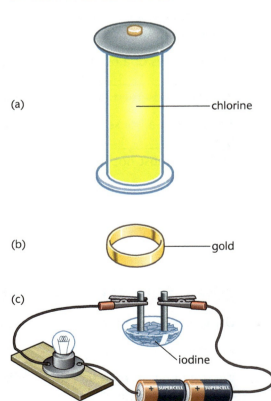

■ Why metals are so useful

Metals have many useful properties. So we use them to make many things.

3 Look at the drawings of the nail and the electrical cable. Write down <u>two</u> properties of steel and <u>two</u> properties of copper which make them suitable for these jobs.

[The 'Do you remember?' box on the opposite page may help you.]

The insides of wires are made of copper.

A nail is made of steel.

■ Making metals more useful

We can mix metals together to get the properties we want. We call a mixture of metals an <u>alloy</u>.

4 (a) What two elements are mixed to make bronze?

(b) Why do you think the helmet was made from bronze rather than copper?

This bronze helmet was made from copper mixed with a little tin to give a much harder metal.

■ Carbon – a very useful non-metal

There are two forms of the element carbon: diamond and graphite. While diamonds are expensive, graphite is cheap.

5 (a) Why are diamonds used as tips for some drills?

(b) Why is graphite used in pencils?

6 Which do you think is more common, diamond or graphite? Give a reason for your answer.

Diamond is the hardest natural substance.

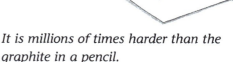

It is millions of times harder than the graphite in a pencil.

WHAT YOU NEED TO REMEMBER (Copy and complete using the **key words**)

Metals and non-metals

Most of the elements are _____.

All metals are good conductors of heat and _____, but most non-metals do not _____ heat or electricity.

Elements which are gases at room temperature are all _____.

1.3 Solids, liquids and gases

There are millions of different materials. But we can put them all into a small number of groups by looking at their properties.

One way of doing this is to say whether something is a <u>solid</u>, a <u>liquid</u> or a <u>gas</u>. These are called the <u>three states of matter</u>.

1 Look at the picture. Then write down the name of <u>one</u> solid, <u>one</u> liquid and <u>one</u> gas.

■ **Solids**

Solids stay the same <u>shape</u>.

Unless it gets hotter or colder, a solid also stays the same size. It takes up the same amount of space. We say that its **volume** stays the same.

2 The diamonds in the photograph have been part of the Crown Jewels for about 100 years. The hooks are fixed on to hold the diamonds in place. Explain why they are as easy to put in place now as they were when they were first made.

These diamonds were cut from the largest diamond ever found. (They are shown smaller than they are in real life.)

■ **Liquids**

You can pour a liquid from one container to another. So liquids do <u>not</u> have a **shape** of their own. They fill up the container from the bottom and take on its shape.

But liquids do stay the same volume unless they get hotter or colder.

3 (a) Describe how the shape of the liquid changes when it is poured into the different containers shown in the drawing. Use the words 'ball-shaped', 'tube-shaped', and 'cubic'.

   (b) What happens to the volume of the liquid as it is poured into the different containers?

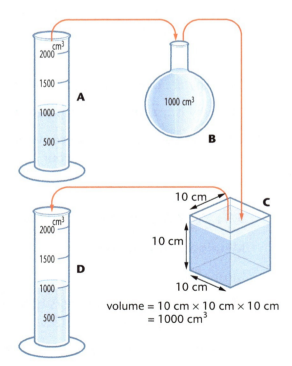

■ Gases

Like a liquid, a gas does not have its own shape. But a gas is different from a liquid because it spreads out into all the **space** in the container.

4 Look at the diagrams. How do we know that the brown gas spreads out to fill all the space when the tap is opened?

tap closed   tap open

gas   vacuum
        (no gas or air
        in flask)

■ Other ways of telling them apart

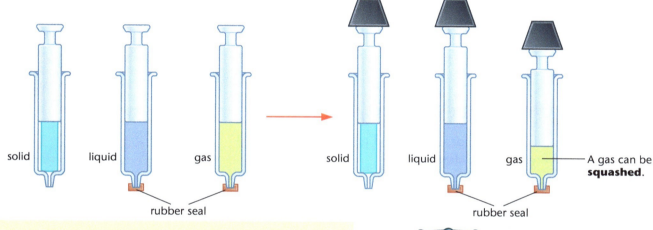

solid   liquid   gas   solid   liquid   gas — A gas can be **squashed**.

rubber seal   rubber seal

5 Look at the drawings.

(a) Write down another way in which a gas is different from a solid or a liquid.

(b) Look at the gas and water taps. Write down <u>one</u> way in which a gas and a liquid are alike but different from a solid.

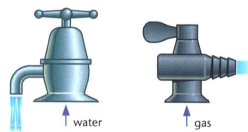

water   gas

Liquids and gases can **flow**.

1.4 Making models of matter

A model is similar to the real thing in some ways. But it is different in other ways.

In science, we use models to help us understand how things are.

1 Look at the pictures.

(a) Write down <u>one</u> way that the model aircraft is the same as the real aircraft.

(b) Write down <u>two</u> differences between the model and the real one.

DO YOU REMEMBER? from *Core Science 1*

Scientists think that solids, liquids and gases are all made of very tiny **particles**.

We can make models of solids and liquids. We do this using particles which are big enough to see.

This scale model of Concorde:
- *is exactly the same shape;*
- *is 100 times shorter;*
- *weighs a million times less.*

■ A model of a solid

The particles in a solid are held together by strong <u>forces</u>. The particles cannot change places. So solids stay the same **shape** and you can't squash them into a smaller space.

2 Look at the model of the solid.

(a) Write down <u>two</u> ways that the model is similar to a real solid.

(b) Write down <u>two</u> differences between the model and a real solid.

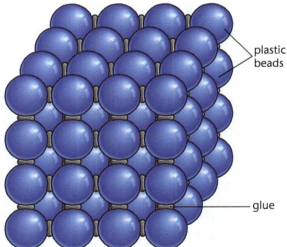

plastic beads

glue

A model of a solid made from plastic beads and glue. The glue holds the beads in position. The beads are billions of times bigger than the particles in a real solid.

A model of a liquid

The particles of a liquid are close together but they can **move** around each other. That means a liquid can flow.

3 **(a)** What happens to the plastic beads in the model liquid when you pour them into the funnel?

(b) Why does this happen?

4 Why can't you pour a solid?

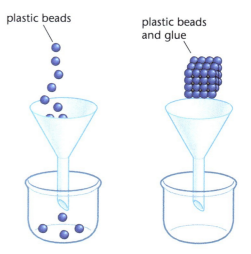

plastic beads

plastic beads and glue

A model of a liquid.   Can you pour a solid?

A model of a gas

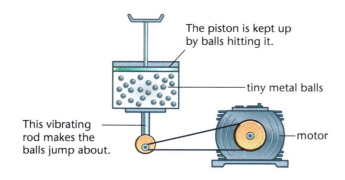

The piston is kept up by balls hitting it.

tiny metal balls

This vibrating rod makes the balls jump about.

motor

A model of a gas.

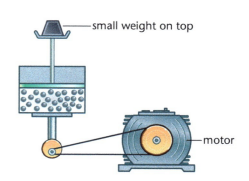

small weight on top

motor

A gas is made of tiny particles flying about in all directions.

There is lots of **space** in a gas so you can squash it into a smaller volume.

The diagrams show a model of what a gas is like.

5 **(a)** Write down <u>two</u> ways that the model is like a real gas.

(b) Write down <u>two</u> differences between the model gas and a real gas.

WHAT YOU NEED TO REMEMBER (Copy and complete using the **key words**)

Making models of matter

Solids have their own _____ because the particles cannot move around.
Liquids and gases flow because their particles can _____ around each other.

You cannot squash liquids and solids easily because there is no space between their _____.
You can squash a gas because there is _____ between the particles.

More about models of matter: C+ 1.11 to 1.15

1.5 Getting warmer, getting colder

Solids and liquids stay the same volume if we don't let them heat up or cool down.

If we heat them up they get bigger. We say they **expand**. If we cool them down they get smaller. We say they **contract**.

The diagrams show an experiment with a metal bar.

1 Why do you need the roller and pointer in this experiment?

2 What causes the pointer to move:

(a) clockwise?

(b) anti-clockwise?

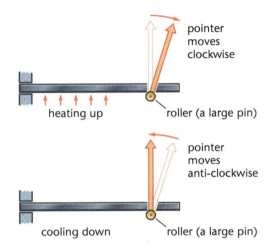

The length of the metal bar doesn't change very much. The roller and pointer magnify the change so you can see it.

■ Avoiding a problem with expansion

This motorway bridge rests on metal rollers. When the bridge sections expand on hot days, the rollers allow them to move.

3 **(a)** Why is a gap left between the sections?

(b) What happens to the gap on cold days?

■ Using expansion and contraction

When you look at old houses, you sometimes see a metal plate and a big nut and bolt sticking out of the wall. The diagram shows why they are there.

4 Look at the pictures. The walls on the old house are bending. Explain how we can use a tie rod to make them straight again. Use the words <u>expansion</u> and <u>contraction</u> in your answer.

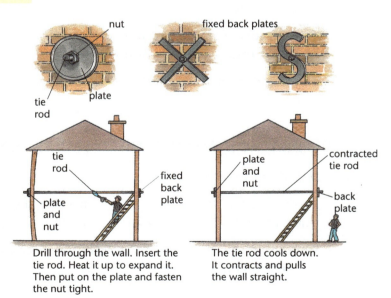

Drill through the wall. Insert the tie rod. Heat it up to expand it. Then put on the plate and fasten the nut tight.

The tie rod cools down. It contracts and pulls the wall straight.

Before   *After*

Expansion and contraction of liquids

If you heat up a liquid, such as mercury, it expands. If you cool down a liquid, it contracts.

5 Write down the name of a piece of equipment that uses these changes.

6 Room temperature is usually about 20°C. What happens to the mercury in a thermometer:

   (a) when the temperature falls to 0°C?

   (b) when the temperature rises to 40°C?

The hot water system in your home has an expansion pipe. The diagram shows where this is.

7 What is the expansion pipe for?

Heating up a gas

A gas such as air will try to expand when it is heated up.

8 **(a)** What is the volume of air in the syringe at 20°C?

   (b) What is the volume of the same air at 100°C?

   (c) What is the increase in volume?

We can stop the air expanding by pushing on the piston of the syringe.

9 Copy and complete this sentence.

To stop a gas from _____ when it is heated, you must increase the _____.

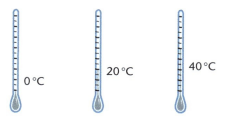

A mercury-in-glass thermometer.

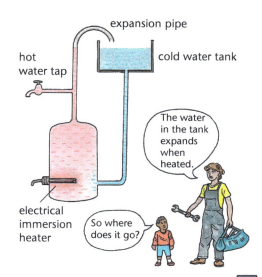

expansion pipe

cold water tank

hot water tap

The water in the tank expands when heated.

electrical immersion heater

So where does it go?

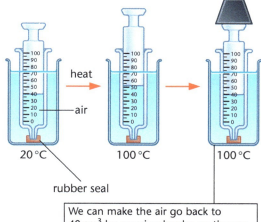

heat

air

20°C   100°C   100°C

rubber seal

We can make the air go back to 40 cm³ by pressing harder on the gas. We say that we increase the **pressure**.

WHAT YOU NEED TO REMEMBER (Copy and complete using the **key words**)

Getting warmer, getting colder

When we heat solids, liquids or gases, they normally _____.

When solids, liquids and gases cool down, they normally _____.

If we stop a gas expanding when it gets hot, we get an increase in _____.

More about expansion: C+ 1.16

1.6 Mixtures

Sometimes the different things in a mixture are big enough to see. For example, you can see the different things in muesli.

	Expensive muesli	Cheap muesli
nuts	30%	5%
dried fruit	35%	25%
oats	30%	55%
sugar	5%	15%

1 Look at the table. Then copy and complete the sentences.

Cheap muesli contains more _____ and _____ than expensive muesli.

Expensive muesli contains more _____ and _____ than cheap muesli.

A mixture contains different amounts of the things that are mixed. We say that we can mix them in different **proportions**.

■ **Mixing metals**

We often mix metals together to get the properties we want. Look at the diagrams.

2 (a) What metal is gold mixed with?

(b) Why is gold mixed with this metal?

You can mix gold with different amounts of silver.

3 (a) How much silver is there in 22 carat gold?

(b) Why is 9 carat gold cheaper than 22 carat gold?

■ **Mixing a solid and a liquid**

Tipp-Ex is a mixture of a white solid and a liquid. When you use it, the liquid evaporates. The white solid is left behind on the paper.

4 Look at the diagram.

(a) What happens to the Tipp-Ex if you leave it for a while?

(b) Why must you shake the Tipp-Ex before you use it?

Gold is a very soft metal. We mix it with silver to make it hard.

22 carat gold contains only a small amount of silver (less than 10%).

9 carat gold contains a lot of silver (more than 60%). This makes it cheaper.

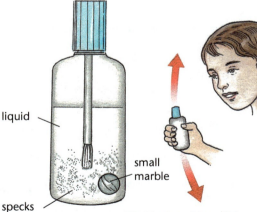

liquid

small marble

specks of white solid

The white solid settles to the bottom.

To mix the white solid and the liquid you must shake the the bottle. The marble helps to mix them properly.

Dissolving a solid in a liquid

The specks in Tipp-Ex are big enough to scatter white light. So the Tipp-Ex looks white.

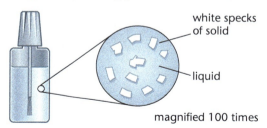

white specks
of solid

liquid

magnified 100 times

But when you mix glucose and water, the glucose seems to disappear. We say that it <u>dissolves</u>.

5 Look at the diagram. Then copy and complete the sentences.

When glucose dissolves in water, glucose _____ are mixed up with water _____.
The glucose seems to disappear because the molecules are too _____ to scatter white light.

6 The glucose solution is made from 1 spoonful of glucose in 200 cm³ of water. Write down <u>two</u> ways that you could you make a weaker glucose solution. (We call a weaker solution 'more dilute'.)

A mixture of gases

Air is also a **mixture**. The diagram shows the two main gases in air.

7 What are the main gases in the air?

8 Copy and complete the sentence.

In air there are about 4 molecules of _____ for every molecule of _____.

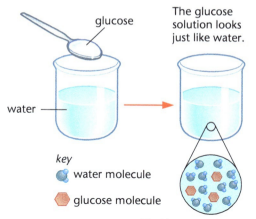

glucose

The glucose solution looks just like water.

water

key
water molecule
glucose molecule

magnified by more than a billion times

*Water and glucose are both made of **particles** (molecules). These molecules are too small to see.*
When glucose dissolves in water, the glucose molecules are mixed up with the water molecules.

Air is a mixture of gases.

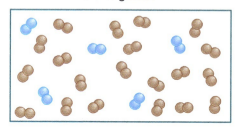

key
molecules of oxygen
molecules of nitrogen

The mixture also contains smaller amounts of argon and carbon dioxide.

WHAT YOU NEED TO REMEMBER (Copy and complete using the **key words**)

Mixtures

You can mix things together in different amounts. We say that they can be mixed in different _____.

When you dissolve a solid in a liquid, the _____ of the solid and the liquid get mixed together.

Air is a _____ of gases.

1.7 Making pure white sugar

We don't find pure white sugar in the world around us. Sugar is **mixed** up with lots of other things in plants such as sugar cane.

Sugar cane is a special kind of grass. It grows in countries where the weather is hot and damp. Children in these countries love chewing sugar cane because it's got so much sugar in it. But it's also very woody, like bamboo. You certainly wouldn't like sugar cane splinters sprinkled on top of your breakfast cereal!

Harvesting sugar cane in Cuba.

■ The refining of sugar

The diagrams show how you might **separate** sugar from sugar cane in your school laboratory.

1 Write the following sentences in a sensible order. The first one is already in place.

   Crush the sugar cane.

   ■ Cool the evaporated juice so that the sugar forms crystals.
   ■ Mix the crushed sugar cane with water.
   ■ Separate the sugar crystals from the molasses.
   ■ Gently evaporate most of the water from the juice.
   ■ Purify the sugar crystals by re-dissolving in water and re-crystallising.
   ■ Filter off the wooden bits of cane from the juice.

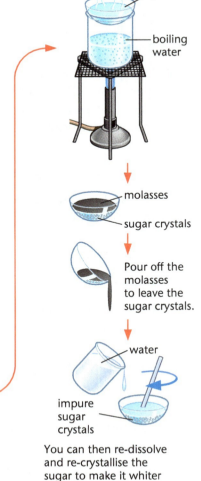

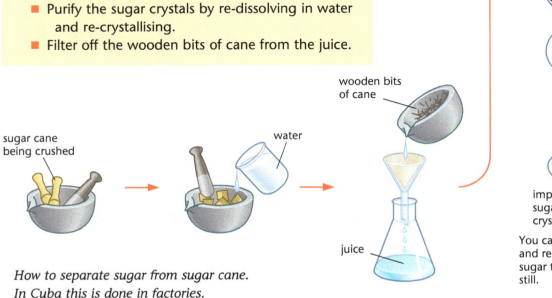

How to separate sugar from sugar cane. In Cuba this is done in factories.

How much sugar dissolves in water?

A lot of sugar will dissolve in a small amount of water. Exactly how much sugar **dissolves** depends upon two things.

■ The **more** water we use, then the more sugar dissolves. The graph shows how much sugar dissolves in 100 grams of water.

■ The **hotter** the water, the more sugar dissolves. For example, at 20°C, 205 g of sugar dissolves in 100 g of water.

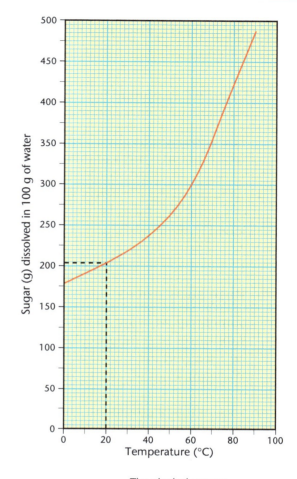

2 (a) How much sugar dissolves in 100 g of water at 0°C?

(b) How much sugar dissolves in 100 g of water at 80°C?

(c) How much sugar would dissolve in 300 g of water at 20°C?

3 Copy and complete the sentences.

The solubility of sugar is the number of _____ of sugar which will dissolve in 100 g of _____.

As the temperature of the water rises, the solubility of sugar _____.

Using the molasses

Molasses is a black sticky liquid. We sometimes call it black treacle.

Some of the molasses is fermented with yeast. This makes a weak solution of alcohol. The diagram shows how this is made into a stronger drink called rum. This works because alcohol boils off at a lower temperature than water. This process is called <u>fractional distillation</u>.

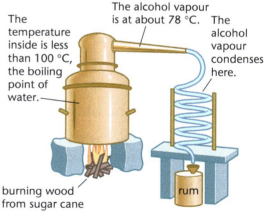

The temperature inside is less than 100 °C, the boiling point of water.

The alcohol vapour is at about 78 °C. The alcohol vapour condenses here.

burning wood from sugar cane

rum

Making rum.

WHAT YOU NEED TO REMEMBER (Copy and complete using the **key words**)

Making pure white sugar

We get sugar from plants such as sugar cane. The sugar is _____ up with many other things. To get pure white sugar, we need to _____ it from these other things. We can do this because sugar _____ in water.

We can make more sugar dissolve by using _____ water, or _____ water.

1.8 Separating mixtures

In the world around us, we often find many different substances all mixed up together.

The photographs show some examples of things which are **mixtures** of different substances.

1 Write down <u>three</u> different things that are mixtures of substances. Try to list some of the substances found in these mixtures.

air

rocks and soil

sea

Mixtures in the world around us.

Pure substances

Sometimes we want to **separate** the different substances in a mixture. We want each substance by itself and not mixed with anything else. We want what we call **pure** substances.

In hot dry countries, people get pure water from sea-water.

2 Look at the photographs. Then copy and complete the table.

Pure substance	What you could get it from
oxygen	
	sea-water

Pure oxygen is used in hospitals and industry. We get pure oxygen from the air.

The case of the blackcurrant jelly

Sometimes we just want to find out what substances are in a mixture.

Paula loves jelly but she has to be very careful. She is allergic to E122, a dye used to colour many food items.

The diagram shows how a food scientist could test the colour in a jelly Paula wants to eat.

3 Should Paula eat the jelly? Explain your answer.

4 What do we call this process for separating colours?

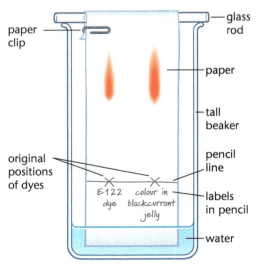

paper clip — glass rod

paper

tall beaker

original positions of dyes

pencil line

E122 dye — colour in blackcurrant jelly

labels in pencil

water

Separating colours like this is called <u>chromatography</u>.

■ How to separate substances

To separate a mixture of substances, we need to know the **properties** of the different substances.

A factory floor is swept at the end of each day. The sweepings contains sawdust, iron filings, copper filings and salt.

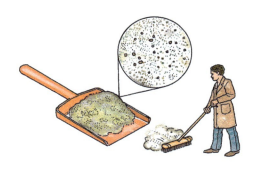

5 Look at the table of properties. Then write down how you would use apparatus in the drawings:

    (a) to separate the iron filings from the sweepings;

    (b) to separate the sawdust and then the sand;

    (c) to separate the salt and water.

Substance	Property
salt	dissolves in water
sand	does not dissolve in water
iron	attracted to a magnet
pure water	boils at 100°C
sawdust	floats on water

Use these properties as clues to separate the mixture of sweepings.

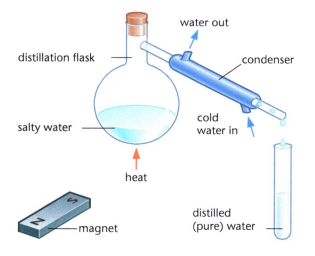

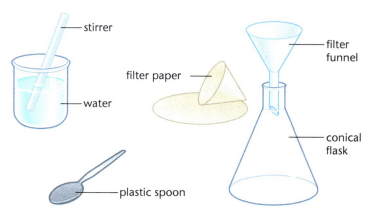

Scientists also want pure substances. They can then find out how they react to make new substances.

6 Salt water boils at a higher temperature than pure water. How would a scientist know that the distilled water was pure?

WHAT YOU NEED TO REMEMBER (Copy and complete using the **key words**)

Separating mixtures

Most substances in the world around us are parts of _____.

A substance that is not mixed up with other substances is called a _____ substance.

To get a pure substance, we need to _____ it from other substances.
We can do this because different substances have different _____.

1.9 What is density?

REMEMBER

We choose materials that have the right properties for the jobs we want them to do.

An important property of a material is how <u>dense</u> it is.

1 (a) Look at the balance in the drawing. What is the mass of 1 cm^3 of steel?

(b) Look at the bowl of water. What mass of water is there in the bowl?

(c) Which has the more mass – the bowl of water or the spoon?

(d) Which has the more mass – 1 cm^3 of water or 1 cm^3 of steel?

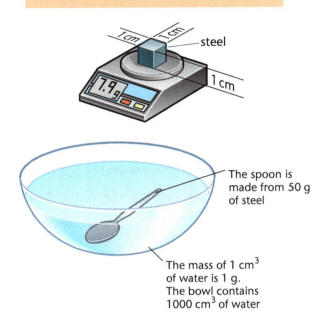

The spoon is made from 50 g of steel

The mass of 1 cm^3 of water is 1 g.
The bowl contains 1000 cm^3 of water

To compare fairly how 'heavy' materials are, we should weigh the same **volume** of each one.

We can work out the density of a material like this:

$$\text{density} = \frac{\textbf{mass}}{\textbf{volume}} \text{ or mass} \div \text{volume}$$

So, for example, the density of steel is $7.9 \div 1 = 7.9 \, \text{g/cm}^3$.

The density of water is 1 g/cm^3. We say that steel is **denser** than water.

2 (a) Work out the density of each of the other materials shown in the picture.

(b) Write down the materials in the order of their densities, starting with the lowest.

1.74 g butter   1.76 g bone   1.76 g cork

■ **Why are gases less dense than solids and liquids?**

Steam is about a thousand times less dense than ice or water. The diagrams show why.

3 Copy and complete the sentence.

Gases are less dense than solids or liquids because their _____ are a lot further apart.

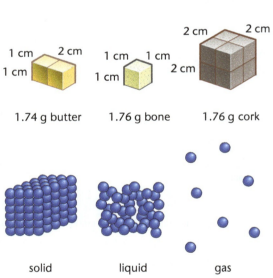

solid   liquid   gas

The same particles make up a substance in its solid, liquid and gas states.

WHAT YOU NEED TO REMEMBER (Copy and complete using the **key words**)

What is density?

A piece of steel weighs more than the same _____ of water.
So we say that steel is _____ than water.

The density of a material is its _____ divided by its volume.

1.10 Density of gases

We write down the **density** of a gas in the same way as for solids and liquids.

1 (a) What is the normal density of air?

(b) How many times denser is water than air?

2 A room is 10 m × 5 m × 3 m. Each cubic metre (m^3) is 1000 litres.

(a) What is the volume of the room in m^3?

(b) What is the volume of the room in litres?

(c) What is the mass of the air in the room?

◼ A gas for balloons

To make a balloon rise through the air, we use a gas that is lighter than air.

3 Which gas in the table will lift a balloon:

(a) fastest through the air?

(b) safest through the air?

Give a reason for each answer.

◼ Changing density by squeezing a gas

Unlike solids and liquids, we can **squeeze** the particles of a gas **closer** together.

4 Look at the drawing. If we squeeze the gas so that its volume is halved, what will happen to:

(a) the number of particles per cm^3?

(b) the density of the gas?

5 Can the density of a solid or a liquid be changed in this way? Explain your answer.

REMEMBER

Density = mass ÷ volume

The density of water is 1 g/cm^3 or 1000 g/litre.

The density of air is 1.3 g/litre at normal temperature and pressure.

At normal temperature and pressure	Density (g/litre)	Other properties
hydrogen	0.09	burns easily
helium	0.18	does not burn
carbon dioxide	1.98	does not burn
air	1.3	allows other things to burn

The balloon rises because it is filled with a gas that is lighter than air.

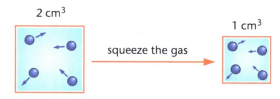

Squeezing the particles closer together increases the number of particles per cm^3. This makes each cubic centimetre weigh more and so the density increases.

WHAT YOU NEED TO REMEMBER (Copy and complete using the **key words**)

Density of gases

When you _____ a gas, the particles move _____ together. This increases the _____ of the gas.

1.11 What makes a solid melt?

The diagrams show the particles in a solid and a liquid.

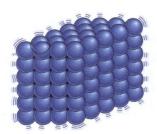

*In a solid, the forces between particles are big enough to stop them moving about. The only way they can move is to **vibrate**.*

In a liquid, the forces between particles hold them close together but do not stop them moving around.

1 Copy the table. Then complete it using the words 'yes' and 'no'.

	Solids	Liquids
Are there forces between the particles?		
Do these forces stop the particles moving around?		

■ Heating a solid

To change a solid into a **liquid**, you need to heat it. The diagrams below show you what happens to the particles.

2 What happens at first to the particles in a solid when you heat the solid up?

3 What happens to the particles when the solid melts?

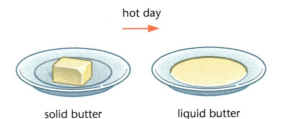

hot day

solid butter   liquid butter

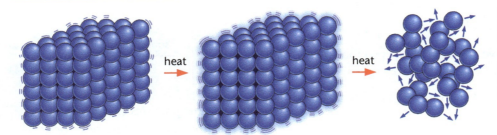

heat   heat

Giving energy to the particles makes them vibrate **faster**.

Eventually the vibrations become so strong that the attractive forces can't hold the particles in position any more. So the particles start to move around.

The solid has **melted**.

WHAT YOU NEED TO REMEMBER (Copy and complete using the **key words**)

What makes a solid melt?

When you heat up a solid, you make its particles vibrate _____.

The particles start to move around if they _____ strongly enough.
The solid has changed into a _____. It has _____.

1.12 Why do liquids evaporate?

When a liquid **evaporates**, it changes into a gas.

The diagrams show the particles in a liquid and in a gas.

1 Write down:

(a) one similarity between the particles in a liquid and in a gas;

(b) one difference between the particles in a liquid and in a gas.

Particles in a liquid can travel about. But forces of attraction hold them close together.

Gas particles are a long way apart. They don't affect each other except when they collide. They can move anywhere in the space available.

How a liquid evaporates

The diagram shows how a liquid evaporates.

2 Copy and complete the sentences.

Particles can escape from the _____ of a liquid. To do this they must be moving _____ enough.

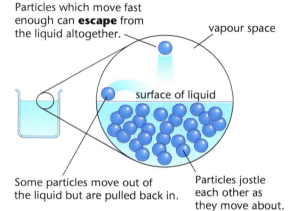

Particles which move fast enough can **escape** from the liquid altogether.

vapour space

surface of liquid

Some particles move out of the liquid but are pulled back in.

Particles jostle each other as they move about.

*In a hot liquid, more of the particles have enough **energy** to escape.*

Evaporation and temperature

Heating a liquid makes it evaporate faster.

An evaporating liquid can also cool things down.

3 When we get out of the sea, we often feel colder than when swimming. Explain why.

To escape, water particles need energy. They get this from your body.

WHAT YOU NEED TO REMEMBER (Copy and complete using the **key words**)

Why do liquids evaporate?

When a liquid changes into a gas, we say that it _____.

A liquid evaporates as faster moving particles _____.

Heating speeds up evaporation because more particles have enough _____ to escape.

.13 Melting, boiling and temperature

When you heat up a solid, its temperature rises. The energy transferred to the particles makes them vibrate faster.

But when the solid is melting (changing to a liquid), its **temperature** stays the same. The energy transferred to the particles makes them **break away** from their fixed positions.

When all the solid has melted, the temperature starts to rise again. The energy transferred to the particles makes them move around faster.

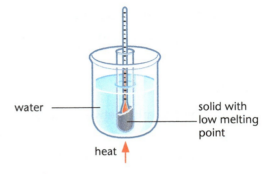

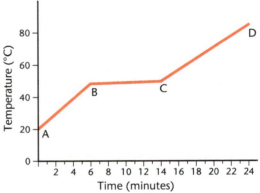

Graph of heating up a solid.

1 (a) Look at the graph. Then copy and complete the table.

Part of graph	What is happening to the temperature of the substance?	What is happening to the particles of the substance?
A to B		
B to C		
C to D		

(b) What state is the substance between C and D (a solid, a liquid or a gas)?

■ Boiling

When a liquid is boiling, it does not get any hotter.

2 (a) What happens to the energy you supply to a boiling liquid?

(b) What does the liquid become?

When a liquid boils, all the energy is transferred to particles to make them escape.

WHAT YOU NEED TO REMEMBER (Copy and complete using the **key words**)

Melting, boiling and temperature

When a solid is melting or a liquid is boiling, its _____ doesn't change.

The energy transferred to a melting solid makes the particles _____ _____ from their fixed positions.

The energy transferred to a boiling liquid makes its particles _____.

1.14 How does a gas fill its container?

The particles in a gas are a long way apart. There is hardly any force of attraction between them.

Gas particles:

- move about very fast in all directions;
- don't travel very far before they bump into each other;
- bounce off the walls of the container.

This is called rapid, **random** motion.

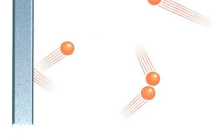

Particles in a gas move about very fast.

1 Look at the diagrams.

(a) Why does the brown gas spread out through all the space in its container?

(b) Why does it take quite a long time for this to happen?

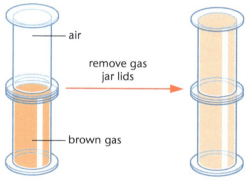

air

remove gas jar lids

brown gas

1 hour later

■ Diffusion

This rapid, random motion of gas molecules causes a gas to spread out as far as it can. We say that the gas **diffuses**.

We can compare how fast different gases diffuse by using a porous pot. Gas molecules can pass through the pot in both directions.

2 Which gas diffuses fastest, hydrogen or air?

3 What would happen if the hydrogen was in the pot and the air in the beaker?

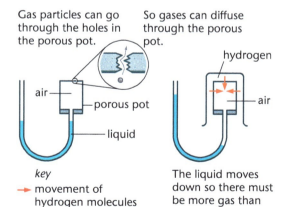

Gas particles can go through the holes in the porous pot.

So gases can diffuse through the porous pot.

hydrogen

air

porous pot

air

liquid

key
→ movement of hydrogen molecules

The liquid moves down so there must be more gas than before in the pot.

WHAT YOU NEED TO REMEMBER (Copy and complete using the **key words**)

How does a gas fill its container?

The particles of a gas move about with rapid, _____ motion.
So a gas spreads out into all the space it can. We say that the gas _____.

.15 How can you change gas pressure?

You can squeeze a gas into a smaller **space**. When you do this you can feel the gas pressure pushing back.

The diagrams show why squeezing the gas changes its pressure.

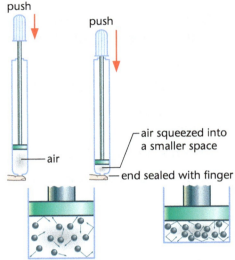

push

push

— air squeezed into a smaller space

— air

— end sealed with finger

Particles hitting the piston give the gas its pressure.

The particles are squeezed closer together. They hit the piston more often. So there is a bigger pressure.

1 Copy and complete the sentences.

When you squeeze a gas into a smaller space, it has a bigger _____. This is because the particles hit the _____ more often.

■ Increasing temperature, increasing pressure

Another way to increase gas pressure is to increase its **temperature**.

2 Heating a gas increases its pressure. Write down <u>two</u> reasons why.

3 What could happen if the gas pressure inside a container gets too big?

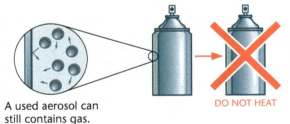

A used aerosol can still contains gas.

DO NOT HEAT

Never heat a used aerosol can up. It might burst with the pressure.

If a gas is hotter, the particles move faster. They hit the container **harder** and more **often**. So the pressure is bigger.

WHAT YOU NEED TO REMEMBER (Copy and complete using the **key words**)

How can you change gas pressure?

You can increase the pressure of a gas:
- ■ by squeezing it into a smaller _____;
- ■ by increasing its _____, which makes its particles hit the sides of the container _____.

Both squeezing and heating the gas make its particles hit the sides of the container more _____.

1.16 Why do solids expand when they are heated?

A solid keeps its shape unless we make a large force act on it. This is because the particles in a solid pull each other together.

These **forces** of attraction are quite big. So they hold the particles in the same positions.

1 How can you change the shape of a solid?

2 Explain why the particles in solids cannot move around from one point to another.

If you don't hit a nail straight, the large force will change its shape.

■ What happens when we heat a solid?

The particles in a solid can't move around each other. But they still have energy so they wobble about in the same place. We say that they **vibrate**.

When we heat up a solid, we give the particles more energy.

The diagram shows what happens then.

3 An iron nail is 40 mm at room temperature. When it has been heated, it is 40.05 mm long. Explain what has happened. Use words like <u>particles</u>, <u>vibrating</u>, and <u>colliding</u> in your answer.

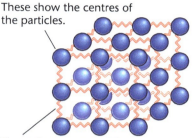

These show the centres of the particles.

The springs represent the attractive forces between them.

In a solid, each particle attracts the particles around it. This holds the particles in position.

Particles in a solid can vibrate.

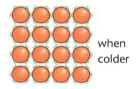
when colder

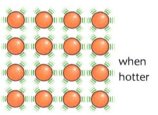
when hotter

*When particles have more energy, they make bigger vibrations. Each particle collides with its neighbours and takes up more space. So the solid **expands**.*

WHAT YOU NEED TO REMEMBER (Copy and complete using the **key words**)

Why do solids expand when they are heated?

The particles in a solid are held in position by strong _____ of attraction.
The particles can't move about but they can _____.

When a solid is heated, the vibrating particles bang into each other and take up more space, so the solid _____.

2.1 Two sorts of change

Gold and magnesium are both metals.
The diagrams show how these metals change when you heat them in air.

1 Copy the table and complete it using the words 'yes' and 'no'.

	Is a new substance produced?	Is it easy to change back again?
Melting gold		
Burning magnesium		

We can put all changes into two groups:

■ **chemical** changes make new substances;

■ **physical** changes do not make any new substances.

2 What kind of change is:

(a) melting gold?

(b) burning magnesium?

Physical changes are usually easier to change back again. We say that they are easier to **reverse**.

■ Ice, water and steam

You can change ice into water and water into steam. These changes are called changes of **state**.

The diagram shows how this happens.

3 (a) Are any new substances formed during these changes?

(b) Give a reason for your answer.

4 Are the changes easy to reverse?

5 Are the changes physical or chemical?

Changes of state are physical changes.

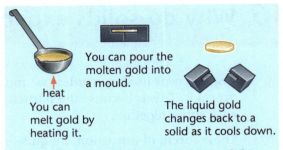

You can melt gold by heating it.

You can pour the molten gold into a mould.

The liquid gold changes back to a solid as it cools down.

You can easily change gold from a solid to a liquid and back again as many times as you want.

Magnesium is a shiny silver-coloured metal.

If you heat magnesium in a Bunsen flame, it burns with a very bright white flame.

A white powdery substance is produced. It is hard to get magnesium back again.

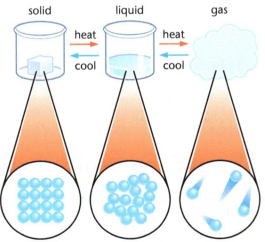

The particles in ice, water and steam are exactly the same. So they are the <u>same</u> chemical substance in a different <u>state</u>.

Dissolving a solid in water

The diagram shows what happens when you dissolve solid copper sulphate in water and then try to separate them again.

6 (a) Is dissolving a solid in water a physical or chemical change ?

(b) Give reasons for your answer.

Mixing things together and separating **mixtures** are physical changes.

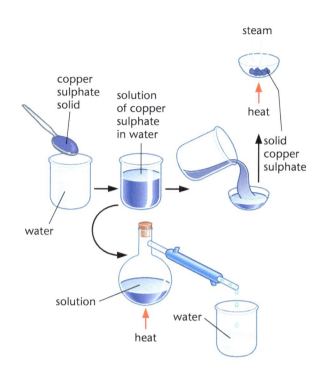

Reacting magnesium with acid

The diagrams below show what happens when magnesium reacts with dilute hydrochloric acid.

7 (a) What two new substances are formed in the reaction?

(b) Is the reaction a physical or a chemical change?

Chemical **reactions** produce chemical changes.

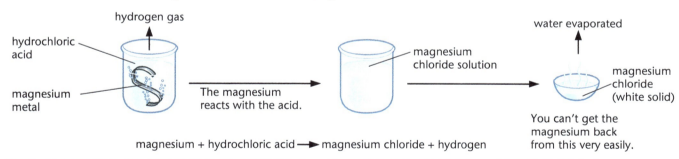

magnesium + hydrochloric acid ⟶ magnesium chloride + hydrogen

WHAT YOU NEED TO REMEMBER (Copy and complete using the **key words**)

Two sorts of change

We call changes that make new substances _____ changes.
Changes that do not make new substances are _____ changes.

Two examples of physical change are changes of _____ , and separating _____ .

Physical changes are usually easier to _____ than chemical changes.

Chemical changes are produced by chemical _____ .

More about chemical and physical changes: C+ 2.15, 2.16

2.2 Chemical reactions

When magnesium metal burns in air, changes happen. A white powdery substance is produced. It is hard to get the magnesium metal back again from this powder.

> **1 (a)** Are these physical or chemical changes?
>
> **(b)** Give a reason for your answer.

Chemical changes are produced by chemical <u>reactions</u>.

There are many different kinds of chemical reactions. Burning is just one kind. Burning is often called <u>combustion</u>.

■ Burning

When a match burns, a chemical reaction takes place.

> **2** Look at the diagram.
>
> **(a)** What is the wood of the match reacting with when it burns?
>
> **(b)** What new substances are produced?

Reactions with **oxygen** are called **oxidation** reactions. So combustion, or burning, is an oxidation reaction.

But oxidation reactions do not always involve burning.

> **3 (a)** Describe an oxidation reaction that doesn't involve burning.
>
> **(b)** How can you slow down this reaction?

DO YOU REMEMBER?
from *Core Science 1*

Chemical changes always make new substances.

Physical changes never make new substances.

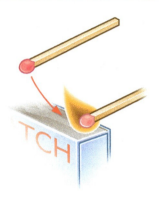

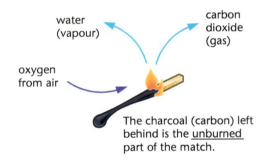

water (vapour)

carbon dioxide (gas)

oxygen from air

The charcoal (carbon) left behind is the <u>unburned</u> part of the match.

Fats like butter or margarine go 'off' if you keep them too long. This is because they react with the oxygen from the air. This reaction is slower when the fat is cold. That's why it's best to keep it in the fridge.

Splitting up chemicals by heating them

If you heat some substances, they split into different substances. The diagrams show what happens when you heat copper carbonate.

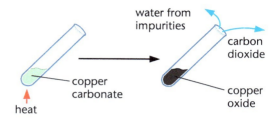

4 What substances does copper carbonate split up into when it is heated?

5 How can you tell that the gas given off is carbon dioxide?

Splitting up a substance by **heating** it is called thermal decomposition.

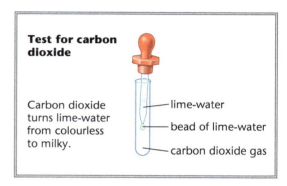

Test for carbon dioxide

Carbon dioxide turns lime-water from colourless to milky.

lime-water
bead of lime-water
carbon dioxide gas

Splitting up chemicals using electricity

You can split up some substances by passing an **electric current** through them. You have to dissolve the substance in water or melt it first. The diagram shows what happens when you pass an electric current through copper chloride solution.

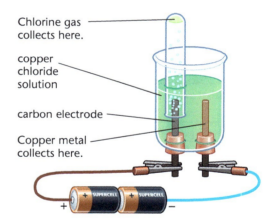

Chlorine gas collects here.

copper chloride solution

carbon electrode

Copper metal collects here.

(Note: most of the chlorine gas that is produced in the reaction shown dissolves in the copper chloride solution.)

6 What two substances are produced when you pass electricity through the copper chloride solution?

7 How can you show that the gas produced is chlorine?

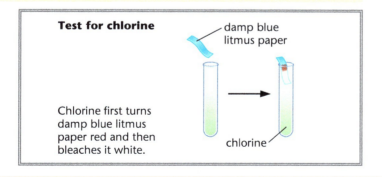

Test for chlorine

damp blue litmus paper

Chlorine first turns damp blue litmus paper red and then bleaches it white.

chlorine

WHAT YOU NEED TO REMEMBER (Copy and complete using the **key words**)

Chemical reactions

Another name for burning is combustion. When things burn they react with _____.
So we also call burning an _____ reaction.

In a thermal decomposition reaction, you split up a substance by _____ it.

In electrolysis, you split up a substance by passing an _____ _____ through it.

2.3 Elements and atoms

There are millions of different substances. But they are made from about 90 simple substances joined together in different ways.

These simple substances are called **elements**.

■ How do we know which substances are elements?

1 Write down two things you can do to try to split up a substance.

If you <u>can</u> split a substance up, it <u>isn't</u> an element.

If you <u>can't</u> split a substance up, it <u>is</u> probably an element.

2 Look at the diagrams on this page. Then copy and complete the table using the words 'yes' and 'no'.

Substance	Can you split it up?	Is it an element?
copper chloride		
copper		
chlorine		
mercury oxide		
mercury		
oxygen		

3 How do you know that heating mercury oxide produces oxygen gas?

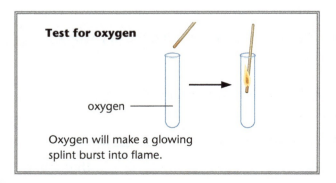

Test for oxygen

oxygen

Oxygen will make a glowing splint burst into flame.

DO YOU REMEMBER?
from *Core Science 1*

There are two main ways of splitting up a substance:
■ heating it;
■ dissolving it in water or melting it, and then passing an electric current through it.

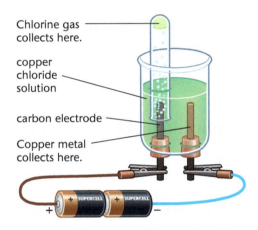

Chlorine gas collects here.

copper chloride solution

carbon electrode

Copper metal collects here.

You can split up copper chloride. But you can't split copper or chlorine into anything simpler.

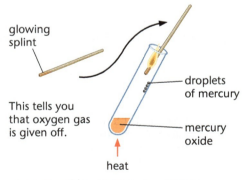

glowing splint

This tells you that oxygen gas is given off.

droplets of mercury

mercury oxide

heat

mercury oxide → mercury + oxygen

You can split up mercury oxide. But you can't split mercury or oxygen into anything simpler. (Note: Mercury is very poisonous. This experiment must be done only by the teacher using a fume cupboard.)

■ Getting copper from copper carbonate

The diagram shows how you can get copper metal starting from copper carbonate.

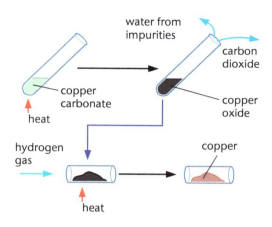

4 Copy and complete the sentences.

We heat copper carbonate to get copper _____.

Then we heat copper oxide with _____ gas. The copper oxide changes to _____.

In this reaction, hydrogen takes the oxygen out of the copper _____ and joins with oxygen to form water.

■ What are elements made of?

An element is made of tiny particles called **atoms**.

An element is a simple substance. This is because it is made up of the **same** kind of atom.

5 Look at the top diagram. Write down the chemicals that you know are not elements.

6 How is an argon atom different from a helium atom?

Helium is an element. Helium atoms are all the same size as each other.

Argon is an element. Argon atoms are bigger and heavier than helium atoms.

*Atoms of different elements are **different** from each other.*

■ The element chart

Scientists put the elements into a special chart called the periodic table.

7 Are there more metals or more non-metals amongst the elements?

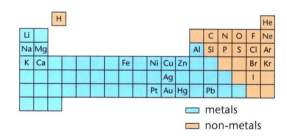

WHAT YOU NEED TO REMEMBER (Copy and complete using the **key words**)

Elements and atoms

We call simple substances _____.

Elements are made up of very small particles called _____.

All the atoms in one element are the _____ kind.

Atoms of different elements are _____.

More about elements: C+ 2.9

2.4 Compounds

We know that there are only about 90 elements that are found in nature. But elements can join together. They make millions of different substances called **compounds**.

1 How many different pairs of letters can you make from A, B and C?

AB AC ...

The more letters we have, then the more pairs we can get.

2 How many different pairs of letters can you make from A, B, C and D?

AB AC ... ... CD

When elements join together to make compounds, their different atoms 'stick' to each other. We say that atoms join together by making chemical <u>bonds</u>.

3 Look at the diagrams. Then copy and complete the table.

Name of substance	What atoms is it made of?	Element or compound?
copper		
copper oxide		
water		
hydrogen		
oxygen		

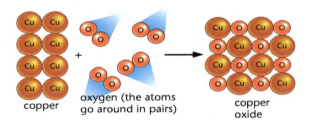

copper   oxygen (the atoms go around in pairs)   copper oxide

■ Differences between compounds and mixtures

A **mixture** of hydrogen and oxygen is very dangerous. The diagram shows why.

4 Copy and complete the sentences.

A flame will make a mixture of hydrogen and oxygen _____. The atoms of hydrogen and oxygen _____ together. This makes a _____ called water.

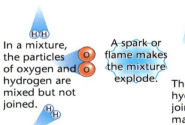

In a mixture, the particles of oxygen and hydrogen are mixed but not joined.

A spark or flame makes the mixture explode.

The oxygen and hydrogen atoms join together to make a compound called water.

■ Compounds and their elements are different

The **properties** of a compound are very different from the properties of its elements.

For example, hydrogen and oxygen are both gases. The compound they produce when they react is the liquid we call water.

Look at the picture.

Mercury oxide

5 Copy and complete the sentences using these words: mercury, solid, oxygen, liquid, gas.

Mercury oxide is a red _____. It is made from the elements _____ and _____.

Mercury is a silver-coloured _____. Oxygen is a colourless _____.

methane

water

■ Names of compounds

You can often tell what elements are in a compound from its name.

The name <u>mercury oxide</u>, for example, tells us that it is a compound of the elements <u>mercury</u> and <u>oxygen</u>.

The names of some compounds don't tell you what elements they contain. You just have to remember.

6 Copy and complete the table by writing down the elements in each of the compounds.

ammonia

Compound	Elements in the compound
mercury oxide	mercury and oxygen
water	
magnesium oxide	
methane	
ammonia	
copper chloride	

WHAT YOU NEED TO REMEMBER (Copy and complete using the **key words**)

Compounds

Substances made from atoms of different elements joined together are called _____.

A substance made from different atoms <u>not</u> joined together is called a _____.

Compounds have different _____ from the elements they are made from.

More about compounds: C+ 2.9 to 2.12

2.5 Elements reacting with oxygen

DO YOU REMEMBER?
from *Core Science 1*

Compounds called <u>oxides</u> contain oxygen joined to a different element.

Many elements will burn in oxygen to make oxides. The atoms of the element join up with atoms of oxygen.

1 (a) What is the everyday name for hydrogen oxide?

(b) Write down the name of <u>two</u> other oxides.

Hydrogen oxide

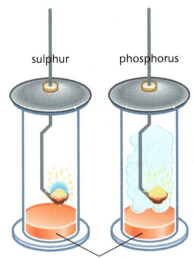

sulphur   phosphorus

litmus solution after the reactions

▪ Burning non-metallic elements

Many non-metallic elements burn in oxygen to make **oxides**.

The diagrams show what these oxides do to litmus solution.

2 Copy and complete the sentences.

Some non-metal oxides make litmus solution go _____. This tells you that these non-metal oxides are _____.

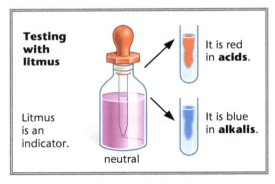

Testing with litmus

It is red in **acids**.

Litmus is an indicator.

It is blue in **alkalis**.

neutral

▪ Burning metallic elements

Metallic elements also burn in oxygen to make <u>water</u>.

Some metal oxides dissolve in water. The diagrams show what these metal oxides do to litmus solution.

3 Copy and complete the sentences.

Metal oxides that dissolve in water make the litmus go _____. This tells you that these metal oxides are _____.

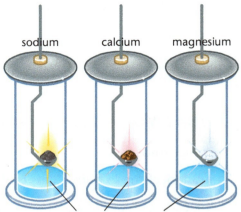

sodium   calcium   magnesium

litmus solution after the reaction

sodium + oxygen ➔ sodium oxide
calcium + oxygen ➔ calcium oxide
magnesium + oxygen ➔ magnesium oxide

How oxygen got its name

More than 200 years ago, a Frenchman called Lavoisier was doing experiments with a 'new kind of air'.

He found that non-metals burned brightly in this gas to make acids. So he called the gas 'oxygen'. It means 'acid maker'. The elements sodium, calcium and magnesium were not discovered until after Lavoisier died.

4 Explain why Lavoisier called the 'new kind of air' oxygen.

5 Why is the name not really very suitable?

Carbon – metal or non-metal?

Diamond and graphite are very different forms of the element carbon. They have some of the properties of non-metals. But they also have some properties of metals.

6 Look at the pictures and then copy and complete the table.

Form of carbon	Conducts heat?	Conducts electricity?	Is the oxide acidic?
diamond	yes		
graphite (carbon rod)	no		

7 Copy and complete the sentences.

Both forms of carbon burn in oxygen to make an oxide that turns litmus red. So carbon must be a _____.

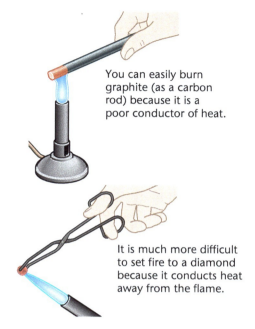

You can easily burn graphite (as a carbon rod) because it is a poor conductor of heat.

It is much more difficult to set fire to a diamond because it conducts heat away from the flame.

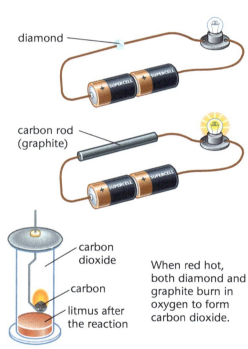

diamond

carbon rod (graphite)

carbon dioxide

carbon

litmus after the reaction

When red hot, both diamond and graphite burn in oxygen to form carbon dioxide.

WHAT YOU NEED TO REMEMBER (Copy and complete using the **key words**)

Elements reacting with oxygen

When we burn elements in oxygen, we get compounds called _____.

Some non-metallic elements make oxides that dissolve in water to make _____.

Some metals make oxides that dissolve in water to make _____.

More about reactions: C+ 2.13

2.6 Metals reacting with acids

Most metals will burn in oxygen to make oxides.

Many metals will also react with dilute **acids**.

How fast do they react?

Some pupils studied the reaction between dilute hydrochloric acid and the metals zinc, iron, and magnesium. The balloons are to catch any gas that is made in the reactions.

1 How did the pupils make sure that their experiment was fair?

2 At the end of the experiment:

   (a) which balloon was biggest?

   (b) which metal reacted fastest?

   (c) which balloon did not get much bigger?

   (d) which metal reacted slowest?

The metal that reacts fastest is the <u>most reactive</u> metal.

3 Write down the three metals in order of their reactivity, putting the most reactive first and the least reactive last.

A list of metals in order of their reactivity is called a <u>reactivity series</u>.

Adding more metals to the reactivity series

The diagrams tell you about the reactions of gold and copper.

4 Add gold and copper to your reactivity series.

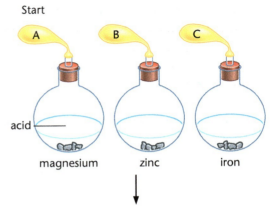

Start

A   B   C

acid

magnesium   zinc   iron

There is the same amount of acid and the same amount of metal in each flask.

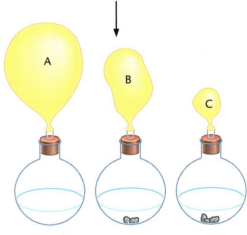

A   B   C

5 minutes later

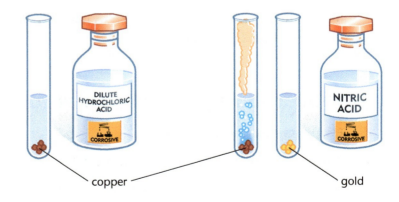

copper

DILUTE HYDROCHLORIC ACID
CORROSIVE

NITRIC ACID
CORROSIVE

gold

Copper does not react with dilute hydrochloric acid.

Concentrated nitric acid will react with copper, but not with gold.

■ What new substances are produced?

The diagrams tell you about the substances produced when zinc reacts with dilute hydrochloric acid.

5 What <u>two</u> substances are produced in the reaction?

6 How do we know that the gas produced is hydrogen?

hydrogen gas

zinc chloride solution

hydrochloric acid

zinc

■ Word equations

Here is a convenient way of writing down what happens in the reaction between zinc and dilute hydrochloric acid.

zinc + hydrochloric acid → zinc **chloride** + hydrogen

This is called a <u>word equation</u>.

The metal compounds produced in reactions like this are called **salts**. So we can write:

metal + acid → a salt + hydrogen

7 What salt would be produced in the reaction between magnesium and hydrochloric acid?

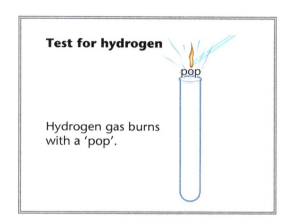

Test for hydrogen

pop

Hydrogen gas burns with a 'pop'.

WHAT YOU NEED TO REMEMBER (Copy and complete using the **key words**)

Metals reacting with acids

Most metals react with dilute _____. The reactions produce a gas called _____. They also produce compounds called _____.

We can write down the reaction between zinc and hydrochloric acid like this:

_____ + dilute hydrochloric acid → zinc _____ + hydrogen

More about the reactivity series: C+ 2.14

2.7 Displacement reactions

A more **reactive** metal will push a less reactive metal out of a **solution** of one of its compounds. We say that the more reactive metal <u>displaces</u> the less reactive one. We call this sort of reaction a **displacement** reaction.

The diagram shows you an example of this.

> 1 Copy and complete the following.
>
>   zinc + copper nitrate → zinc nitrate + _____
>   (metal)   (solution)   (solution)   (metal)
>
> This reaction shows that zinc is a more _____ metal than copper.

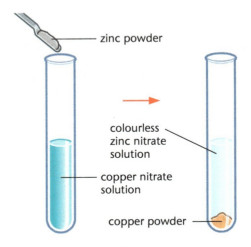

zinc powder

colourless zinc nitrate solution

copper nitrate solution

copper powder

■ Looking at displacement reactions

A group of pupils does an experiment.

To each 1 cm square piece of zinc, they add 2 drops of a solution of different metal compound.

They watch for small crystals of the metal from the solution growing on the surface of the zinc square.

The illustration shows crystals of lead. These grow on the surface of the zinc. This happens because zinc is more reactive than lead. Zinc particles go into the solution and push out the lead particles.

Look at the results. Where crystals have grown, the drawings are shaded.

> 2 Copy and complete the results table for this experiment.
>
> 3 (a) Write down a list of metals that are less reactive than zinc.
>
>   (b) Which metal may be more reactive than zinc?
>
>   (c) How could you find out for sure?

At the start

zinc   magnesium nitrate

copper nitrate   lead nitrate   tin nitrate

zinc metal

magnified lead crystal

lead nitrate solution

magnesium nitrate

copper crystals   lead crystals   tin crystals

A few minutes later.

Solution of metal nitrate	Did crystals form on zinc?
copper	✓
lead	
magnesium	
tin	

More displacement reactions

The pupils test 1 cm square pieces of tin in the same way.

4 (a) Which <u>two</u> metals does tin displace?

(b) Which <u>two</u> metals are less reactive than tin?

tin

copper nitrate | lead nitrate | magnesium nitrate | zinc nitrate

copper crystals | lead crystals

The pupils test other metal squares – copper, lead, and magnesium. They put these results, and the results from the first two experiments, into a table.

Looking at results

The most reactive of these metals is the one that displaces the most metals (gets the most ticks).

Solution of metal nitrate	Metals				
	zinc	tin	magnesium	lead	copper
copper	✓	✓	✓	✓	
lead	✓	✓	✓		✗
magnesium	✗	✗		✗	✗
tin	✓		✓	✗	✗
zinc		✗	✓	✗	✗

Key: ✓ indicates that crystals formed on the metal.

5 Write out these metals in the order of their reactivities, starting with the most reactive and going down to the least reactive.

A list of metals in the order of their reactivities is called a **reactivity series**.

Two very reactive metals

Sodium and calcium are very reactive metals. But you can't use them to displace other metals from solutions.

6 Explain why.

7 Add sodium and calcium to your reactivity series.

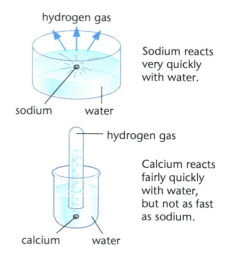

hydrogen gas

Sodium reacts very quickly with water.

sodium | water

hydrogen gas

Calcium reacts fairly quickly with water, but not as fast as sodium.

calcium | water

WHAT YOU NEED TO REMEMBER (Copy and complete using the **key words**)

Displacement reactions

Some metals are more _____ than others.

A reactive metal will push a less reactive metal out of a _____ of one of its compounds. We call this type of chemical change a _____ reaction.

A list of metals in order of their reactivities is called a _____ _____.

2.8 Carrying out tests

■ Three common gases

Oxygen, hydrogen and carbon dioxide are all gases. All of them are colourless and all of them have no smell. So if we get a colourless gas in a chemical reaction we need to <u>test</u> it to find out what it is.

The diagrams show the **chemical tests** for these gases, but they don't tell you which is which.

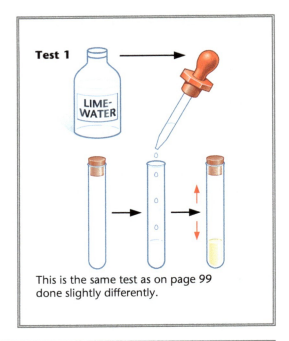

Test 1

LIME-WATER

This is the same test as on page 99 done slightly differently.

1 Copy and complete the sentences.

We use lime-water to test for

_____ _____.

This gas makes the lime-water go

_____.

[See page 99 if you are not sure.]

We use a lighted splint to test for

_____.

This gas burns with a slight _____.
[See page 107 if you are not sure.]

We use a glowing splint to test for

_____.

This gas makes the glowing splint

_____.

[See page 100 if you are not sure.]

Test 2

Test 3

Using litmus

Litmus is a very useful dye. It can tell us whether a solution is an acid or an alkali or neutral (like water). We say that litmus is an <u>indicator</u>.
We can also use litmus to test for a gas called chlorine.

2 Look at the diagrams. Then copy and complete the table.

Colour of litmus	What this tells you
red	
purple	
blue	
white	

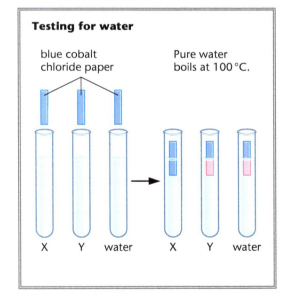

Using litmus

LITMUS

in acid   in water (neutral)   in alkali

damp litmus paper

chlorine gas

Testing for water

Many colourless liquids are neutral. So just because a liquid turns litmus purple, it does <u>not</u> mean that the liquid is water.

We can also test liquids with blue cobalt chloride paper.

3 (a) What colour does the paper turn in water?

(b) What can you say about liquid X?

Many solutions contain water and would change the colour of the cobalt chloride.

4 How could you prove whether liquid Y is <u>pure</u> water?

Testing for water

blue cobalt chloride paper

Pure water boils at 100 °C.

X   Y   water   X   Y   water

WHAT YOU NEED TO REMEMBER (Copy and complete using the **key words**)

Carrying out tests

When we want to find out what a substance is, we carry out chemical _____.
Most tests are _____ changes.

You need to know what each of these tests tells you.

2.9 Different kinds of mixtures

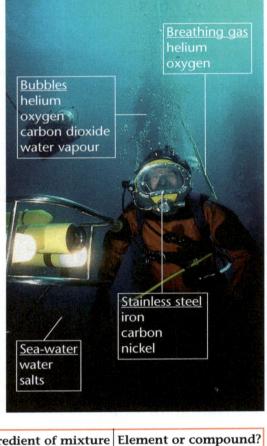

Bubbles
helium
oxygen
carbon dioxide
water vapour

Breathing gas
helium
oxygen

Stainless steel
iron
carbon
nickel

Sea-water
water
salts

We know that elements can react and join together to make new substances. We call these substances chemical compounds. But if we put two or more elements together, and they do not react, then what we have is a **mixture** of elements.

Look at the picture of the diver and also at the table below.

1 Write down the name of <u>one</u> mixture made up of <u>elements</u> that are:

(a) solids   **(b)** gases.

■ Mixtures of compounds

Pure compounds just contain the single compound. But just as we can have a mixture of elements, so we can have a mixture of different **compounds**.

2 Write down <u>one</u> mixture of different <u>compounds</u> given in the picture.

3 Explain why we do <u>not</u> say sea-water is a pure compound.

■ Mixtures of elements and compounds

We can also **mix** different kinds of substances together, such as elements and compounds.

4 Write down <u>one</u> mixture in the photograph which contains both elements and compounds.

5 Copy and complete the table on the right.

Name of mixture	Ingredient of mixture	Element or compound?
stainless steel	iron	element
	carbon	_____
	_____	_____
breathing gas	helium	_____
	_____	element
bubbles	helium	element
	oxygen	_____
	carbon dioxide	_____
	water vapour	compound
_____	water	compound
	salts	compound

WHAT YOU NEED TO REMEMBER (Copy and complete using the **key words**)

Different kinds of mixtures

We can have a _____ of elements, or of _____.
We can also _____ elements and compounds together.

2.10 More about compounds and mixtures

We can <u>mix</u> hydrogen and oxygen gases together in any amounts. This makes mixtures of the same substances but in different **ratios**.

The drawings show two mixtures of hydrogen and oxygen gas being made.

1 (a) Copy and complete the table.

Mixture	Number of hydrogen molecules for each oxygen molecule	Ratio of hydrogen molecules to oxygen molecules
A		
B		

(b) Mixture C contains 5 million hydrogen molecules and 1 million oxygen molecules. Add an extra row to your table to show this information.

So a mixture of hydrogen and oxygen can be in <u>any</u> proportions.

Hydrogen and oxygen reacting

The diagram shows what happens when hydrogen and oxygen react.

2 Copy and complete the sentences.

Hydrogen burns in oxygen to form a compound called _____. In each molecule of water there is 1 atom of _____ and 2 atoms of _____.
So, in water, the ratio of hydrogen atoms to oxygen atoms is always _____.

In water, as in all other compounds, the ratio of atoms is always the **same**. We say that compounds have a fixed **composition**.

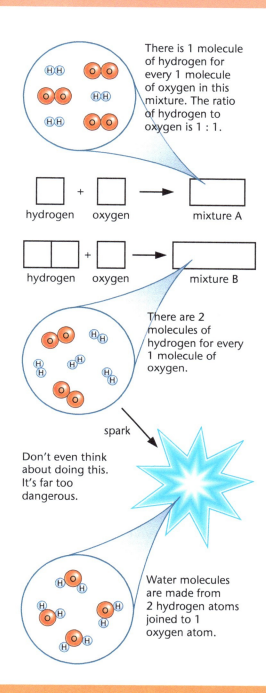

There is 1 molecule of hydrogen for every 1 molecule of oxygen in this mixture. The ratio of hydrogen to oxygen is 1 : 1.

hydrogen + oxygen → mixture A

hydrogen + oxygen → mixture B

There are 2 molecules of hydrogen for every 1 molecule of oxygen.

spark

Don't even think about doing this. It's far too dangerous.

Water molecules are made from 2 hydrogen atoms joined to 1 oxygen atom.

WHAT YOU NEED TO REMEMBER (Copy and complete using the **key words**)

More about compounds and mixtures

In a mixture, elements can be mixed together in different _____.

But in a compound, the atoms of the different elements are always joined together in the _____ ratio. We say that compounds have a fixed _____.

2.11 Simple chemical formulas

Every element has a chemical symbol. This is a quick way of writing down an element.

1 Write down these elements in a list: carbon, chlorine, copper, hydrogen, oxygen, sodium, sulphur and zinc. Alongside each name write down the symbol for that element.
[An old name for sodium is 'natrium'.]

We can use chemical symbols to show the atoms in a compound.

The diagrams show the atoms in sodium chloride and in water.

2 Copy and complete the table.

Compound	Ratio of atoms in the compound	Formula
sodium chloride	1 sodium atom for every 1 _____ atom	
water	2 _____ atoms for every 1 oxygen atom	
carbon dioxide	2 oxygen atoms for every 1 _____ atom	
	1 copper atom for every 1 oxygen atom	

The box tells you the formulas of some more compounds.

3 (a) Copy and complete the sentence.

In hydrogen chloride there is 1 atom of hydrogen for every 1 atom of _____.

(b) Write a similar sentence about each of the other compounds in the box.

REMEMBER

In a chemical compound, the atoms of different elements are always in the same ratio.

The symbols for some elements

H	C	Cl	Cu
Na	O	S	Zn

---

sodium chloride NaCl

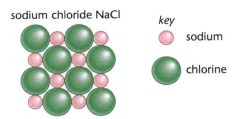

key
● sodium
● chlorine

Sodium and chlorine atoms are in the ratio 1 : 1. So the formula for sodium chloride is NaCl.

```
Cl — Na — Cl — Na
 |     |     |     |
Na — Cl — Na — Cl
 |     |     |     |
Cl — Na — Cl — Na
 |     |     |     |
Na — Cl — Na — Cl
```

key
○ hydrogen
water
● oxygen

Hydrogen and oxygen atoms are in the ratio 2 : 1. So the formula for water is H_2O.

The formulas of some compounds

hydrogen chloride	HCl
copper sulphide	CuS
copper chloride	$CuCl_2$
sodium oxide	Na_2O

WHAT YOU NEED TO REMEMBER

Simple chemical formulas

You should be able to use the formula of a compound to tell you what elements are in the compound and the ratio of their atoms.

2.12 More complicated chemical formulas

Most of the compounds we have seen so far have been compounds of two elements only.

Some compounds we have met before involve three elements.

1 Read the box about formula and rules then write down how many atoms of each of these elements there are in one molecule of glucose:

(a) carbon (b) hydrogen (c) oxygen

2 Now do the same for the elements in the formulas of:

(a) nitric acid HNO_3

(b) sulphuric acid H_2SO_4

Element	Symbol
hydrogen	H
carbon	C
chlorine	Cl
copper	Cu
sodium	Na
oxygen	O
sulphur	S
zinc	Zn

Formula rules

Rule 1: The symbol of the element by itself means one atom of the element. For example, in hydrochloric acid (HCl), there is one hydrogen atom.

Rule 2: If there is a number after the symbol, this says how many atoms there are of the element. For example, in glucose:

$$C_6H_{12}O_6$$

This tells us there are 6 atoms of carbon. 12 atoms of hydrogen How many atoms of oxygen?

Rule 3: If there are brackets, the number just after the brackets multiplies everything inside. $Zn(NO_3)_2$

This multiplies everything inside by 2.

■ The 'ate' compounds

Compounds containing a metal always start with the name of the metal. If they also contain oxygen and another non-metal, the name often ends in 'ate'.

Look at the names and formulas of some 'ate' compounds.

3 For each of the 'ate' compounds shown, write down how many atoms there are for each element in the formula.

4 Write down the names of the elements in the following compounds:

potassium nitrate, copper carbonate, zinc sulphate

5 Explain how the name of an 'ate' compound depends upon the name of the other non-metal.

Some 'ate' compounds

zinc carbonate	$ZnCO_3$
copper sulphate	$CuSO_4$
zinc nitrate	$Zn(NO_3)_2$

WHAT YOU NEED TO REMEMBER

More complicated chemical formulas

You need to be able to work out which elements are in a compound (and what numbers of atoms they have) just as you have for the compounds on this page.

2.13 Energy changes in chemical reactions

■ Reactions that give out energy

When things burn, **energy** is given out.

The diagram shows what happens when hydrogen burns.

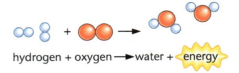

hydrogen + oxygen ⟶ water + energy

> **1** Copy and complete the sentence.
>
> When hydrogen burns, _____ atoms join up with _____ atoms to make _____ of water.

When atoms of two elements join together, the reaction usually gives out energy.

■ Reactions that take in energy

To **split** a compound into simpler substances, we usually have to put energy in.

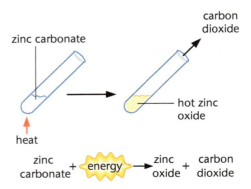

zinc carbonate

carbon dioxide

hot zinc oxide

heat

zinc carbonate + energy ⟶ zinc oxide + carbon dioxide

> **2** What can you do to zinc carbonate to split it into simpler substances?

■ Now try these

The diagrams show two more reactions.

> **3 (a)** Copy the word equation for each reaction.
>
> **(b)** Add energy to the correct side of each equation.

hydrogen + chlorine ⟶ hydrogen chloride
(Hydrogen burns in chlorine.)

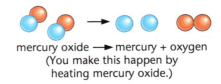

mercury oxide ⟶ mercury + oxygen
(You make this happen by heating mercury oxide.)

WHAT YOU NEED TO REMEMBER (Copy and complete using the **key words**)

Energy changes in chemical reactions

When the atoms of two elements join together, the reaction usually gives out _____.

Reactions which _____ up compounds take energy in.

2.14 More about the reactivity series

Reactivity series for metals

sodium		most reactive
calcium		
magnesium		
aluminium		
zinc		
iron		
lead		
copper		least reactive

As we go from the top to the bottom of the reactivity series, the metals become less reactive.

1 For each of the following pairs of metals, write down which one is the more reactive.

(a) calcium or sodium

(b) magnesium or zinc

(c) iron or copper

(d) lead or calcium

■ Reaction with water

sodium	very fast reaction with cold water
calcium	fast reaction with cold water
magnesium	burns when heated in steam
aluminium	no reaction
zinc	reacts when heated in steam
iron	reacts when heated to red heat in steam
lead	dissolves very slowly over many years
copper	no reaction

2 (a) Which metal does not react as you would expect?

(b) This metal is used to make window frames. Explain why it can be used like this.

■ Putting hydrogen into the reactivity series

We can make metals above copper react with water or with acids to give **hydrogen**.

So we can put hydrogen into the reactivity series even though it is not a metal. This shows which metals are more reactive than hydrogen and which are not.

3 Copy out the reactivity series from the top of the page with hydrogen in its place.

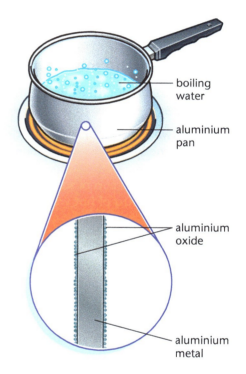

boiling water

aluminium pan

aluminium oxide

aluminium metal

Aluminium is a reactive metal. So it quickly gets covered with a thin layer of aluminium oxide. This layer is very tough. It protects the aluminium underneath.

WHAT YOU NEED TO REMEMBER (Copy and complete using the **key words**)

More about the reactivity series

We sometimes include _____ in the series even though it is not a metal.

2.15 Physical change and mass

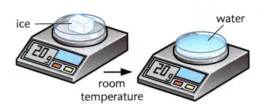

Melting ice is a physical change. Dissolving sugar in water is also a physical change. This is because no new substances are made.

1 What happens to the total mass:

(a) when ice melts?

(b) when sugar dissolves in water?

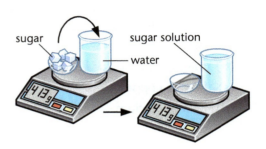

■ Why does the mass stay the same?

Water and sugar, like everything else, are made of particles.

When we melt ice or dissolve sugar in water, we still have exactly the same number of particles.

2 Leo is making a cup of soup. He adds 100g of soup powder to 500g of hot water and stirs until all the powder dissolves.

(a) What is the mass of his soup?

(b) Explain your answer. Use the words 'particles' and 'mass' in your answer.

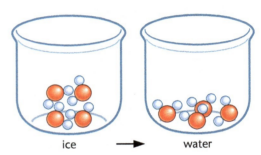

The molecules are not shown to scale.

*If we still have exactly the same **particles**, then we have exactly the same **mass**.*

■ Why does mass sometimes seem to change?

If you leave a beaker of water for a few days, the mass of the water does seem to change.

Water molecules escape from the beaker into the air. You would have to weigh the whole Earth to show that there was no change in mass!

3 (a) Explain how puddles 'dry up' once it's stopped raining.

(b) What happens to the mass of the puddle? Explain your answer.

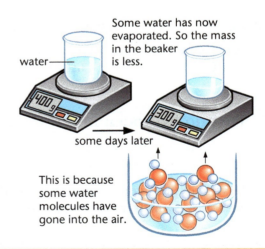

Some water has now evaporated. So the mass in the beaker is less.

some days later

This is because some water molecules have gone into the air.

WHAT YOU NEED TO REMEMBER (Copy and complete using the **key words**)

Physical change and mass

In a physical change you still have the same substances made from the same _____.
So in a physical change there is no change in _____.

2.16 Chemical change and mass

In chemical reactions, atoms of different elements join together in **different** ways to make new substances.

But all the **atoms** must still be there. So the **mass** of the new substances must be exactly the same as the mass of the substances you start with.

■ Explaining apparent changes in mass

In many chemical reactions, the mass does seem to change. We need to be able to explain why.

1 What seems to happen to the mass:

  (a) when a candle burns?

  (b) when magnesium burns?

2 Explain each of these changes of mass.

■ Testing your explanations

To check that mass doesn't change when something burns, you need to burn it inside a sealed container.

The experiment shown in the diagram was done by the famous chemist called Lavoisier more than 200 years ago.

3 (a) Write in a word equation for the reaction shown in the diagram.

  (b) Explain why there is no change in mass.

4 Look again at the magnesium reaction. What mass of oxygen combined with the magnesium?

Hydrogen reacts with oxygen to make water. But there are still the same atoms, so there is no change in mass.

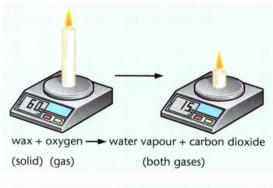

wax + oxygen ⟶ water vapour + carbon dioxide
(solid) (gas)   (both gases)

heat strongly

magnesium ribbon

magnesium + oxygen ⟶ magnesium oxide
(solid)   (gas)   (solid)

You lift the lid of the crucible a little way every minute or so to let air in so that the magnesium can burn. You put the lid back down to trap as much of the magnesium oxide ash as possible. This is what you need to weigh.

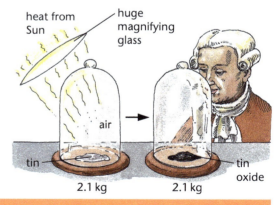

heat from Sun

huge magnifying glass

air

tin

tin oxide

2.1 kg   2.1 kg

WHAT YOU NEED TO REMEMBER (Copy and complete using the **key words**)

Chemical change and mass

In chemical reactions, there is no change in _____.
This is because there are still the same _____.
They are just joined together in _____ ways.

119

3.1 Different kinds of rocks

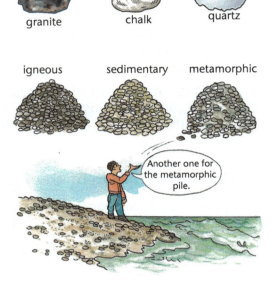

Rocks make up the ground we walk on. They make up the crust of the Earth and all its hills and mountains. They make up every single pebble that we find on the beach. Even the tiny grains of sand came from rocks that have been broken up.

There are thousands of different types of rock. To help us to think about all these different rocks, we divide them into groups.

1 Look at the picture. Then write down the three groups that scientists sort rocks into.

■ Igneous rocks

'Igneous' in the Greek language means 'fire'. **Igneous** rocks were once so hot that they were molten. The rocks formed when this molten material cooled down.

Basalt and granite are both igneous rocks.

2 What are igneous rocks and where are they made?

3 (a) Write down <u>one</u> way that basalt and granite look different.

(b) Which one cooled down quickly and which one cooled down slowly?

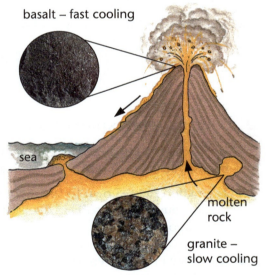

The longer the rock takes to solidify, the bigger the crystals are.

■ Sedimentary rocks

Sedimentary rocks start off with bits of mud, sand and shells, falling to the bottom of the sea or a lake.

4 What do we call the bits which settle out?

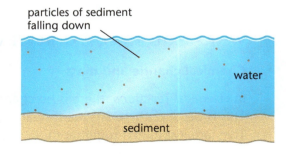

Each layer of sediment gets covered up by new **layers**. As more layers settle on top, the pressure on the lower layers increases. Minerals from the water stick the bits together. It's a bit like squeezing damp soil together to make a solid ball.

5 Look at the three pictures of sedimentary rocks. Which one was made from the remains of animals?

Metamorphic rocks

When rocks are heated and put under pressure, they slowly change. This happens deep inside the Earth's crust. It takes hundreds of thousands of years. The changed rocks are called **metamorphic** rocks.

6 Look at the pictures. Then copy and complete the table.

Sedimentary rock	Metamorphic rock	How the rock has changed
limestone		
	slate	

7 Why are sapphires and rubies so expensive?

Heat and pressure makes aluminium and oxygen, contained in some rocks, turn into sapphires and rubies. This happens only very rarely.

sandstone

chalk

conglomerate

Sedimentary rocks.

limestone

Heat and pressure →

marble

mudstone

Heat and pressure →

slate

These metamorphic rocks are harder and denser than the sedimentary rocks they are made from.

WHAT YOU NEED TO REMEMBER (Copy and complete using the **key words**)

Different kinds of rocks

When molten rock cools down _____ rocks are formed.

_____ rocks form at the bottom of lakes and seas.
They are made up of sediment that builds up in _____.

Heat and pressure can change rocks. We call the new rocks _____ rocks.

121

3.2 Heating up the rock cycle

We don't normally think about rocks moving around. But over millions of years, they do. The centre of the Earth is hot. This energy makes the rocks move around and go through a series of changes. We call this the **rock cycle**.

Weathering breaks up the surface rocks.

Magma rapidly solidifies to form basalt (an igneous rock).

Magma slowly crystallises to form granite (an igneous rock).

Bits of rock are swept down to the sea.

Sedimentary rock forms.

Heat and pressure changes rocks.

metamorphic rock

magma (molten rock)

1 Copy and complete the rock cycle below.

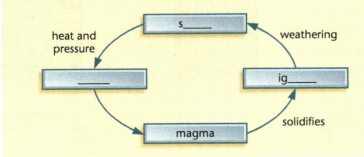

2 Write down <u>four</u> different kinds of weather that can break down rocks.

The rock cycle and the weather

Most of the energy in the rock cycle comes from under the Earth's crust. But the **weather** also plays a big part in breaking down rocks on the top of the Earth's crust.

Frost, wind, rain and the Sun all play a part in breaking down rocks.

■ Why is it hot inside the Earth?

When the Earth first formed, it was very cold. But **radioactive** substances in the rocks release a tremendous amount of thermal energy. This melted most of the rocks. These molten rocks make up the **magma** inside the Earth.

Thousands of millions of years later, radioactive substances are still releasing energy. So the centre of the Earth is still very **hot**. On the outside is a **crust** of solid rock.

3 Copy the diagram of the Earth. Replace the labels on the diagram with:

crust   iron and nickel core   magma (molten rock)

4 At the bottom of the deepest hole drilled into the Earth's crust, the temperature is 246 °C. Explain why the temperature is a lot higher than at the Earth's surface.

■ Free hot water

In some places, water trickles down to hot rocks in the Earth's crust. Some water changes to steam. This forces hot water back to the surface.

5 Look at the photographs. Then copy and complete the sentences.

Water heated by hot rocks can make _____ and _____ springs.

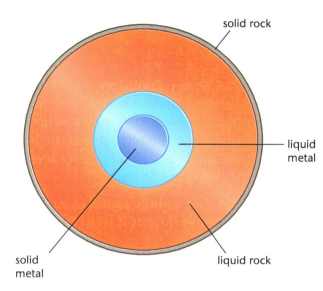

solid rock

liquid metal

liquid rock

solid metal

The structure of the Earth.

A geyser is a mixture of steam and boiling water. In Iceland people use this <u>geothermal</u> energy to heat their homes and provide hot water.

The water in this lake comes from a thermal spring.

WHAT YOU NEED TO REMEMBER (Copy and complete using the **key words**)

Heating up the rock cycle

We live on the Earth's _____.

As we go deeper into the Earth's crust, it gets very _____.

Between the crust and the core, the Earth consists of molten rock called _____.

Rocks slowly move around all the time. We call this the _____ _____.
The energy for this movement comes from _____ substances and from the _____.

More about the rock cycle: C+ 3.9

3.3 Getting metals out of rocks

In 1869, two Englishmen were walking in the Australian outback. One of them stubbed his toe against a rock. They saw a yellow gleam through the dust on the rock. It was the largest nugget of pure gold the world has ever seen. They called it the 'Welcome Stranger'.

Gold isn't usually found in such large pieces. But it's always 'just as it is' in the ground.

We call gold a **native** metal.

1 Why was gold one of the very first metals to be used by humans?

2 What does the nugget's age tell you about how reactive gold is?

■ Other native metals

We sometimes find other unreactive metals in the ground as native metals. But getting these metals from the ground is usually very hard work.

Metals that we find native

copper
mercury
silver
platinum
gold   least reactive

3 What metals do we sometimes find native?

4 Why is getting the gold from the ground usually very hard work?

■ Metals and ores

We find most metals joined to other elements as compounds. Rocks containing metals or metal compounds are called **ores**.

Early people found very little copper as a native metal. But they did discover that heating certain rocks in a charcoal fire gave copper.

The 'Welcome Stranger' weighed about 71 kg and contained 70 kg of pure gold. The gold in the nugget was millions of years old.

In the gold mines of South Africa, there are only about 14 grams of gold per tonne of crushed rock.

native copper

5 (a) What does copper look like?

(b) What does the copper ore called malachite look like?

(c) Can you see any actual copper metal in the copper ore? Explain your answer.

malachite

Malachite is an ore for copper because it contains copper carbonate.

Getting metals from their ores

When you heat copper ore with charcoal you get copper metal. A new substance is produced so there has been a <u>chemical</u> change. A chemical <u>reaction</u> has happened.

When we use a chemical reaction to get a metal out of its ore, we call this **smelting**.

Most iron ores contain iron joined with oxygen. To get the iron, we need to remove the oxygen. It is much harder to get iron out of its ore than copper. It needs a higher temperature. So we use a **blast furnace**.

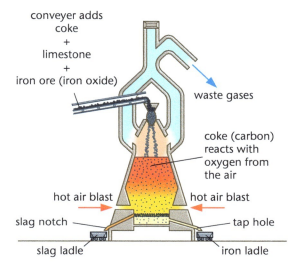
conveyer adds coke + limestone + iron ore (iron oxide)

waste gases

coke (carbon) reacts with oxygen from the air

hot air blast · hot air blast

slag notch · tap hole

slag ladle · iron ladle

6 What makes the high temperature of the blast furnace?

Some metals are more reactive than others. If a metal is more reactive, it is harder to get the metal out of its ore. This is why many metals were not discovered until scientists could split up metal compounds using **electricity**.

7 Name a metal that might be smelted using electricity.

Reactivity series of some metals

sodium	most reactive
magnesium	
aluminium	
zinc	
iron	
lead	
copper	
silver	
gold	least reactive

WHAT YOU NEED TO REMEMBER (Copy and complete using the key words)

Getting metals out of rocks

A metal found in the ground as itself is said to be _____.

Rocks that contain metals or metal compounds are called _____.

When we use a chemical reaction to get a metal out of its ore, we call this _____.

We smelt iron in a _____ _____.

More reactive metals are smelted using _____.

More about smelting: C+ 3.10

125

3.4 Corroding metals

If a metal is more reactive, it is harder to get it out of its ore. But that's not the only problem. If a metal is more reactive, it will react faster with substances such as oxygen. We call this **corrosion**.

1 Look at the photograph. Why do archaeologists hardly ever find complete Viking swords?

This Viking sword is about a thousand years old. It is very rare. Archaeologists usually only find the wooden handles of Viking swords.

■ Rusting and the motor car

The average life of a motor car in the UK used to be only about seven years. After that, most cars were so rusty they were fit only for scrap.

Rusting takes place when iron or steel is in contact with both air and **water**. Rusting is an example of what we call corrosion.

Look at the photograph of the car exported to California soon after it was made.

Compare it with the photograph of the car that stayed in Britain.

2 **(a)** Which vehicle shows the most rusting?

(b) Write down a reason why this is so.

This car was exported to California soon after it was made. The climate there is warm and dry.

■ How can rusting be prevented?

Most ways of slowing rusting down put some kind of **barrier** between the iron and the air and water.

3 Explain what the barrier is in each of these pictures.

This photograph shows a close up of a car made in the same year but which stayed in Britain.

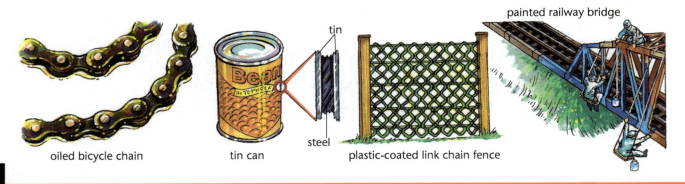

oiled bicycle chain   tin can   plastic-coated link chain fence   painted railway bridge

tin

steel

■ Improving the barrier

One of the best ways of preventing steel from rusting is to coat the steel with **zinc**. We call this <u>galvanised steel</u>. Galvanising steel makes it more expensive.

Look at the table. It shows the guarantees modern cars carry against rusting.

4 Why do cars last longer now than in the 1960s?

5 What makes the guarantees different?

6 Why aren't all the steel parts of all cars galvanised?

A coating of zinc is better than paint or plastic.
It protects the steel even when there is a scratch in the coating.

Make of car	Percentage of galvanised steel in car body	Anti-rusting guarantee in years
A	100	10
B	50	6
C	35	5
D	70	8

■ Corrosion of other metals

The less reactive a metal is, the less likely it is to **corrode** or tarnish.

Look at the pictures of gold and silver.

7 What does the picture tell you about gold? Give a reason for your answer.

8 What does the picture tell you about silver?

9 Which of these two metals is more reactive, silver or gold? Explain your answer.

This wedding ring has been in and out of water 'lots of times' every day for thirty years.

some weeks later

WHAT YOU NEED TO REMEMBER (Copy and complete using the **key words**)

Corroding metals

Rusting is a special case of _____.
Rusting takes place when iron or steel is in contact with both air and _____.

Most methods of slowing down rusting use a _____.
One of the best barriers is _____.

The less reactive a metal is, the less likely it is to _____.

3.5 Acids and alkalis

Acids are often made in the air. For example, whenever a volcano erupts, it throws tonnes of **acidic** gases into the air.

Whenever lightning flashes, the energy from the flash makes oxygen and nitrogen from the air react. This produces acidic gases called <u>nitrogen oxides</u>.

1 Look at the diagrams. Then copy and complete the table.

	Acidic gas produced	Acid produced
volcanoes		
lightning		

■ **Alkalis**

The opposites of acids are **alkalis**. These are not as common as acids. But we can easily make alkalis from two substances we find in the Earth's crust.

2 What alkali is made:

(a) from salt?

(b) by heating limestone?

(c) from both salt and limestone?

■ **Making useful substances from alkalis**

Alkalis are very useful.

Early houses had only very primitive windows. For example, the Romans used very thin leather smeared with oil.

3 Roman windows were good for some purposes but not for others. Explain why.

4 (a) What material do we use now for windows?

(b) What alkalis are used to make this material?

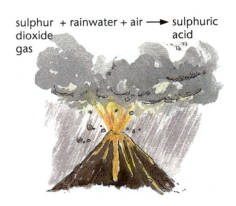

sulphur + rainwater + air ⟶ sulphuric
dioxide   acid
gas

nitrogen + oxygen + water ⟶ nitric acid

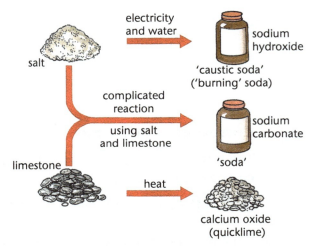

salt

electricity and water ⟶ sodium hydroxide
'caustic soda' ('burning' soda)

complicated reaction using salt and limestone ⟶ sodium carbonate
'soda'

limestone

heat ⟶ calcium oxide (quicklime)

Roman windows let light through, but you could not see through them clearly.

sand + quicklime + soda ⟶ furnace ⟶ glass

■ More things made from alkalis

Until the 19th century, people made soap by boiling fat with wood ashes. Soap was very expensive. So most people did not wash themselves with soap very often.

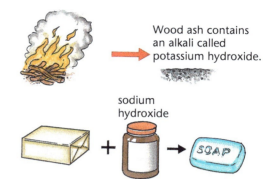

Wood ash contains an alkali called potassium hydroxide.

5 (a) Why were wood ashes used to make soap?

(b) What alkali do we use today to make soap?

People have used natural fibres like wool, cotton, silk and linen for thousands of years. Rayon was the first artificial fibre.

6 What alkali do we use to make it?

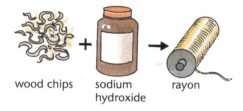

sodium hydroxide

How we make soap today.

wood chips   sodium hydroxide   rayon

How rayon is made.

■ Acidic, neutral or alkaline?

Many plants contain natural **dyes** that change **colour** in acids and alkalis. Chemists call these dyes, **indicators**. They tell us whether a substance is an acid or an alkali. They can also tell us whether a substance is <u>neutral</u>.

7 Why are the flowers in the photographs different colours?

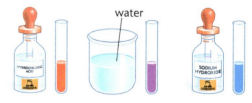

More acidic soil   …less acidic soil

■ Litmus

Litmus is a very well known indicator that comes from a kind of plant called a lichen.

8 What colour is litmus with:

(a) acids?   **(b)** alkalis?   **(c)** neutral solutions?

The test tubes contain litmus mixed with each of the other substances.

WHAT YOU NEED TO REMEMBER (Copy and complete using the **key words**)

Acids and alkalis

Sulphur dioxide from volcanoes and nitrogen oxides from lightning are _____ gases.

The opposites of acids are _____.

Chemists tell the difference between acids and alkalis by using _____.
These are often natural _____. In acids and alkalis, they change _____.

3.6 Acids in the soil

For farmers and gardeners, the most important part of the Earth's crust is the layer of soil on the top.

They sometimes test the soil with a special indicator called <u>universal indicator</u>.

This tells them more than just whether the soil is acidic or alkaline. It also tells them <u>how</u> acidic or alkaline it is.

The indicator measures **pH** (said 'pea-aitch').

1 Copy and complete the following.

_____ pH numbers = more acidic
_____ pH numbers = more alkaline
A pH number of 7 = _____

Getting rid of soil acidity

When soil is too acidic, many plants will not grow. Some plants, such as cabbages, grow better in slightly alkaline soil. Gardeners add lime (calcium hydroxide) to their soil. Lime is an alkali. This neutralises or takes away the acid in the soil.

2 Farmer Giles wants to plant potatoes, peas, sugar beet, maize and cabbages.

Copy the plan of the farm and write what he should plant on each field.

Using fertilisers

Adding fertilisers to the soil helps plants like wheat to grow.

3 What happens to the acidity of the soil if the farmer uses fertilisers year after year?

4 Farmers using fertilisers need to add lime to the fields. Explain why.

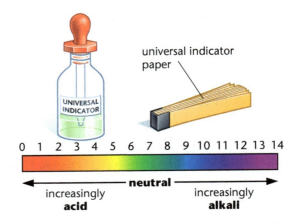

universal indicator paper

0 1 2 3 4 5 6 7 8 9 10 11 12 13 14

increasingly **acid** ← neutral → increasingly **alkali**

Crop	Best pH for plant
potatoes	5
peas	5.5
maize	6
sugar beet	6.5
cabbage	7–8

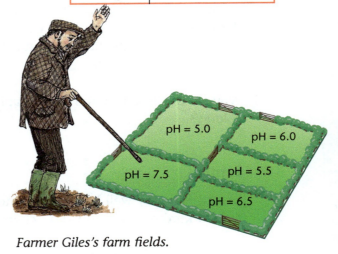

pH = 5.0
pH = 6.0
pH = 7.5
pH = 5.5
pH = 6.5

Farmer Giles's farm fields.

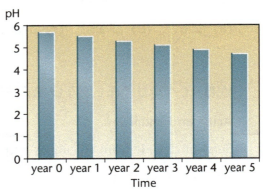

How using fertiliser for several years affects the acidity of soil.

What new substances does neutralisation make?

Neutralisations are chemical reactions. Like all chemical reactions, they make new substances.

When an alkali neutralises an acid, we get a **salt** and **water**.

5 The diagram shows an experiment where sodium hydroxide was added to hydrochloric acid drop by drop.

   (a) Write down the pH in each flask. [Use the chart opposite.]

(b) Which flask shows the end of the neutralisation reaction?

(c) What two substances does the reaction make?

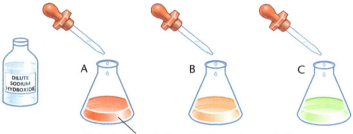
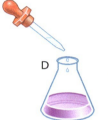

dilute hydrochloric acid plus universal indicator

The salt produced in the reaction between this acid and this alkali is called sodium chloride.

Another way to neutralise soil

Farmers can also neutralise the soil in their fields by spreading crushed limestone on it.

Limestone is calcium carbonate. When a carbonate neutralises an acid, you get a salt, water and **carbon dioxide** gas.

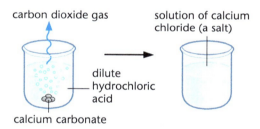

carbon dioxide gas

solution of calcium chloride (a salt)

dilute hydrochloric acid

calcium carbonate

All metal carbonates react with acid in the same way as calcium carbonate.

6 Copy and complete the word equation for this reaction.

_____ acid + calcium _____ → calcium _____ + _____ + _____ _____

WHAT YOU NEED TO REMEMBER (Copy and complete using the **key words**)

Acids in the soil

We use universal indicator to measure _____.
A pH of 7 means that the solution is _____.

When the pH is less than 7, we have an _____.
When the pH is more than 7, we have an _____.

When an alkali neutralises an acid, we get a _____ and _____ only.
When a carbonate neutralises an acid, we get a salt, water and _____ _____.

More about salts: C+ 3.11

3.7 Weathering rocks

Gold miners in ancient Egypt needed to break up rocks to get the gold. So they built fires to heat up the rock faces deep inside the mines. The rock expanded. They then threw cold water on to the hot rock. The rock cooled suddenly, contracted and shattered. The miners could then get at the bits of gold in the rock.

Something similar happens in deserts.

Imitating nature in an ancient Egyptian gold mine.

1 What happens to the stones of the gibber deserts

(a) during the day? (b) at night?

2 Explain how the Egyptain gold miners were 'imitating nature'.

Australian gibber plains. The stones range from about 30 cm across down to small pebbles. The Sun's heat causes them to expand and the cold of the night causes them to contract. This cracks the stones into smaller and smaller pebbles.

■ Wind

When the **wind** blows hard in a desert, it makes a sandstorm. When bits of sand hit the surface of a rock, they gradually wear it away. We say that they scour away the rock.

3 Why is the rock in the picture shaped like a mushroom?

In sandstorms, the air close to the ground contains the most sand. So this air scours the rock most.

■ Water

Water gets into cracks in the rocks. When the temperature drops, the water freezes. Water expands when it freezes. This can force a crack to become wider and wider. Eventually the rock splits.

Water rushing down a mountainside carries with it small bits of rock. These grind away at other rocks, wearing them down.

4 A large rock from the top of a mountain can eventually end up as a lot of small rounded pebbles at the bottom of the mountain. Describe how this happens.

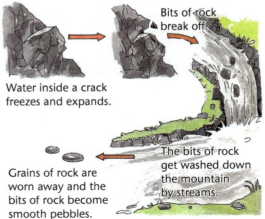

Bits of rock break off.

Water inside a crack freezes and expands.

The bits of rock get washed down the mountain by streams.

Grains of rock are worn away and the bits of rock become smooth pebbles.

■ Rivers of ice

In cold climates, huge rivers of **ice** flow down mountains. These are called <u>glaciers</u>. The huge weight of the ice grinds away at the rock.

5 If a glacier moved at about two metres a year, how long would it take to travel 1 kilometre?

The action of the Sun, wind, water and ice breaks down rocks into smaller pieces. This is called **erosion**.

It is the weather that causes the surfaces of rocks to break up. We call this **weathering**.

Glaciers contain millions of tonnes of ice. They slide down at a few metres per year. They carve out entire valleys. They carry thousands of tonnes of ground up rocks with them.

■ Chemical weathering

Carbon dioxide dissolves in rainwater to make it slightly acidic. Rainwater very slowly reacts with rocks that contain carbonates. We call this **chemical weathering**.

6 Is the chemical weathering of limestone a fast or slow process? Explain your answer.

Chemical weathering takes place faster when the air is polluted with other acidic gases. These are mainly sulphur dioxide and nitrogen oxides from burning fuels.

7 (a) Where is the air more polluted with acidic gases – in the countryside or in the town?

(b) Where is chemical weathering fastest?

This is known as a limestone pavement. Every 500 years, the rainwater dissolves another 1 cm of limestone. The rainwater reacts chemically with the limestone. The new substance formed dissolves in the water. The gaps between the slabs become deeper as the rainwater drains through them.

Motor vehicles produce acidic gases.

WHAT YOU NEED TO REMEMBER (Copy and complete using the **key words**)

Weathering rocks

Rocks being broken down into smaller pieces is called _____.
This is caused by the Sun, the _____, water and _____.
Because erosion is caused by the weather, we call it _____.

Chemical reactions can also attack rocks; we call this _____ _____.

More about ice and water: C+ 3.12, 3.13

3.8 Looking after the environment

We live on top of the Earth's crust. But this is only part of our environment. The air in the Earth's atmosphere and the water in rivers, lakes and seas, are also part of our environment. How we live and what we do also affects these parts of our environment.

The air and the water in our environment have improved in some ways over the last 40 years. The air is cleaner because coal is no longer burnt in most homes and factories. Our rivers and streams are cleaner because we now try to stop factories and sewage works from discharging waste straight into the waterways.

An industrial town in the 1950s.

1 How did many ordinary people pollute the air before the 1960s?

2 How did factories damage the environment?

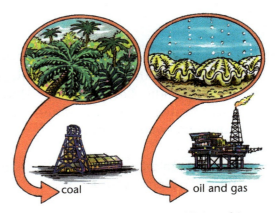

Fossil fuels are the remains of living things. These remains are found underground. They were changed by heat and pressure into what they are now – coal, gas or oil.

■ Using fossil fuels

Fossil fuels are our main source of **energy**.

3 (a) Write down <u>three</u> fossil fuels.

(b) Why are they called fossil fuels?

Each of the pictures shows a fossil fuel (or a fuel made from a fossil fuel) being used.

4 Give <u>one</u> example of how each of these fuels is used:

coal petrol diesel gas wax

All these fuels contain carbon and **hydrogen**.

5 When petrol burns, what new <u>substances</u> do the following make?

(a) carbon atoms (b) hydrogen atoms

6 What else do these burning fuels release?

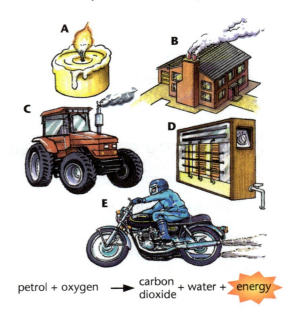

petrol + oxygen → carbon dioxide + water + energy

■ Pollution from cars

The invention of the motor car was one of the biggest changes that happened in the last 100 years. Cars give us a freedom to travel around.

The Strand, London, in 1887.

7 What is the main difference between the two photographs of the same street?

8 What does the graph tell us about the use of the motor car?

When a car burns petrol or diesel, it doesn't only produce carbon dioxide and **water**. It also makes small amounts of poisonous gases such as carbon monoxide and **nitrogen oxides**. Diesel engines also give out smoke containing carbon particles that enter deep into our lungs. All of this pollution can damage our health.

Car engines and exhausts are being improved all the time to reduce the amount of pollution they cause. But the number of cars keeps on increasing.

9 Will the pollution from cars get worse or get better? Explain your answer.

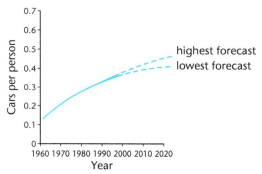

The Strand, London, in the 1990s.

Forecast of car ownership in Britain to 2020.

■ Controlling a burning fuel

For burning to take place, three things must be present. We can show this in what is called the <u>fire triangle</u>.

10 Look at the fire triangle. Write down <u>three</u> ways in which a fire can be put out.

The fire triangle has three sides. Take away one of the sides, and the triangle collapses and the fire goes out.

WHAT YOU NEED TO REMEMBER (Copy and complete using the **key words**)

Looking after the environment

Fossil fuels contain carbon and _____.
When fossil fuels such as petrol burn, they release carbon dioxide and _____.

The useful thing that we get from fossil fuels is _____.

The motor car also produces small amounts of carbon monoxide and _____ _____.

More about pollution: C+ 3.14, 3.15

3.9 More about the rock cycle

The diagram shows you what you already know about the rock cycle.

If rock gets very hot, it may melt and form magma.

1 Does this change take in or give out energy?

When magma solidifies, it forms igneous rock.

2 Does this change take in or give out energy?

But there are some things that this simple rock cycle diagram doesn't explain. For example, the rocks at the tops of very high mountains are often **sedimentary** rocks.

3 Why can't the rock cycle diagram explain this?

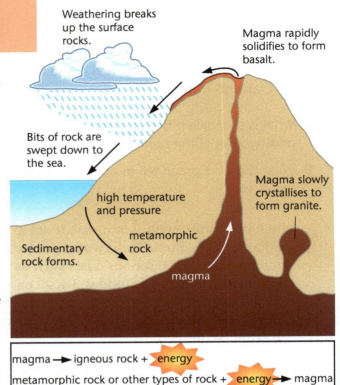

Weathering breaks up the surface rocks.

Magma rapidly solidifies to form basalt.

Bits of rock are swept down to the sea.

high temperature and pressure

metamorphic rock

Magma slowly crystallises to form granite.

Sedimentary rock forms.

magma

magma → igneous rock + energy

metamorphic rock or other types of rock + energy → magma

This rock from the top of a mountain contains fossils. So it must be a sedimentary rock.

How do sedimentary rocks get to the tops of mountains?

The Earth's crust is split into different sections or 'plates'. These plates float around on the hot, liquid magma beneath.

When two plates collide, one of them can be pushed up to form **mountains**.

4 (a) What type of rocks do we sometimes find at the top of mountains?

(b) Explain how the fossils came to be in the rock.

5 How did sedimentary rocks get to the top of mountains?

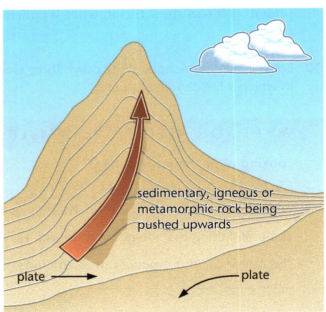

sedimentary, igneous or metamorphic rock being pushed upwards

plate

plate

Making more sedimentary rocks

All types of rock can be pushed up to form new mountains. These rocks are gradually broken down and eventually form new sedimentary rocks.

The diagrams show how.

6 Copy and complete the flow chart below. Use the information from the diagrams to help you.

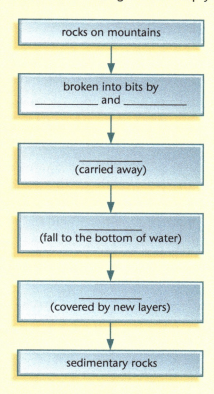

7 Write down three ways in which rocks are transported down a mountain.

Rocks are broken into bits by **weathering** and **erosion**.

avalanche   stream   glacier

Small bits of rock are carried down mountains. This is called **transportation**.

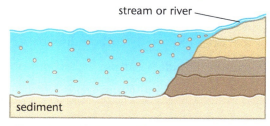

stream or river

sediment

Bits of rock fall as sediment to the bottom of lakes and sea. This is called **deposition**.

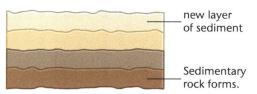

new layer of sediment

Sedimentary rock forms.

Old layers of sediment are covered by new layers. This is called **burial**.

WHAT YOU NEED TO REMEMBER (Copy and complete using the **key words**)

More about the rock cycle

When plates in the Earth's crust collide, rocks are slowly pushed up to form _____.

The rocks at the top of the new mountain can be igneous, metamorphic or _____.
These rocks are then broken down by _____ and _____.
They are carried down the mountainside; this is called _____.
At the bottom of the mountain they form a sediment; this is called _____.
Later new rock is formed as the sediment gets covered up; this is called _____.

3.10 Smelting metals

Look at the formulas of the ores in the box.

1 What do these two ores have in common?

■ How easy is it to smelt a metal?

To get a metal out of one of its compounds, we have to remove the non-metals. This needs energy. The more **reactive** the metal is, then the more **energy** we must put in to extract each atom of the metal.

2 To extract the same number of atoms of metal, which ore needs the most energy, Fe_2O_3 or Al_2O_3? Explain your answer.

To extract iron from iron oxide, we heat it in a blast furnace with **carbon** (coke).

> **Reactions in a blast furnace**
>
> carbon + oxygen → carbon dioxide + energy
>
> carbon dioxide + carbon → carbon monoxide
>
> carbon monoxide + iron oxide → iron + carbon dioxide

3 (a) Write down the reaction that provides the energy.

(b) Write down the reaction that takes the oxygen away from the iron oxide.

■ Extracting aluminium

4 Aluminium is the most common metal in the Earth's crust. But it was not extracted until 1827. What does this tell you about aluminium?

We use **electricity** to get aluminium.

> **The chemical formula of an ore tells you:**
> - what elements are in the chemical compound;
> - how many atoms of each element are in the formula.
>
> Fe_2O_3 contains 2 atoms of iron for every 3 atoms of oxygen, and Al_2O_3 contains 2 atoms of aluminium for every 3 atoms of oxygen.

> **Reactivity series of metals**
>
> | | |
> |---|---|
> | sodium | most reactive |
> | magnesium | extracted with |
> | aluminium | electricity |
> | zinc | |
> | iron | can be extracted |
> | lead | with carbon |
> | copper | |
> | silver | found native |
> | gold | least reactive |

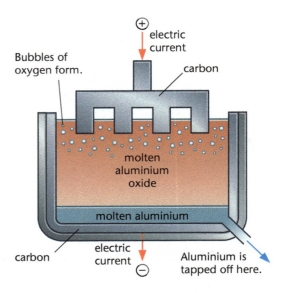

Bubbles of oxygen form.

electric current

carbon

molten aluminium oxide

molten aluminium

carbon

electric current

Aluminium is tapped off here.

WHAT YOU NEED TO REMEMBER (Copy and complete using the **key words**)

Smelting metals

The more _____ the metal, the more _____ is needed to extract it.
We smelt metals in the middle of the reactivity series, like iron, with _____.
But for metals higher in the reactivity series, like aluminium, we use _____.

3.11 More about salts

When an acid and an alkali react together, they make a salt and water.

1 Look at the word equation.

(a) What salt is produced in this reaction?

(b) What kind of reaction is it?

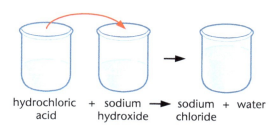

hydrochloric + sodium → sodium + water
acid   hydroxide   chloride

In a salt, you always put the name of the metal first.

Making different salts

The type of salt you get in a reaction depends on what acid and what alkali you use.

2 What salt do you get when the following react together?

(a) nitric acid and sodium hydroxide

(b) sulphuric acid and potassium hydroxide

Which acid? Which salt?

Hydrochloric acid makes **chlorides**.

Nitric acid makes **nitrates**.

Sulphuric acid makes **sulphates**.

Another way to make salts

A reactive metal can push the hydrogen out of acids. The new compound formed is a salt.

magnesium + sulphuric → magnesium + hydrogen
               acid   sulphate

3 Write a word equation to show the reaction of:

(a) zinc with sulphuric acid.
(b) magnesium with hydrochloric acid.

 copper sulphate   sodium chloride   iron sulphate

solution of salt A

Looking at salts

Iron salts are usually pale green or yellow. Copper salts are usually blue. Most other salts are white.

4 Look at the pictures. Match the labels with the salts A, B and C.

crystals of salt B

crystals of salt C

WHAT YOU NEED TO REMEMBER (Copy and complete using the **key words**)

More about salts

Hydrochloric acid makes salts called ＿＿＿＿＿＿. Sulphuric acid makes salts called ＿＿＿＿＿＿.
Nitric acid makes salts called ＿＿＿＿＿.

3.14 Carbon dioxide and the greenhouse effect

Go into a greenhouse on a cold winter's day and you could be pleasantly surprised. The temperature is almost always warmer than outside. The diagram shows why.

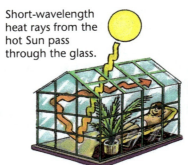

Short-wavelength heat rays from the hot Sun pass through the glass.

Long-wavelength heat rays from the greenhouse cannot escape.

1 How does the greenhouse stay warmer inside than outside?

Some gases in the atmosphere – **carbon dioxide** and methane – act like the glass of the greenhouse. They let the heat rays from the Sun pass through. But they absorb the longer wave heat rays given off by the Earth and send some of that heat back to Earth.

2 How does the greenhouse effect work for the Earth?

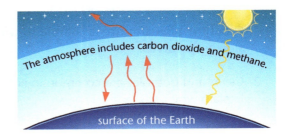

The atmosphere includes carbon dioxide and methane.

surface of the Earth

■ Level of carbon dioxide in the atmosphere

Until about 150 years ago, there was about 0.03% of carbon dioxide in the air. This had been roughly the same for millions of years.

But for the last 150 years or so, we have burned **fossil fuels** at an increasing rate. This releases more carbon dioxide into the air. Today, the level of carbon dioxide is about 0.035% and is still rising.

Carbon dioxide doesn't do any harm directly. But with more carbon dioxide in the air, we expect the greenhouse effect to increase. The Earth's average **temperature** may be 1 to 2 °C warmer in the near future. This might affect our weather and cause more of the ice at the North and South poles to melt.

increasing areas of desert

melting of the polar ice

3 (a) What might happen because of an increased greenhouse effect?

(b) Explain how this might happen.

rising sea levels

longer and more frequent famines

What might happen if the Earth gets warmer.

WHAT YOU NEED TO REMEMBER (Copy and complete using the **key words**)

Carbon dioxide and the greenhouse effect

One of the greenhouse gases is _____ _____.

The amount of carbon dioxide in the air increases because we burn _____ _____.

An increase in the greenhouse effect will raise the Earth's average _____.

3.15 Waste and pollution

One of the problems that all villages, towns and cities have, is getting rid of waste.

Two ways that help solve the problem are:

■ some kind of rubbish collection;

■ a sewage system.

But this waste doesn't just **disappear**.

> **1** What happens to the household waste that we put into the dustbin?
>
> **2** Where would the waste that we flush down the sewer finish up if it wasn't treated?

sewage treatment plant

river

sea

■ Waste gases

When we burn waste, it does look as if we've got rid of it altogether. But we haven't really. The diagram shows why.

> **3** What happens to the waste that seems to disappear when you burn it?
>
> **4** Why can't waste ever just disappear?

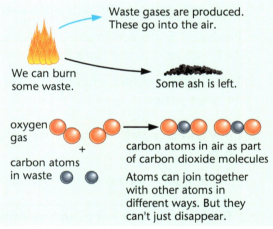

Waste gases are produced. These go into the air.

We can burn some waste.

Some ash is left.

oxygen gas

carbon atoms in waste

+

carbon atoms in air as part of carbon dioxide molecules

Atoms can join together with other atoms in different ways. But they can't just disappear.

■ How can we prevent pollution?

All the waste we produce has to go somewhere here on Earth. That's why there's a problem with pollution.

> **5** Hardly any matter leaves the Earth. What are the only <u>two</u> ways that this can happen?

The only way we can prevent pollution is to change all our waste into **harmless** substances. Then we can let them into the air or put them into the ground or into our rivers, lakes and seas.

Space rockets move fast enough to escape from Earth. The only other things that can move this fast are hydrogen molecules.

WHAT YOU NEED TO REMEMBER (Copy and complete using the **key words**)

Waste and pollution

Waste is a problem because it can never just _____.

To prevent pollution, we must change waste into _____ substances.

1.1 The Sun and the Earth's satellites

When it is daytime on one half of the Earth, it is night on the other half. The diagram shows why.

1 Copy and complete the sentences.

Light travels in _____ lines.
So the side of the Earth that faces away from the Sun is in _____.

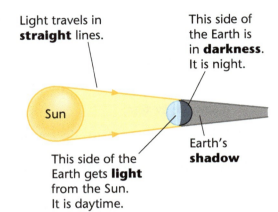

Light travels in **straight** lines.

This side of the Earth is in **darkness**. It is night.

Sun

This side of the Earth gets **light** from the Sun. It is daytime.

Earth's **shadow**

■ Day and night

The Earth spins on its axis once every 24 hours.

Places on Earth are in the light for part of each 24 hours and in the dark for the rest.

The diagram shows where Britain is during a 24-hour period.

2 Copy and complete the table using the following words.

coming light   going dark   mid-day   midnight

Time	What's happening in Britain
06:00	
12:00	
18:00	
00:00	

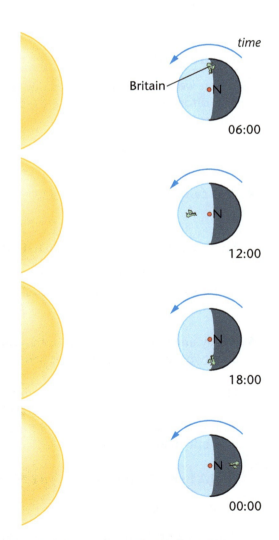

time

Britain

•N

06:00

•N

12:00

•N

18:00

•N

00:00

Looking down on the Earth for 24 hours in mid-March.

Moonlight

The Sun is very hot. So it gives out **light** as well as heat.

The Moon doesn't send out its own light. But we can still see it. The diagram shows why.

3 Why can we see the Moon?

The Moon goes round the Earth. We say that the Moon **orbits** the Earth. We also say that the Moon is a **satellite** of the Earth.

Watching other satellites

Humans have put lots of small satellites into orbit around the Earth. We can sometimes see these satellites in the night sky. They look like stars but you can see them moving.

4 Satellites don't give out their own light. So how can we see them?

The diagram shows a satellite in different positions as it orbits the Earth.

5 (a) Why can't you see the satellite from Earth when it is in position A?

(b) You <u>can</u> see the satellite from Earth when it is in position B. Explain why.

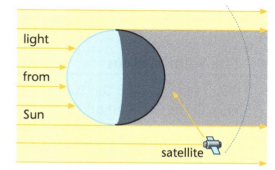

light from Sun

light **reflected** from Moon

Britain

When the Moon is in the position shown, it looks like this from Britain.

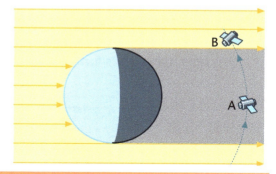

light from Sun

satellite

B

A

WHAT YOU NEED TO REMEMBER (Copy and complete using the **key words**)

The Sun and the Earth's satellites

The Sun gives out its own _____.

Light travels in _____ lines.

The side of the Earth that faces away from the Sun is in _____. This is because it is in the Earth's _____.

The Moon _____ the Earth. We say that it is a _____ of the Earth.

We can see the Moon and other satellites because light from the Sun is _____ from them.

More about shadows: C+ 1.9

1.2 The solar system and the stars

The Sun is about 400 times further away from Earth than the Moon is.

The Sun's diameter is about 400 times bigger than the Moon's diameter.

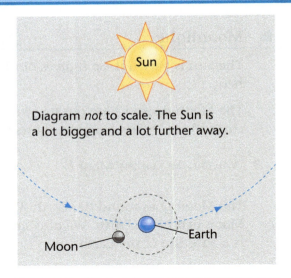

Diagram *not* to scale. The Sun is a lot bigger and a lot further away.

1 Copy and complete the sentence.

   The Moon is much nearer to _____ than the Sun is.

2 The Sun and the Moon both look the same size from Earth. Explain why.

■ The solar system

Other planets orbit the Sun just like the Earth does. We call the Sun and all its planets the <u>solar system</u>.

3 Which two planets are nearer to the Sun than the Earth is?

4 (a) Which planet is the next furthest away from the Sun than the Earth?

   (b) How many times further away is it than the Earth?

Planet	Average distance from Sun (millions of kilometres)
Mercury	58
Venus	108
Earth	150
Mars	225
Jupiter	780
Saturn	1430
Uranus	2870
Neptune	4500
Pluto	5900

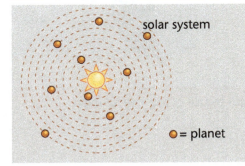

solar system

○ = planet

Diagram *not* to scale. The stars are a lot further away.

■ Stars

The **Sun** is a star.

All the other stars are <u>much</u> further away from Earth than the Sun is.

5 Many stars give out a lot more light than the Sun. But they look a lot fainter. Explain why.

Stars give out their own light. The Sun is our nearest star. The next nearest star is about a quarter of a million times further away from the Earth than the Sun is.

How we see planets

We can sometimes see other planets from Earth. The diagram shows how.

6 Why can we sometimes see other planets?

Planets and stars both look like small points of light in the night sky.

Stars stay in fixed patterns called **constellations**. But planets seem to move slowly through the constellations of stars.

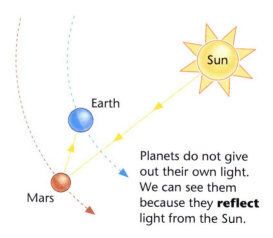

Planets do not give out their own light. We can see them because they **reflect** light from the Sun.

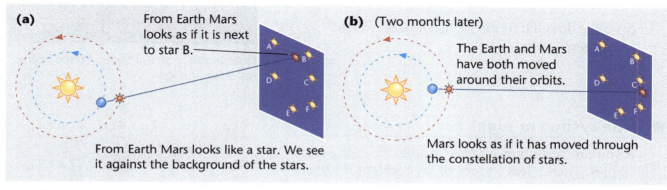

(a) From Earth Mars looks as if it is next to star B.

From Earth Mars looks like a star. We see it against the background of the stars.

(b) (Two months later)

The Earth and Mars have both moved around their orbits.

Mars looks as if it has moved through the constellation of stars.

7 Copy and complete the sentences.

Planets seem to _____ through the constellations of stars.

In diagram (a), Mars looks as if it is next to star _____.

Two months later, Mars looks as if it is next to star _____.

8 During each night the constellations of stars seem to move across the sky. Why is this?

The Earth **spins** round in one direction.

The stars and planets seem to move in the opposite direction.

More about movements in space: C+ 1.10

147

1.3 Driving at night

At night there is no light from the Sun.

In towns, street lights come on at night. But cars still need lights so that other people can see them.

Outside of towns, cars need headlights so that drivers can see where they are going.

1 Look at the diagram.

   (a) Explain how the driver sees the bend sign.

   (b) Why does the headlight beam have straight edges?

■ Safe cycling at night

If you are cycling at night, it is safer to wear pale clothes. There's less chance of an accident if drivers can see you easily.

2 Why can drivers see pale clothes more easily?

3 What happens to most of the light that falls on dark clothes?

The photograph shows some other ways to make cycling at night safer.

4 Write down <u>three</u> other things cyclists can do to make sure they are easy to see at night.

Cars and bicycles have rear lights so that people behind them can see them more easily in the dark.

DO YOU REMEMBER?
from *Core Science 1*

We can see some things because they give out their own light.

We can see other things because they reflect light that comes from something else.

Light travels in straight lines. So the beam has straight edges.

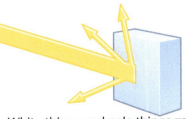

White things and pale things **reflect** most of the light that falls on them.

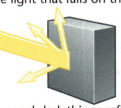

Black things and dark things reflect very little of the light that falls on them. They absorb most of the light.

Cyclists need to be easy to see at night.

Car mirrors

Car drivers need to see the traffic behind them as well as the traffic in front of them. They do this using mirrors.

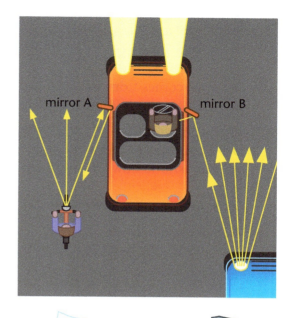

mirror A   mirror B

5 Look at the diagram.

(a) Which mirror does the driver of the red car use to see the car that is overtaking her?

(b) When the driver of the red car looks at mirror A she can't see the cyclist that she is overtaking. Explain why.

(c) What should the driver do to mirror A as soon as she gets the chance?

What's special about mirrors?

A mirror and a piece of white paper both reflect most of the light that falls on them. But you can't see things in a piece of white paper.

A mirror and a piece of white paper reflect light in different ways. The diagrams show how.

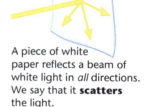
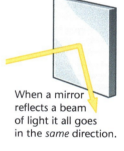

A piece of white paper reflects a beam of white light in *all* directions. We say that it **scatters** the light.

When a mirror reflects a beam of light it all goes in the *same* direction.

6 Copy and complete the sentences.

A piece of white paper reflects a beam of light in all _____.

A mirror reflects a beam of light in just _____ direction. The beam is reflected at the same _____ as it strikes the mirror.

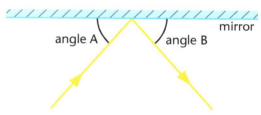

angle A   angle B   mirror

The mirror reflects a beam at the same angle as it strikes the mirror.
So angle A and angle B are **equal**.

WHAT YOU NEED TO REMEMBER (Copy and complete using the **key words**)

Driving at night

White or pale surfaces _____ light better than black or dark surfaces.

A piece of white paper reflects light in all directions; it _____ the light.

The diagram shows how a mirror reflects a beam of light.

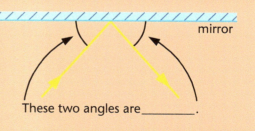

mirror

These two angles are_____.

More about mirrors: C+ 1.11

1.4 Colour

Daylight comes from the Sun. It doesn't look coloured, so we say that it is <u>white</u> light.

Although light from the Sun looks white, it is in fact a **mixture** of many different colours. The diagram shows how we know this.

> **1** Copy and complete the sentences.
>
> We can use a prism to _____ white light into colours. The band of colours that we get is called a _____.

■ Why daffodils look yellow

In daylight, daffodil flowers look yellow. The diagram shows why.

> **2** Why do daffodil flowers look yellow?
>
> **3** Why do the stems and leaves of daffodils look green?

■ How to make daffodils look black

If you look at a daffodil flower through a blue filter, it looks black. The diagram shows why.

> **4** Copy and complete the sentences.
>
> The blue filter lets through mainly _____ light. But the daffodil flower doesn't _____ any blue light. So it looks _____.
>
> **5** The daffodil stem looks dark but not black. Explain why.

You can split white light into colours using a transparent prism. We say that the prism **disperses** the white light.

We call these bands of colour a **spectrum**.

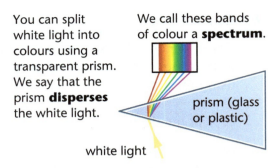

prism (glass or plastic)

white light

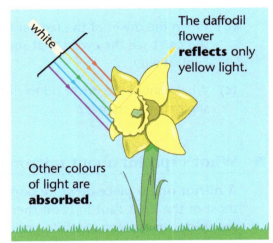

The daffodil flower **reflects** only yellow light.

Other colours of light are **absorbed**.

A daffodil through a blue filter.

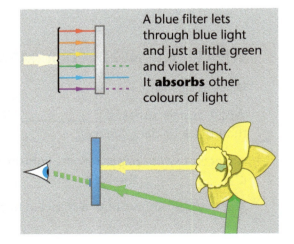

A blue filter lets through blue light and just a little green and violet light. It **absorbs** other colours of light

■ Daylight and artificial light

Some street lights definitely look yellow.

Light bulbs and fluorescent tubes seem to give out white light. But the mixture of colours isn't quite the same as it is in daylight.

The bar graphs show the differences.

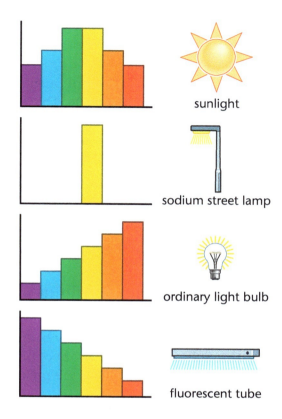

sunlight

sodium street lamp

ordinary light bulb

fluorescent tube

6 Copy and complete the table.

Type of light	Mixture of colours
sunlight	more or less the same amount of all _____ slightly more in the _____ of the spectrum
sodium street light	only _____ light
ordinary light bulb	more of the colours at the _____ end of the spectrum
fluorescent tube	more of the colours at the _____ end of the spectrum

■ Looking at colours in artificial light

Things often look a different colour in artificial light than they do in daylight.

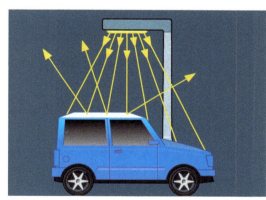

7 A blue car has a white roof. The car is parked under a sodium street light.

(a) What colour will the roof of the car look?

(b) What colour will the bonnet of the car look?

WHAT YOU NEED TO REMEMBER (Copy and complete using the **key words**)

Colour

White light is a _____ of many different colours.

We can split white light into a _____ using a glass or plastic prism.
We say that the prism _____ the white light.

An object looks coloured because it _____ only some of the colours in white light.
The other colours from the white light are _____.

A coloured filter only lets some colours pass through; it_____ other colours.

More about mixing colours: C+ 1.12

1.5 What prisms do to light

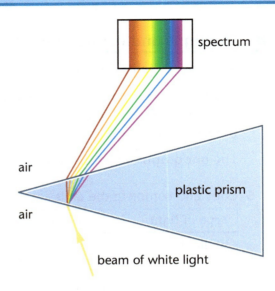

spectrum

You can use a transparent prism to split white light into a spectrum of colours. The diagram shows what happens.

air

plastic prism

air

beam of white light

1 Copy and complete the sentences.

The beam of light passes from the air into the _____ that the prism is made from. Then it travels through the _____. Finally, it passes out of the plastic and back into the _____.

■ What happens to light as it goes into and out of the prism?

Some pupils shine a narrow beam of blue light through a prism. The beam of blue light bends as it passes into and out of the prism. We say that it is **refracted**.

The diagram shows what happens.

A line at right angles to the edge of a prism is called a **normal**.

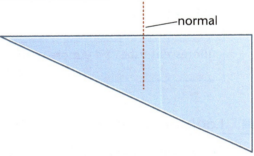

normal

We can use normals to say which way light is refracted (bent).

2 Copy and complete the sentences.

When the beam of light goes into and out of the prism, it is _____.

When it goes into the prism, the light is refracted towards the _____.

When it comes out of the prism, the light is refracted _____ from the normal.

The prism splits a beam of white light up into colours. This is because the prism refracts some colours more than others.

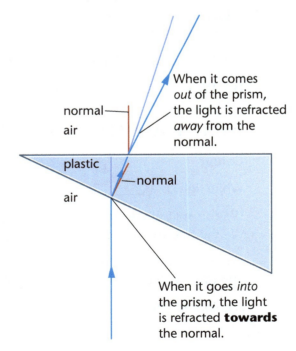

normal

air

When it comes *out* of the prism, the light is refracted *away* from the normal.

plastic

normal

air

When it goes *into* the prism, the light is refracted **towards** the normal.

■ Which colour does a prism refract most?

The diagram shows what happens to beams of red light and violet light as they pass through a prism.

> **3** Copy and complete the sentences.
>
> Violet light and red light are both _____ when they go into and out of a prism. But violet light is refracted _____ than red light.

Violet light is refracted more than any other colour of light. Red light is refracted less than other colours.

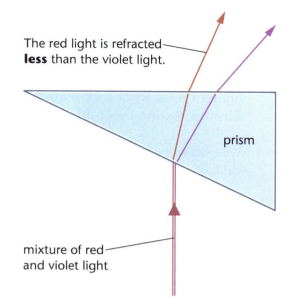

The red light is refracted **less** than the violet light.

prism

mixture of red and violet light

■ How the prism makes a complete spectrum

The different colours in white light are all refracted different amounts. So when a beam of white light goes through a prism a spectrum is formed.

> **4** Copy and complete the following. Put the colours of the spectrum in the right order.
>
>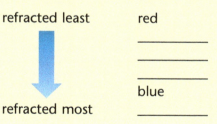
>
> refracted least   red
> _____
> _____
> _____
> blue
> refracted most   _____

There are lots of colours in a spectrum. We usually group them into six or seven broad bands.

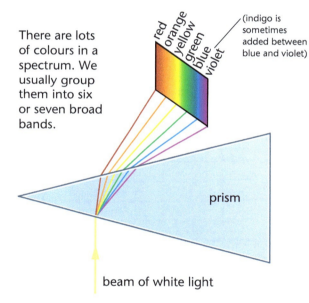

red orange yellow green blue violet

(indigo is sometimes added between blue and violet)

prism

beam of white light

WHAT YOU NEED TO REMEMBER (Copy and complete using the **key words**)

What prisms do to light

When light passes from one substance into another, it is _____.

normal
air
glass or plastic

This beam of light is refracted away from the _____.

glass or plastic
air
—normal

This beam of light is refracted _____ the normal.

Light at the red end of the spectrum is refracted _____ than light at the violet end of the spectrum.

More about using prisms: C+ 1.13

1.6 'Bent' rulers and 'shallow' water

When you look into water, things can look different from what they really are. The diagrams show two examples of this.

1 Write down <u>two</u> ways that you can be tricked when you look into water.

This ruler is straight

But if you dip it into water it looks **bent**.

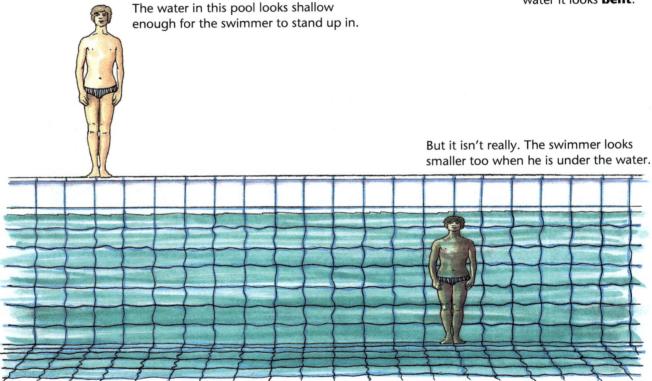

The water in this pool looks shallow enough for the swimmer to stand up in.

But it isn't really. The swimmer looks smaller too when he is under the water.

■ Why does the water trick you?

Light bends when it comes out of water into **air**. We say that it is **refracted**. This makes things look different.

2 Copy and complete the sentences.

A narrow beam of light is often called a _____. When a ray of light passes from water into air, it is refracted away from the _____.

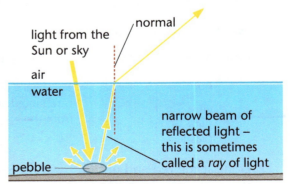

light from the Sun or sky

normal

air

water

narrow beam of reflected light – this is sometimes called a *ray* of light

pebble

We see this pebble because it reflects light that falls on it.

154

■ Why water looks shallower than it is

Water looks **shallower** than it really is because light is refracted as it comes out of the water. The diagram shows what happens.

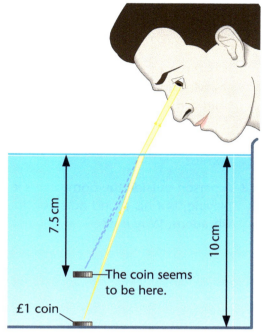

The coin seems to be here.

£1 coin

7.5 cm

10 cm

3 Copy and complete the sentences.

Light is refracted as it passes from water into _____. So water which is 10 centimetres deep only looks _____ centimetres deep.

■ Why a ruler looks bent

Water always looks only three-quarters as deep as it really is. So part of a ruler which is 2 cm below the surface looks as if it is only 1.5 cm below. The same sort of thing happens to all the other parts of the ruler.

The diagram shows where four different parts of the ruler seem to be.

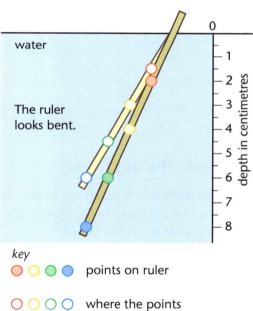

water

The ruler looks bent.

0
1
2
3
4
5
6
7
8

depth in centimetres

4 Copy and complete the table.

How far under water parts of the ruler really are	How far under water parts of the ruler seem to be
2 cm	1.5 cm
4 cm	
6 cm	
8 cm	

These points are joined on the diagram. They show you why the ruler looks bent.

key

●○●○ points on ruler

○○○○ where the points *seem* to be

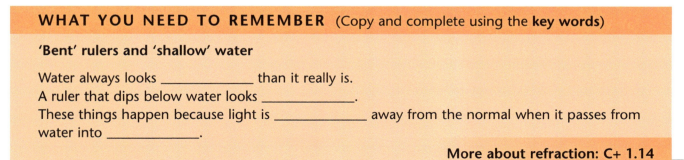

WHAT YOU NEED TO REMEMBER (Copy and complete using the **key words**)

'Bent' rulers and 'shallow' water

Water always looks _____ than it really is.
A ruler that dips below water looks _____.
These things happen because light is _____ away from the normal when it passes from water into _____.

More about refraction: C+ 1.14

1.7 A rock band on the Moon

It is the year 2120. Humans have been living on the Moon for 100 years. To celebrate, they decide to hold a rock concert in the Big Dome.

1 Why do people on the Moon have to live inside domes?

2 A person outside the dome can see the band playing, but his sound detector doesn't pick up any vibrations. Why not?

There is no air on the Moon.

Inside the Big Dome

Two friends are listening to the rock band inside the dome. They are a long way from the band, at the opposite side of the dome.

They see the drummer hit the cymbals. A fraction of a second later they hear the sound. Then they hear faint echoes of the sound.

3 (a) Why is there a delay between seeing the drummer hit the cymbal and hearing the sound?

(b) Why do they hear faint echoes?

Sound is **reflected** from hard surfaces.

sound vibrations travelling through the air

Light travels through air very fast. Sound travels a lot **slower**.

■ Making the sound louder

Rock music is often played very loud. We say that the sounds are <u>amplified</u>.

You can look at sound vibrations using an oscilloscope. You can then see the difference between a loud sound and a quieter one.

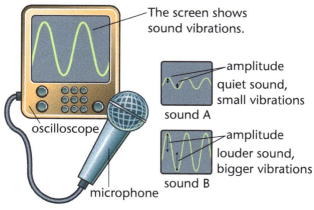

The screen shows sound vibrations.

amplitude
quiet sound, small vibrations
sound A

amplitude
louder sound, bigger vibrations
sound B

oscilloscope

microphone

*We say that the vibrations in sound B have a bigger **amplitude**.*

4 What do you need to be able to look at sound vibrations?

5 Copy and complete the sentences.

Sound B is _____ than sound A. This is because the vibrations have a bigger _____.

6 Rock musicians quite often have damaged hearing. Explain, as fully as you can, how this can happen.

DO YOU REMEMBER?
from *Core Science 1*

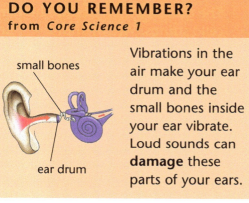

small bones

ear drum

Vibrations in the air make your ear drum and the small bones inside your ear vibrate. Loud sounds can **damage** these parts of your ears.

■ Back on Earth

During the concert, the dome is on the dark side of the Moon. Back on Earth, people can't possibly hear the band, but they <u>can</u> see the laser lights from the dome.

7 Copy and complete the sentence.

People on Earth can see the laser lights on the Moon because light can travel through a _____.

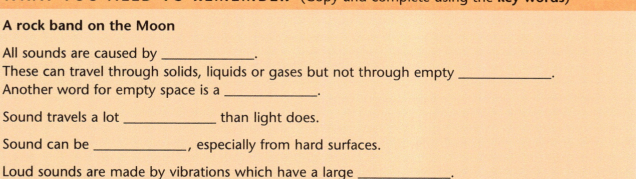

empty space (a vacuum)

dark side of the Moon (in shadow)

laser light

I'll see you on the dark side of the moon ♪

Earth

WHAT YOU NEED TO REMEMBER (Copy and complete using the **key words**)

A rock band on the Moon

All sounds are caused by _____.
These can travel through solids, liquids or gases but not through empty _____.
Another word for empty space is a _____.

Sound travels a lot _____ than light does.

Sound can be _____, especially from hard surfaces.

Loud sounds are made by vibrations which have a large _____.
Loud sounds can _____ your ears.

More about the speed of sound: C+ 1.15

1.8 Two different stringed instruments

The photographs show an electric guitar and a cello.

1 (a) Which parts of the guitar and the cello vibrate to make sounds?

(b) What must you do to make these parts vibrate?

High notes and low notes

The guitar strings produce higher notes than the cello strings. We say that the notes played by the guitar have a higher **pitch**.

Sounds from the guitar have a higher pitch because the vibrations are faster. The number of vibrations each second is called the **frequency**. So sounds from the guitar have a higher pitch because they have a higher frequency.

2 Copy and complete the sentence.

Vibrations that have a high frequency produce sounds which have a _____ pitch.

The box shows what the frequency of a vibrating string depends on.

> To get vibrations with a higher frequency:
>
> - you can make a string tighter;
> - you can make a string shorter;
> - you can use a thinner string.

3 The cello plays notes with a lower pitch than the guitar.

(a) What two differences between the strings that you can see would explain this?

(b) What else affects the pitch of the note that a string plays?

When playing a guitar, you pluck the strings to make them vibrate.

When playing a cello (you say this 'chello'), you use a bow to make the strings vibrate.

■ Tuning a guitar

Each string on a guitar has to be tuned so that it plays exactly the right note.

4 How do you tune the strings?

5 One of the strings of a guitar is out of tune. The pitch is too low. What should you do to make it in tune?

You turn the keys to make the strings tighter or slacker.

■ Playing a guitar

You can play many different notes on the same string of a guitar.

6 (a) What must you do to get different notes?

(b) Explain why this works.

■ What notes can we hear?

The frequencies of sound that people can hear depend on their age. The information in the box tells you what happens.

An elderly guitarist can hear the highest pitched notes he plays on his guitar. But he can't hear the very high pitched note a grasshopper makes.

7 Why can't the guitarist hear the grasshopper?

DO YOU REMEMBER?
from *Core Science 1*

Most children can hear sounds with frequencies between 20 and 20 000 hertz (20–20 000 Hz).

As you get older, the highest frequency you can hear gradually falls to about 10 000 Hz, or even lower.

WHAT YOU NEED TO REMEMBER (Copy and complete using the **key words**)

Two different stringed instruments

If a string vibrates faster, we say that it has a higher _____.

Vibrations with a high frequency produce sounds with a high _____.

You also need to know what is in the 'Do you remember?' box.

More about frequency: C+ 1.16

1.9 Another look at shadows

We get shadows because light travels in straight lines. Light can't get round things that are in the way.

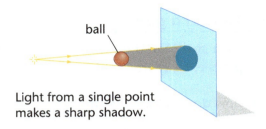

ball

Light from a single point makes a sharp shadow.

■ Looking at the edges of shadows

Shadows cast by light from a light bulb are blurred at the edges. The diagram shows why.

1 Copy and complete the sentences.

Light from a bulb doesn't all come from a single _____.

In the centre of the shadow, no light from the bulb gets past the object so there is a _____ shadow.

At the edges of the shadow, light from part of the bulb gets past the object so there is only a _____ shadow.

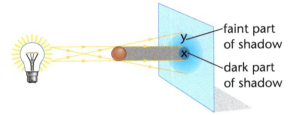

faint part of shadow

dark part of shadow

Light from a bulb doesn't all come from one point.

The shadow now has a blurred edge.

■ What you see if you're in the faint part of the shadow

The diagram shows what you see if your eye is at position Y in the faint part of the shadow.

2 Copy and complete the sentence.

From the faint part of the shadow you see just the _____ of the bulb.

3 Draw what you would see from position X in the shadow.

The diagram shows what happens during an eclipse of the Sun.

4 Copy and complete the table.

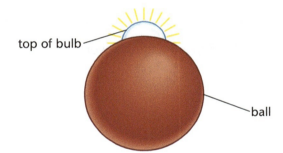

top of bulb

ball

What you can see from Y.

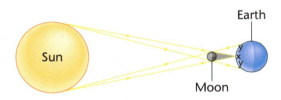

Earth

Sun

Moon

An eclipse of the Sun happens when the Earth is in the Moon's shadow.

x = total eclipse   y = partial eclipse

At a place on Earth in the dark part of the shadow ...	... there is a _____ eclipse.
At a place on Earth in the faint part of the shadow ...	... there is a _____ eclipse.

WARNING!

It is <u>very</u> dangerous to look directly at the Sun, even during an eclipse.

WHAT YOU NEED TO REMEMBER

Another look at shadows

You will need to use Core ideas in different ways like you have on this page.

1.10 Some astronomical speeds

Even when you are standing still, you are moving very fast. This is because the Earth is moving in two ways.

The spinning Earth

You are moving all the time because the Earth is spinning all the time. How fast you move depends on where you are on the Earth.

1 How fast, in kilometres per hour, does a person move because of the Earth's spin:

  (a) at the equator?   **(b)** in London?

  (c) at the north pole?

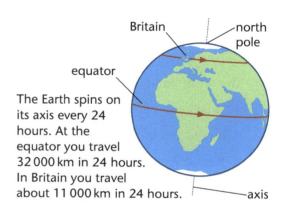

The Earth spins on its axis every 24 hours. At the equator you travel 32 000 km in 24 hours. In Britain you travel about 11 000 km in 24 hours.

The orbiting Earth

The Earth takes a year to orbit the Sun. But it travels a long way in this time. So it still moves quite fast.

2 How fast does the Earth move round its orbit, in kilometres per hour?

The Earth travels about 1 billion kilometres around its orbit in a year (365¼ days).

How fast does light travel?

The Earth travels a billion kilometres in a year. Light travels a billion kilometres in about an hour. This is 300 000 kilometres every second.

A <u>light-year</u> is the distance that light travels in a year. This is a very long way.

Stars are a very long way away. So we can measure the distances to stars in light-years.

3 About how far away is the next nearest star from the Earth:

  (a) in light-years?   **(b)** in kilometres?

solar system

nearest star

It takes more than 4 years for light to travel from the next nearest star to the Earth. We say that this is more than 4 *light-years* away. Diagram *not* to scale.

WHAT YOU NEED TO REMEMBER

Some astronomical speeds

You will need to use Core ideas in different ways like you have on this page.

1.11 Using two mirrors together

Light is reflected from a mirror at the same angle as it strikes the mirror.

You can put two mirrors together at right angles to each other. A ray of light is then reflected from one mirror on to the other mirror.

The first diagram shows what happens to a ray of light that strikes one of the mirrors at 45°.

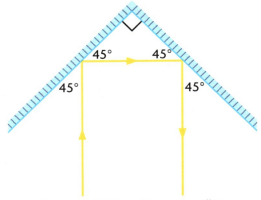

This ray of light ends up travelling in the opposite direction.

> 1 Copy and complete the following.
>
> The ray of light:
>
> ■ strikes one mirror at 45°;
>
> ■ is reflected from this mirror at _____°;
>
> ■ then strikes the other mirror at _____°;
>
> ■ is reflected from this mirror at _____°;
>
> ■ ends up travelling in the _____ direction to the direction it started off.

The second diagram shows what happens to a ray of light that strikes one of the mirrors at 20°.

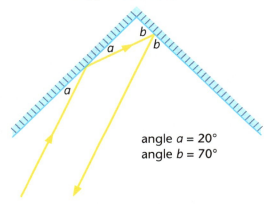

angle $a = 20°$
angle $b = 70°$

All rays of light end up travelling back to where they came from.

> 2 What direction does this ray of light travel in after it has been reflected from both mirrors?

It doesn't matter what direction a ray of light is coming from. After it has been reflected from both mirrors, it ends up travelling back to where it came from.

> 3 Draw a diagram showing how a ray of light that strikes one of the mirrors at 30° is reflected.
>
> 4 Describe an example of when we want light to be reflected back the way it came.

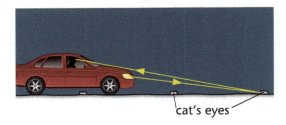

cat's eyes

The lanes on a road are marked with cat's eyes. These have reflectors at right angles inside them. So they reflect light back to where it came from.

WHAT YOU NEED TO REMEMBER

Using two mirrors together

You will need to use Core ideas in different ways like you have on this page.

1.12 Mixing colours

You can split white light into different colours using a prism.

You can then mix all the colours back together again using a second prism.

The diagram shows what happens.

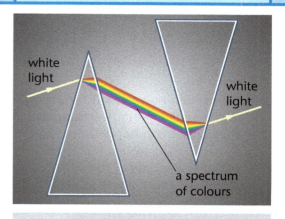

white light

white light

a spectrum of colours

> **1** Copy and complete the sentence.
>
> If you mix together all the colours from a spectrum, you get _____ light back again.

Each part of this colour wheel reflects its own colour of light.

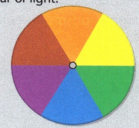

■ Another way to make white light

The diagram shows a colour wheel. If you spin it quickly, the colours seem to disappear and the wheel looks white. The diagrams show why this happens.

As the wheel spins, every colour is reflected in turn. Your eyes see all the colours added together. So the wheel looks white.

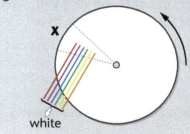

X

white

> **2** Copy and complete the sentences.
>
> The red sector of the colour wheel looks red because it reflects _____ light. The same applies to all of the other coloured sectors of the wheel.
>
> As the wheel rotates, the part of the disc at X reflects first red light, then _____ light, then _____ light, and so on. Altogether it reflects colours from _____ part of the spectrum. So it looks _____.

This mixture absorbs most of the colours. So it looks very dark (usually brownish).

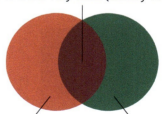

■ Mixing paints

The diagram shows what happens when you mix together red and green paint.

> **3 (a)** What colour do you get?
>
> **(b)** Why do you get this colour?

This paint absorbs most of the colours in white light except red.

This paint absorbs most of the colours in white light except green.

WHAT YOU NEED TO REMEMBER

Mixing colours

You will need to use Core ideas in different ways like you have on this page.

.13 More ways of using prisms

Prisms don't always split white light into a spectrum of different colours. The diagrams show some other things that can happen.

1 Make a large copy of the second diagram. Then label it in the same sort of way as the first diagram.

Using prisms in a periscope

You can use prisms instead of mirrors to make a periscope.

2 Draw a diagram of a periscope with prisms instead of mirrors.

Using prisms in a telescope

To make a telescope, you need to have the right kind of lenses and you need to have them the right distance apart.

The diagrams show two different telescopes made from the same two lenses. These particular lenses need to be 20 cm apart.

3 Copy and complete the sentences.

Binoculars are two _____ side by side. Prisms are often used so that these telescopes are much _____.

Prisms are often used in binoculars. These are two telescopes side by side.

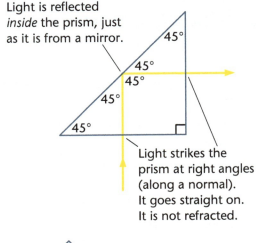

Light is reflected *inside* the prism, just as it is from a mirror.

45° 45° 45° 45° 45°

Light strikes the prism at right angles (along a normal). It goes straight on. It is not refracted.

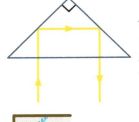

You can use the prism like this to send light back in the opposite direction.

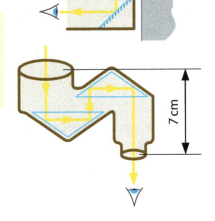

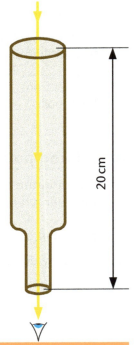

You can use a periscope to see over the top of things.

7 cm

20 cm

Telescopes make far-away things look nearer.

WHAT YOU NEED TO REMEMBER

More ways of using prisms

You will need to use Core ideas in different ways like you have on this page.

1.14 Why glass and plastic look thinner than they are

A piece of glass always looks thinner than it really is. The diagram shows why.

(Don't worry about the very large eye. It just helps to make the diagram clearer.)

1 Copy and complete the sentences.

The glass is really _____ millimetres (mm) thick but it only looks _____ mm thick. This happens because light is _____ as it passes from _____ into _____ .

2 What fraction of its real thickness does the glass seem to be?

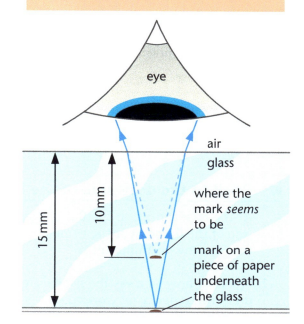

eye

air
glass

15mm

10mm

where the mark *seems* to be

mark on a piece of paper underneath the glass

Measuring how thick plastic looks

The diagram shows a way of measuring how thick a piece of plastic seems to be.

3 Copy and complete the sentences.

You have to move the microscope up _____ mm to bring the mark back into focus. So the mark seems to be _____ mm higher up than it really is.

The plastic is really _____ mm thick, but it only looks _____ mm thick.

4 What fraction of its real thickness does the plastic seem to be?

The microscope is focused on the mark.

You move the microscope up to re-focus the mark.

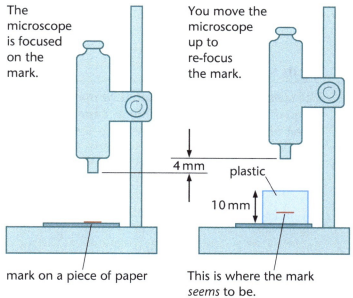

4 mm

plastic

10 mm

mark on a piece of paper

This is where the mark *seems* to be.

.15 The speed of sound

Sound travels quite fast through the air.

But light travels through air <u>very</u> fast indeed. It takes light hardly any time at all to travel a few kilometres.

This gives us a way of measuring the speed of sound. The diagram shows what we can do.

The person with the watch starts it when they see the smoke. They stop the watch when they hear the sound. The watch shows 5 seconds.

1 Copy and complete the following.

The sound travels _____ metres in _____ seconds.

So its speed is _____ ÷ _____

= _____ metres per second

■ Back to the dark side of the Moon

At the rock concert in the Big Dome, people at the far side of the dome hear the cymbal $\frac{1}{3}$ of a second after they see the drummer hit it.

2 Work out how far away the people are from the drummer. (Show your working.)

■ High speed jets

The speed of an aircraft is often compared to the speed of sound. A speed of Mach 2 means twice the speed of sound.

3 What is the speed of Blackbird:

(a) in metres per second?

(b) in kilometres per hour?

Blackbird can reach speeds of around Mach 3.

WHAT YOU NEED TO REMEMBER

The speed of sound

You will need to use Core ideas in different ways like you have on this page.

1.16 More about frequency

We measure frequencies in units called hertz (Hz, for short). A string that makes 110 complete to-and-fro vibrations per second has a frequency of 110 Hz.

The diagram shows the frequencies that the different strings of a guitar are usually tuned to.

1 Copy and complete the table.

String	Frequency (Hz)
1st (thinnest)	329.6
2nd	
3rd	
4th	
5th	
6th (thickest)	

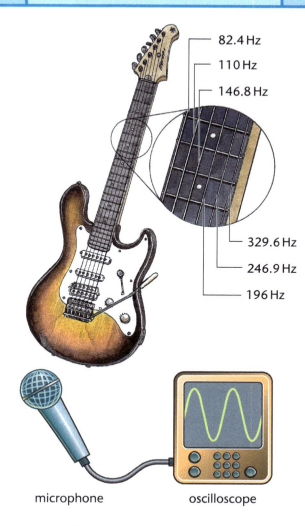

82.4 Hz
110 Hz
146.8 Hz
329.6 Hz
246.9 Hz
196 Hz

■ Measuring frequency

The diagram shows how you can measure the frequency of any sound using a microphone and an oscilloscope.

microphone   oscilloscope

2 (a) How many complete vibrations are shown on the oscilloscope screen?

(b) How much time did it take for this number of vibrations to be made?

(c) How many vibrations would there be in a whole second?

(d) What is the frequency of the sound?

3 (a) The same note one octave higher has double the frequency (400 Hz). Draw what this would look like on the oscilloscope screen.

(b) Which two of the guitar strings play the same note two octaves apart? Explain your answer.

$\bigwedge$ = one complete vibration

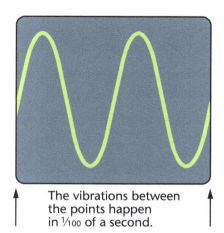

The vibrations between the points happen in $\frac{1}{100}$ of a second.

WHAT YOU NEED TO REMEMBER

More about frequency

You will need to use Core ideas in different ways like you have on this page.

2.1 Things that can attract or repel

■ Magnets

Two magnets can attract each other or they can repel each other. It depends which way round the magnets are.

The diagrams show what happens with two bar magnets.

1 What are the ends of the bar magnets called?

2 Copy and complete the sentences.

Two north poles _____ each other.
Two south poles _____ each other.
A north pole and a south pole _____ each other.

We say that:

■ like poles **repel**;

■ unlike poles **attract**.

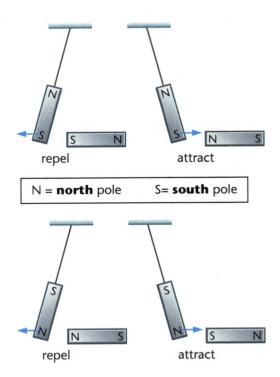

repel   attract

N = **north** pole   S= **south** pole

repel   attract

■ Why the poles of a magnet are called north and south

The diagram shows what happens if a magnet is free to turn.

3 Copy and complete the sentences.

The end of a magnet which points north is called the north seeking _____.

The other end of a magnet points south. So we call it the south _____ pole.

We can use a magnetic _____ to tell us where north and south are.

We often leave out the word 'seeking'.
We call the poles of a magnet the north pole and the south pole.

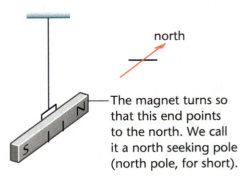

north

The magnet turns so that this end points to the north. We call it a north seeking pole (north pole, for short).

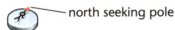

north seeking pole

A magnetic compass is a small magnet balanced on a short point so that it can turn.

■ Electric charges

Two objects that have electric charges either attract each other or repel each other. It depends on what <u>kinds</u> of charge the objects have.

The diagrams show which charges attract and which charges repel.

> **4** There are two types of electrical charge. What are they called?
>
> **5** Copy and complete the sentences.
>
> Two positive charges _____ each other.
> Two negative charges _____ each other.
> A positive charge and a negative charge _____ each other.

We say that:

- ■ **like** charges repel;
- ■ **unlike** charges attract.

■ A simple charge detector

We can use the idea that like charges repel to make a charge detector. This is called an <u>electroscope</u>.

> **6 (a)** What can you <u>see</u> happen when a charged object is brought near to an electroscope?
>
> **(b)** Why does this happen?

DO YOU REMEMBER?
from *Core Science 1*

You can give an object an electric charge by rubbing it with a different material.

Electric charges can be **positive** (+) or **negative** (−).

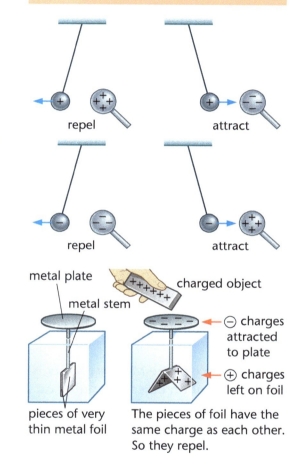

repel   attract

repel   attract

metal plate   charged object
metal stem
⊖ charges attracted to plate
⊕ charges left on foil

pieces of very thin metal foil

The pieces of foil have the same charge as each other. So they repel.

WHAT YOU NEED TO REMEMBER (Copy and complete using the **key words**)

Things that can attract or repel

A magnet has a _____ pole and a _____ pole.
Like poles _____.
Unlike poles _____.

Electric charges can be _____ (+) or _____ (−).
_____ charges repel.
_____ charges attract.

You also need to know what is in the 'Do you remember?' box.

More about magnets: C+ 2.9

2.2 Gravity – a force that attracts

Two magnets or two objects with electric charges may attract each other or they may repel each other. But a force called **gravity** can only attract. It never repels.

There is a force of gravity between <u>any</u> two objects. The objects don't have to be magnets, or have electric charges. The force of gravity between objects happens just because they are made of stuff and have a <u>mass</u>.

The diagrams show another way that the force of gravity is different from the forces between magnets or between objects that have electric charges.

1 Write down <u>two</u> differences between the force of gravity and the forces between magnets or between objects with electric charges.

■ Gravity and weight

Gravity is what gives you weight.

The **weight** of an object on Earth is the force of the Earth's gravity that acts on it.

The force of the Moon's gravity is smaller. So the weight of an object is smaller on the Moon than it is on Earth.

2 Look at the diagram. Then copy and complete the table.

What a 1 kilogram mass weighs	
on Earth	
on the Moon	

3 An astronaut has a mass of 80 kg. What is the astronaut's weight:

(a) on Earth?

(b) on the Moon?

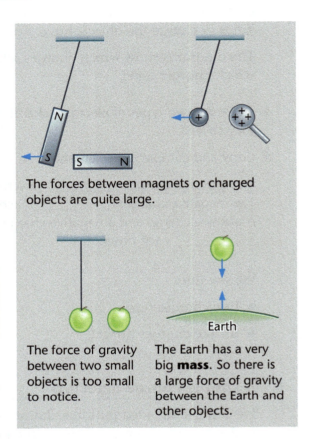

The forces between magnets or charged objects are quite large.

The force of gravity between two small objects is too small to notice.

The Earth has a very big **mass**. So there is a large force of gravity between the Earth and other objects.

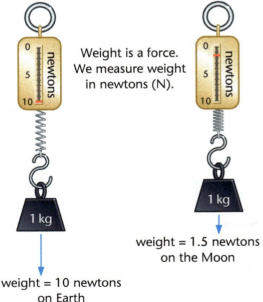

Mass is how much stuff there is. We measure mass in kilograms (kg).

Weight is a force. We measure weight in newtons (N).

weight = 10 newtons on Earth

weight = 1.5 newtons on the Moon

■ Gravity and the solar system

The Sun is made of a lot more stuff than any of the planets. It has a much bigger mass.

The force of gravity between the Sun and the planets holds the solar system together.

4 (a) Why doesn't the Sun's gravity make all the planets fall into the Sun?

(b) Why don't the planets move off into space?

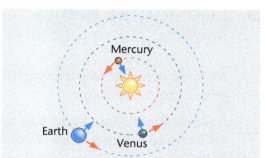

The planets move quickly. So the Sun's gravity doesn't make them fall into the Sun. But the Sun's gravity does stop them moving off into space. So the planets move in orbits round the Sun.

■ Gravity and satellites

The Moon is a <u>satellite</u> of the Earth. This means that it moves in an **orbit** around the Earth.

Humans have put lots of artificial satellites into orbit around the Earth. The diagram shows the forces of gravity acting on an artificial satellite.

5 Why does the Moon move in an orbit round the Earth? Why doesn't it just orbit the Sun like the Earth does?

6 Artificial satellites stay in orbit. Why don't they shoot off into space or fall to Earth?

Satellites move in a circle round the Earth because the force of the Earth's gravity keeps changing the **direction** in which they are moving.

The Moon, the Earth and the Sun

The Moon is a lot nearer to the Earth than it is to the Sun. So the Earth's gravity keeps it in orbit around the Earth.

The Earth and the Moon orbit the Sun <u>together</u>.

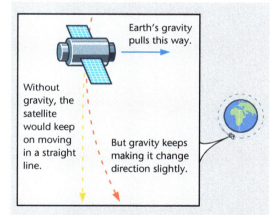

Earth's gravity pulls this way.

Without gravity, the satellite would keep on moving in a straight line.

But gravity keeps making it change direction slightly.

WHAT YOU NEED TO REMEMBER (Copy and complete using the **key words**)

Gravity – a force that attracts

Any two objects attract each other with a force called _____.
This force is very weak unless one (or both) of the objects has a large _____.

The force of gravity that acts on an object is what we call its _____.

Gravity keeps a planet or a satellite moving around its _____.
The force of gravity keeps changing the _____ in which planets and satellites move.

More about gravity and distance: C+ 2.10

2.3 Looking at orbits

A planet needs to keep moving so that it stays in its orbit round the Sun.

A planet that is close to the Sun has to move very fast because the force of the Sun's gravity is very big.

A planet that is further away from the Sun can move more slowly because the force of the Sun's gravity is smaller.

The graph shows how the time it takes for a planet to go once round its **orbit** depends on its distance from the Sun.

REMEMBER

Planets and satellites stay in their orbits because of the combined effects of their speed and the force of gravity.

Planet	Distance	Orbit time
Mercury	0.4	0.25
Venus	0.7	0.6
Earth	1.0	1.0
Mars	1.5	1.9

The planets in this table are too small to show on the graph clearly.

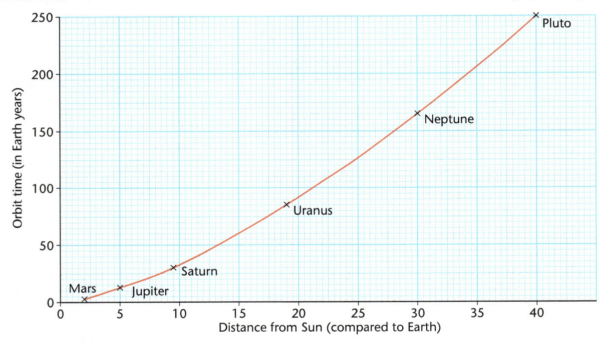

1 Copy and complete the sentence.

A planet that is further from the Sun takes a _____ time to orbit the Sun.

2 Copy and complete the table. Put the planets in order of their distance from the Sun, starting with the nearest.

Planet	Distance from Sun (compared to Earth)	Orbit time (Earth years)
Mercury	0.4	0.25

3 (a) Earth is sometimes called Planet 3. Explain why.

(b) Which planet is Planet 7?

(c) What could you call Mars?

■ Satellites and the Earth's atmosphere

Artificial satellites need to be well above the Earth's atmosphere. The diagrams show why.

> **4** Write down <u>three</u> reasons why satellites need to be in orbit above the Earth's atmosphere.

The Earth's atmosphere gradually fades away. All the weather is in the first 20 kilometres above the Earth's surface.

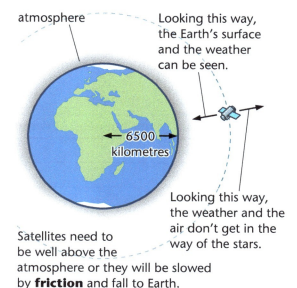

atmosphere

Looking this way, the Earth's surface and the weather can be seen.

6500 kilometres

Looking this way, the weather and the air don't get in the way of the stars.

Satellites need to be well above the atmosphere or they will be slowed by **friction** and fall to Earth.

■ Satellites that watch the Earth

We use satellites to watch the weather on Earth and to watch what's happening on the Earth's surface. These satellites are put into quite **low** orbits so that they can see as much detail as possible.

The graph shows how the orbit time of a satellite depends on its height.

> **5** How long does it take a satellite 15 000 kilometres above the Earth to make an orbit?
>
> **6** How high above the Earth must a satellite be:
>
> **(a)** to have an orbit time of 6 hours?
>
> **(b)** to have an orbit time of 24 hours?

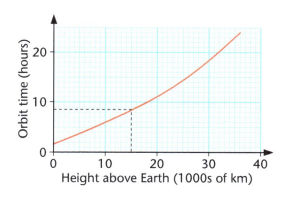

The Earth spins round once every 24 hours. So a satellite in orbit 36 000 kilometres above the equator looks like it isn't moving at all.

WHAT YOU NEED TO REMEMBER (Copy and complete using the **key words**)

Looking at orbits

The further away from the Sun a planet is, the longer is its _____ time.

Artificial satellites need to be above the atmosphere so they aren't slowed down by _____ with the air.

Satellites that are used to watch the Earth are put into quite _____ orbits.

You need to know the order of the planets in the solar system.

More about orbits: C+ 2.11

2.4 Getting things moving

When you start something moving, or when you try to start it moving, a **friction** force acts in the <u>opposite</u> direction.

We sometimes use forces to start things moving.

The diagrams show what happens when some children try to push a box along the floor.

1 Copy and complete the table.

Size of force	What happens	Reason
small		
medium		
large		

To start something moving you need an **unbalanced** force.

The children push the box. It doesn't move.

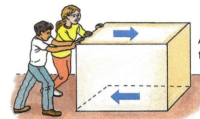

A friction force balances the pushing force.

The children push harder. The box still doesn't move.

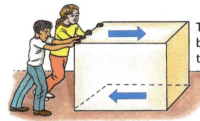

The friction force gets bigger. It still balances the pushing force.

■ **Trying a different surface**

The children push the box off the carpet and on to a polished wooden floor. The diagram shows what now happens.

2 Copy and complete the sentences.

The children can push the box along the polished floor with a _____ force. This is because there is less _____.

3 What happens to the friction force if the children move the box faster?

The children push harder still. Now the box moves.

The friction force can't get any bigger. The pushing force is now bigger than the friction force. There is an unbalanced force. So the box moves.

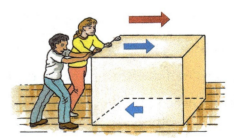

The friction force is smaller than it is on the carpet.

On a polished wooden floor, the box moves with a much smaller pushing force. If the children move the box faster, the friction force stays the same.

Friction with air

When an object moves through the air, there is a friction force between the moving object and the air. This friction force can also be called **air resistance** or drag.

4 Look at the diagrams. Then write down <u>two</u> differences between air resistance and the friction force between two solids which can slide over each other.

Friction with liquids

When an object moves through a liquid, there is a friction force between the object and the liquid. This friction force is like air resistance but it is a lot bigger.

The diagrams show the force needed to pull two different blocks of wood through water.

5 (a) Which block needs the smaller force to pull it through the water?

(b) Why does this block need a smaller force?

6 A fish is a good shape for moving through water. Explain why.

bicycle not moving

no friction with the air

bicycle moving slowly — small amount of friction with the air

bicycle moving faster — **larger** amount of friction with the air

It takes a force of 3 N to pull this block of wood through the water.

It takes a force of only 1 N to pull this block of wood through the water at the same speed.

Block B has a more **streamlined** shape.

As a fish swims along, the water can flow past it very easily. The fish's streamlined shape reduces friction.

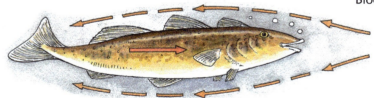

WHAT YOU NEED TO REMEMBER (Copy and complete using the **key words**)

Getting things moving

An object will not start to move unless an _____ force acts on it.

To make an object move, you need a force which is bigger than any _____ force that is also acting.

The friction force when an object moves through air is called _____ _____. When an object moves faster, this air resistance becomes _____.

To reduce the friction force in air or water you need a _____ shape.

More about friction: C+ 2.12

175

2.5 Slowing down

REMEMBER

When something moves, friction forces act in the **opposite** direction.

To keep something moving along at a steady speed you have to keep pushing it. If you don't, it will slow down and then stop.

1 Look at the diagrams. Then copy and complete the sentences.

A car travels at a steady speed when the driving force and the friction forces are

_____.

If the engine stops driving the car, the car _____ down. This is because the friction forces are then _____.

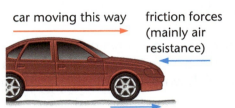

car moving this way friction forces (mainly air resistance)

The driving force and friction forces are **balanced**. So the car keeps moving at a steady speed.

'driving' force pushing car forward (this comes from the engine, through the wheels)

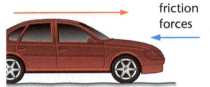

friction forces

The friction forces are now <u>unbalanced.</u> So they slow the car down.

engine no longer pushing car forward

■ Using air resistance to slow things down

It isn't safe to jump out of an aeroplane unless you use a parachute. The diagrams show why.

2 Copy and complete the sentences.

Opening a parachute increases air _____. The parachutist then slows down because the air resistance is _____ than the force of gravity (weight).

As the speed decreases the air resistance becomes _____.

Eventually, the forces become _____ again. This happens when the parachutist is falling at a much _____ speed.

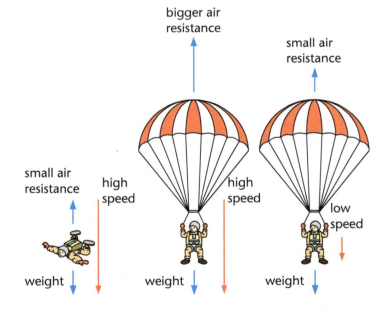

bigger air resistance

small air resistance

small air resistance   high speed   high speed   low speed

weight   weight   weight

Without a parachute a person falls very fast before air **resistance** balances weight.

Opening a parachute increases air resistance. The air resistance is bigger than the weight. So the parachutist slows down.

Eventually the forces <u>balance</u>. The parachutist is falling at a lower speed.

How a skater slows down

There is very little friction on ice. So a skater needs some way of slowing down. The diagram shows how a skater can do this.

3 (a) What does a skater do to slow down?

(b) How does this work?

The toe of the skate has teeth.

The bottom of the skate is smooth so that there is very little friction with the ice.

To slow down, a skater uses the toe of the skate. This is very rough.

large force of friction

Slowing a vehicle down

A driver slows down a car using the brakes. The car's brakes use the friction force between two surfaces which **slide** across each other. The diagram shows what happens.

4 Copy and complete the sentence.

A car's brakes slow the car down because of friction between the brake _____ and the wheel _____.

5 You must be very careful not to get oil on a brake pad or wheel disc. Explain why.

6 Write down <u>two</u> things that happen to the brake pads and wheel discs when they are used to stop a car.

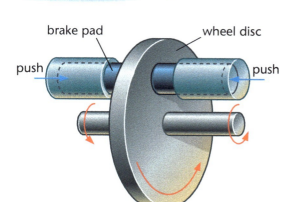

brake pad   wheel disc

push   push

To slow a car down, the brake pads are pressed hard against the wheel disc.

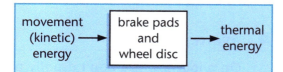

movement (kinetic) energy → brake pads and wheel disc → thermal energy

So the brakes get hot.
Also the pads and the disc wear away and eventually have to be replaced.

More about falling things: C+ 2.13

177

2.6 Looking at speed

Things sometimes move at a <u>steady</u> speed. For example, police officers often walk at a steady speed when they are on the beat.

You can work out a speed like this:

speed = **distance travelled ÷ time taken**

Example

An athlete runs 400 metres in 50 seconds. His speed is

  400 ÷ 50 = 8 metres per second

1 Look at the diagrams. Then work out (in metres per second):

  (a) the speed of the police officers walking along the pavement;

  (b) the speed of the car travelling along the motorway.

■ **Average speed**

On a journey, you don't usually travel at the same speed all the time. But you can still work out your **average** speed.

2 Look at the information on the diagrams about a car journey. Then copy and complete the following.

Distance travelled = _____ miles

Time taken   = _____ hours

Average speed   = _____ ÷ _____

        = _____ miles per hour

3 The driver stopped to see a friend between 10:30 and 11:30. Work out the average speed of the car during this journey, <u>not</u> counting the time taken for this stop.

60 metres

It takes the police officers 30 seconds to walk along the stretch of pavement shown.

When there aren't too many other cars about, you can travel at a steady speed along a motorway. This car travels 1500 metres every minute.

depart   arrive

car milometer

at start   at finish

■ Showing a journey on a graph

The graph shows the distance travelled during different parts of a cycle ride.

A graph like this is called a <u>distance:time</u> graph.

A steep slope on the graph means a **high** speed.

A flat part on the graph means that the cyclist is stopped.

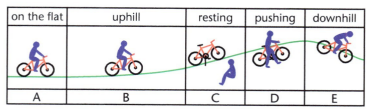

on the flat	uphill	resting	pushing	downhill
A	B	C	D	E

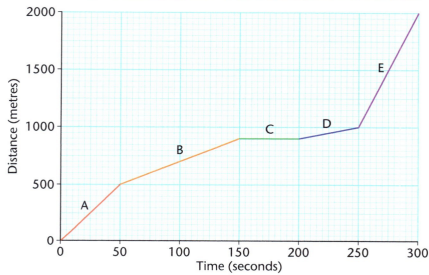

4 Copy and complete the table. Choose from: stopped, very slow, quite slow, quite fast, very fast.

5 Work out the cyclist's speed during part A of the journey.

6 (a) How far does the cyclist travel downhill?

   (b) How long does this take?

   (c) What is the cyclist's speed downhill?

7 What is the cyclist's average speed for the whole journey?

Part of graph	Speed
A	
B	
C	
D	
E	

WHAT YOU NEED TO REMEMBER (Copy and complete using the **key words**)

Looking at speed

You can work out speeds like this: speed = _____ _____ ÷ _____ _____

If the speed changes, the answer you get is the _____ speed.

On a distance:time graph, a steep slope means a _____ speed.

More about measuring speed: C+ 2.14

2.7 Pressure

A gardener is using a new wheelbarrow on some very soft ground. The gardener is pleased that the wheel doesn't sink into the ground as much as the wheel of the old wheelbarrow.

The fat tyre means that the weight is spread over a large **area**. So the tyre doesn't press very hard on the ground. We say that there is only a small **pressure**.

1 Look at the picture of the new wheelbarrow (opposite) and the old one at the bottom of the page. What difference is there between the wheels of the two wheelbarrows?

2 Copy and complete the following.

The new wheelbarrow tyre is fat, so there is a large _____ touching the ground. This means that the pressure on the ground is _____.

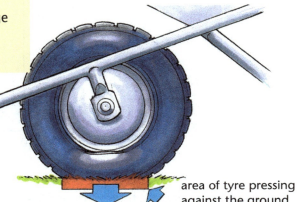

area of tyre pressing against the ground = 80 cm² (square centimetres)

force of wheel on the ground = 400 N (newtons)

■ Working out pressure

To work out the pressure of the wheelbarrow wheel on the ground you need to know:

- the <u>force</u> of the wheel on the ground;

- the <u>area</u> of tyre touching the ground.

The box shows how you can work out the pressure.

The gardener's old wheelbarrow has a narrower wheel. There is only 20 cm² of the wheel touching the ground.

> pressure = **force ÷ area**
>
> For the fat tyre:
>
> pressure = 400 ÷ 80
>   = 5 N/cm² (5 newtons per square centimetre)

3 (a) Work out the pressure of the narrower wheel on the ground with the same load in the wheelbarrow. (So there is the same <u>force</u> between the wheel and the ground.)

(b) How does the pressure of the narrow tyre on the ground compare with that of the fat tyre?

Using a spade

The gardener then uses a spade to dig the ground. The diagram shows how the gardener pushes the blade of the spade into the ground.

> **4** Copy and complete the sentences.
>
> The bottom edge of the blade is quite sharp. It has only a very small _____. This means that it produces a big _____ on the ground.
>
> **5** Work out the pressure of the end of the blade on the ground.
>
> **6** Why does the top edge of the blade need to be wider than the bottom edge?

Getting the right pressure

Sometimes we want to increase pressure. At other times we want to reduce it.

> **7** Explain why a fork:
>
> **(a)** has prongs which are pointed;
>
> **(b)** has a wide rounded handle.
>
> **8** The diagram shows a builder mending a roof. Why is the builder kneeling on a long wide board?

The top edge of the blade is wider than the bottom. So the pressure isn't big enough to cut the gardener's boot or hurt his foot.

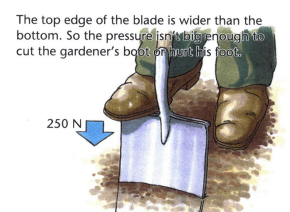

250 N

The bottom edge of the spade is quite sharp. Its area is very small (only 2 cm²).

The pressure of the end of the blade on the ground is large. So the blade goes into the ground easily.

The handle of a fork is wide and rounded.

The prongs of a fork are quite sharp.

DANGER
Fragile roof

WHAT YOU NEED TO REMEMBER (Copy and complete using the **key words**)

Pressure

To reduce the pressure a force produces, you can spread it over a large _____.

Making a force act on a small area produces a large _____.

You can work out a pressure like this: pressure = _____ ÷ _____.

More about pressure: C+ 2.15

2.8 Forces that make things turn

To make something move you need an unbalanced force. But an unbalanced force doesn't always make something move <u>along</u>. It sometimes makes it <u>turn</u> around a **pivot**.

This is what happens with a cat flap. The diagrams show how a cat flap works.

1 Which way does the cat flap turn when the cat pushes it to come into the house?

2 What force makes the cat flap move back again after the cat has gone through?

There is a special name for the turning effect of a force. It is called the **moment** of the force.

Some people have a cat flap fitted to the door. Their cat can then go in and out of the house whenever it wants to.

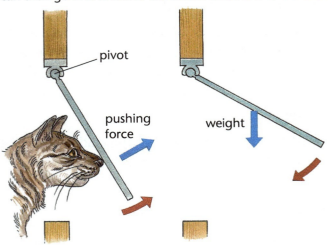

When the cat pushes the flap, it turns about the pivot point. The flap turns anti-clockwise.

After the cat has gone through, the weight of the flap turns it back again, in a clockwise direction.

■ Balanced and unbalanced moments

To make something turn, you need an **unbalanced** turning force or moment.

The diagrams show two see-saws with different turning forces acting on them.

3 Copy and complete the sentences.

The top see-saw moves because there is an anti-clockwise turning force that is

_____.

The bottom see-saw doesn't move because the clockwise moment and the anti-clockwise moment are _____.

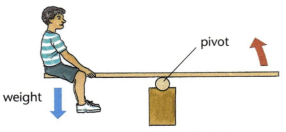

There is an unbalanced anti-clockwise moment. So the see-saw turns anti-clockwise.

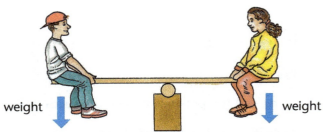

Clockwise and anti-clockwise moments balance. So the see-saw does not move.

■ What does the moment of a force depend on?

There are two ways of getting a bigger turning effect or moment:

- ■ you can use a **bigger** force;

- ■ you can apply a force **further away** from the pivot.

The diagram shows a small lad and his big sister on a see-saw. The see-saw doesn't move because the clockwise and anti-clockwise moments are **balanced**.

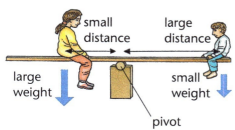

The big sister has a larger weight. But the small lad is further away from the pivot. So they both produce the same moment. The clockwise moment balances the anti-clockwise moment.

4 Explain how the small lad can balance his big sister on a see-saw.

■ Getting a bigger turning effect

To undo a nut you can use a spanner. The force you apply then has a much bigger moment than just using your fingers.

But the nut could be so tight that you still can't undo it. The diagram shows what you could do.

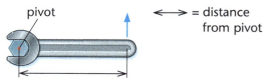

This nut is too tight to slacken with this spanner.

5 Using the pipe you can get a bigger moment with the same force. Explain why.

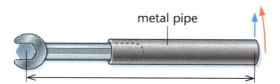

You can add a metal pipe to increase the distance between the force and the pivot.

WHAT YOU NEED TO REMEMBER (Copy and complete using the **key words**)

Forces that make things turn

The point about which something turns is called a _____.
The turning effect of a force is called its _____.

To get a bigger moment:
- ■ you can use a _____ force;
- ■ you can apply a force _____ _____ from the pivot.

For an object to turn there must be an _____ moment acting on it.

An object <u>doesn't</u> turn if the clockwise and anti-clockwise moments are _____.

More about moments: C+ 2.16

2.9 Why do magnets point north and south?

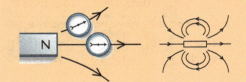

A magnetic compass tells you the direction of the lines of magnetic force in the magnetic field around a magnet.

The needle of a magnetic compass is a small magnet. It is free to turn.

The needle always comes to rest with one end pointing north and the other end pointing south. This happens because the Earth acts like a very big magnet with its own magnetic field.

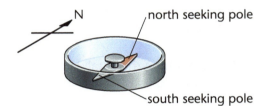

The needle of a magnetic compass points to the north. (So the other end points to the south.)

1 What are the ends of a magnetic compass needle called?

2 Copy and complete the sentences.

One end of a compass needle points _____; the other end points _____. This means that the Earth must have a magnetic _____. The lines of magnetic _____ must run from south to north.

The lines of force in the Earth's magnetic field run from south to north.

■ Why the Earth has a magnetic field

The diagram shows why the Earth has a magnetic field with the lines of force running from south to north.

3 Copy and complete the sentences.

The Earth's core is made of _____ and _____. These metals produce a magnetic _____ just like the one from a _____ magnet.

The Earth spins on its own axis. The Earth's north and south poles are at the ends of this axis.

4 Why doesn't a magnetic compass point exactly to the Earth's north and south poles?

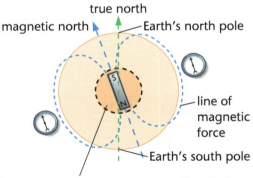

The Earth's core is made of metals called nickel and iron. The core acts just like a bar magnet. This magnet is at an angle to the Earth's axis.

2.10 More about gravity and distance

As a spaceship moves further away from the Earth, the pull of the Earth's gravity on it changes. So the <u>weight</u> of the spaceship changes too. The diagram shows how.

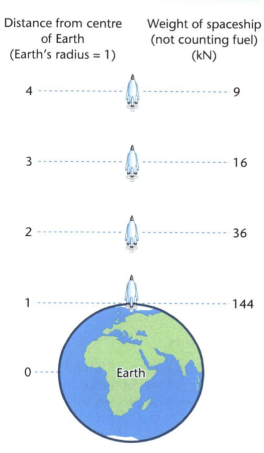

Distance from centre of Earth (Earth's radius = 1) | Weight of spaceship (not counting fuel) (kN)

4 ⋯⋯ 9

3 ⋯⋯ 16

2 ⋯⋯ 36

1 ⋯⋯ 144

0 ⋯ Earth

1 What happens to the weight of the spaceship as it gets further away from Earth?

2 (a) Copy and complete the table.

Distance from centre of Earth	(Distance)^2	Weight	(Distance)^2 × weight
1			
2	2 × 2 = 4	36	144
3			
4			

(b) What will the weight of the spaceship be when its distance is six times the radius of the Earth?

■ A journey to the Moon

A spaceship travels from Earth to the Moon.

The graph shows the force of the Earth's gravity and the force of the Moon's gravity on the spaceship during different parts of the journey.

3 Copy and complete the following.

As the spaceship travels from the Earth to the Moon:
- the pull of the Earth's gravity _____;
- the pull of the Moon's gravity _____.

4 What can you say about the forces acting on the spaceship at position X?

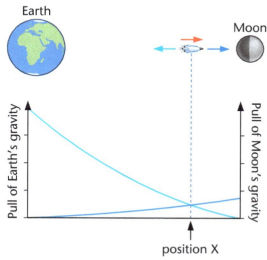

WHAT YOU NEED TO REMEMBER

More about gravity and distance

You will need to use Core ideas in different ways like you have on this page.

2.11 More about orbits

The diagram shows the <u>shape</u> of the orbits of the planets.

1 (a) What shape do the orbits of most of the planets seem to be?

  (b) Which planet has an orbit that looks a different shape?

2 Which planet is furthest from the Sun? (Look carefully at the diagram. The answer isn't as simple as you might think at first.)

In fact, the orbits of all the other planets are <u>ellipses</u> like Pluto's orbit. But they are only a tiny bit different from circles. Pluto's orbit is a lot more elliptical than the orbits of the other planets.

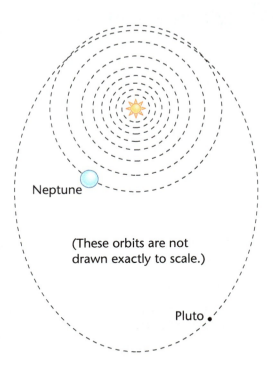

Neptune

(These orbits are not drawn exactly to scale.)

Pluto

■ Comets

Comets are large lumps of rock and ice. They move in <u>very</u> elliptical orbits around the Sun. They are a lot smaller than planets so you can't usually see them.

3 During which part of its orbit can you see a comet?

4 You could see comet Hale-Bopp very clearly during the first few months of 1997. When will it be seen again?

Halley's comet was seen when the Normans invaded England in 1066. It has been seen 12 times since then. The last time was in 1986.

5 (a) About how long does it take Halley's comet to go round its orbit?

  (b) When will it be seen again?

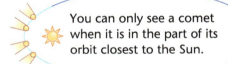

You can only see a comet when it is in the part of its orbit closest to the Sun.

Then you can't see the comet for a long time.

The orbit time for comet Hale-Bopp is about 4000 years.

WHAT YOU NEED TO REMEMBER

More about orbits

You will need to use Core ideas in different ways like you have on this page.

2.12 Comparing forces of friction

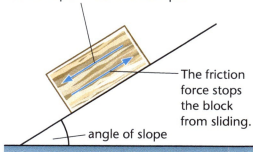

The force of gravity on the block tends to pull it down the slope.

The friction force stops the block from sliding.

angle of slope

■ Friction between sliding surfaces

Suppose you want to compare the friction between different surfaces. The diagram shows how you can do this.

1 Copy and complete the sentence.

The bigger the friction force is, the bigger the _____ of the slope must be before the block starts to slide.

You can increase the angle of the slope until the block *just* slides down.

The table shows the results of some tests.

2 What do these results tell you about the friction between the different types of surface? Answer as fully as you can.

Type of surface on slope	Type of surface on block	Angle of slope when sliding starts
polished wood	polished wood	40°
	rough wood	50°
	sandpaper	60°
rough wood	polished wood	50°
	rough wood	60°
	sandpaper	70°
sandpaper	polished wood	60°
	rough wood	70°
	sandpaper	80°

■ Friction in liquids

The diagrams show how you can compare the friction in water and oil.

3 (a) In which liquid is the friction greater?

(b) How do you know that it is?

Oil is a 'thicker' liquid than water. Things don't fall so easily through oil as they do through water. Oil also doesn't pour as easily as water. Scientists say that oil is a more <u>viscous</u> liquid than water.

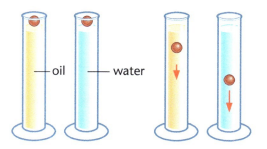

oil   water

Drop beads into oil and water at the same time.

Then watch how fast the beads fall through the liquids.

WHAT YOU NEED TO REMEMBER

Comparing forces of friction

You will need to use Core ideas in different ways like you have on this page.

2.13 Raindrops and other falling things

Drops of rain fall down through the air at a steady speed. The diagram shows why.

1 (a) What <u>two</u> forces act on a falling raindrop?

(b) Why does the raindrop fall at a steady speed?

When things fall, they increase in speed at first. Then they reach a steady speed. We call this steady speed the <u>terminal velocity</u>.

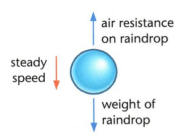

air resistance on raindrop

steady speed

weight of raindrop

The forces on the raindrop are balanced. So it falls at a steady speed.

REMEMBER

The air resistance acting on a moving object depends on its speed. The faster it falls, the bigger the air resistance is.

■ Measuring terminal velocity

There is a lot more resistance when objects fall through a liquid such as water than when they fall through air. So their terminal velocity is smaller.

They also reach their terminal velocity quicker. This makes it easier to measure terminal velocities in water than it is in air.

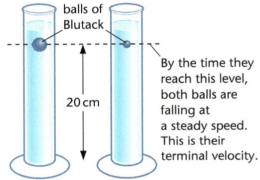

balls of Blutack

20 cm

By the time they reach this level, both balls are falling at a steady speed. This is their terminal velocity.

The large ball takes 4 seconds to fall 20 cm.

The small ball takes 10 seconds to fall 20 cm.

2 Look at the diagrams. Copy and complete the table.

	Terminal velocity (cm per second)
larger ball	
smaller ball	

Drops of rain falling through air behave just like balls of Blutack falling through water.

3 (a) Which falls faster, the large drops of rain in a thunderstorm or the small drops of rain in drizzle?

(b) Explain your answer as fully as you can.

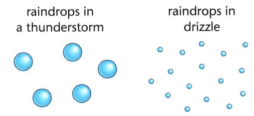

raindrops in a thunderstorm

raindrops in drizzle

Compared to raindrops in a thunderstorm, raindrops in drizzle have:
■ a smaller air resistance;
■ a <u>much</u> smaller weight.

WHAT YOU NEED TO REMEMBER

Raindrops and other falling things

You will need to use Core ideas in different ways like you have on this page.

2.14 Measuring speed

A car has a speedometer to tell the driver how fast it is travelling.

If you are <u>inside</u> a car, you can easily find out how fast you are travelling.

But when the police want to catch speeding motorists, they must be able to measure a car's speed from <u>outside</u> the car. They need to do this quickly without having to work it out.

The police use a speed sensor to measure a car's speed. It sends out waves which are reflected back from the car.

1 (a) How fast is the car in the picture travelling:

    (i) according to the speedometer in the car?

    (ii) according to the police speed sensor?

(b) Suggest a reason for the difference.

Measuring speeds in the lab

If you make a slope at just the right angle, a trolley will move down the slope at a steady speed. This happens when the force pulling it down the slope exactly balances the forces of friction.

The diagrams show four different ways of measuring the speed of the trolley.

Remember: speed = distance ÷ time

2 Copy and complete the table.

Method of measuring speed	What the measured speed is (cm per second)
speed sensor	
hand-operated timer	
automatic timer	
ticker tape	

3 (a) Which result is most different from the others?

(b) Suggest why it is different.

1 This speed sensor measures speed directly.

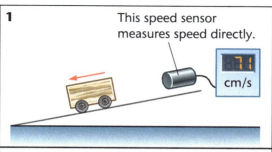

71 cm/s

2 Using a timer that you can start and stop with your finger, you find that the trolley takes 0.5 seconds to travel between these points.

49 cm

3 You can set up a timer to start and stop automatically when the trolley passes the points. Result: 0.7 seconds.

4

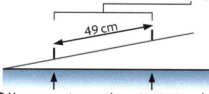

paper strip

The ticker timer makes dots on paper every $\frac{1}{50}$ of a second.

paper strip

6.8 cm in $\frac{1}{10}$ of a second

2.15 More about pressure

standing   sitting

area touching   area touching
ground = 0.05 m²   chair = 0.1 m²

lying down

area touching bed = 0.4 m²

floating

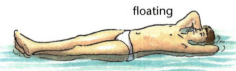

area touching water = 0.5 m²

REMEMBER

Pressure = force ÷ area

◼ Pressure on your body

Your weight is the force of the Earth's gravity on your body.

If you lie down, your weight is spread over a larger area than when you are standing up. So there is a smaller pressure between your body and what it is resting on.

The diagram shows the same person standing, sitting, lying on a bed and floating in water.

1 **(a)** When is the pressure on the person's body:

   (i) least?   **(ii)** greatest?

   (b) Give reasons for your answers.

2 The person's weight is 600 newtons. Work out the pressure on his body in each case.

   Example

   Lying down: pressure = 600 ÷ 0.4
                          = 1500 N/m²

◼ Pressure on a car tyre

The diagrams show a car tyre before and after the driver pumps some more air into it.

3 What difference does pumping air into the tyre make to its pressure on the ground? Explain your answer.

4 The pressure between the hard tyre and the ground is 30 newtons per square centimetre. What is the force of the tyre on the ground?

soft tyre   hard tyre

needs pumping up   pumped up

300 cm²   100 cm²
touching ground   touching ground

force = pressure × area

If the pressure between the soft tyre and the ground is 10 N/cm²,

force = 10 × 300 = 3000 N (newtons)

WHAT YOU NEED TO REMEMBER

More about pressure

You will need to use Core ideas in different ways like you have on this page.

2.16 More about moments

REMEMBER

The turning effect or moment of a force depends on:
- the size of the force;
- the distance of the force from the pivot.

We sometimes need to work out what happens when two turning forces act on a body. To do this, we need to know exactly how big the moment of each force is.

You can work out the moment of a force like this:

moment of force = **size** of force × **distance** of force
from the pivot

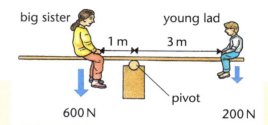

big sister   young lad
1 m   3 m
pivot
600 N   200 N

1 Look at the diagram of the see-saw.

(a) Copy and complete the table.

	Weight (N)	Distance from pivot (m)	Moment (N × m)	Clockwise or anti-clockwise?
big sister				
young lad				

Turning forces balance when:

anti-clockwise = clockwise
moment   moment

(b) Why does the see-saw balance?

■ Calculating moments

The diagram shows a girl weighing herself using 10 kilograms of potatoes.

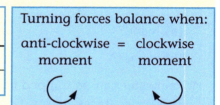

10 kg of potatoes
2.5 m
0.5 m
100 N

2 (a) What is the clockwise moment caused by the weight of the potatoes?

(b) What must the anti-clockwise moment of the girl's weight be?

(c) What is the weight of the girl (in newtons)?

(d) What is the mass of the girl (in kilograms)?

The girl stands quite near to the pivot.

Her friend moves the bucket until the plank balances.

To undo a nut, you must overcome the moment of the friction force.

3 How big is this moment for the nut shown in the diagram?

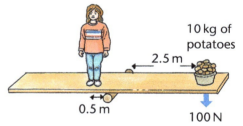

10 cm or 0.1 metre

The nut starts to turn when this force reaches 60 N.

3.1 Energy sources

We get energy from energy <u>sources</u>. The diagram tells you about these energy sources.

1 Copy and complete the sentence.

Most of our energy sources depend upon energy which has come from the _____.

2 We can use energy from the Sun's rays directly to make things warm. Write down <u>two</u> ways of doing this.

3 How does energy from the Sun make:

(a) wind?

(b) waves?

4 Rainwater can be trapped behind dams to make lakes. This water stores energy. Describe how water gets from the sea to the lake behind a dam.

5 Most fuels store energy that has come from the Sun.

(a) Write down the names of <u>four</u> of these fuels.

(b) Which of these fuels are fossil fuels?

(c) Why are they called fossil fuels?

6 Write down the names of <u>three</u> energy sources that do <u>not</u> depend on energy that came from the Sun.

A **renewable** energy source is one that does not get used up. This is because it is being replaced all the time.

7 Copy and complete the table.

Renewable energy sources	Non-renewable energy sources

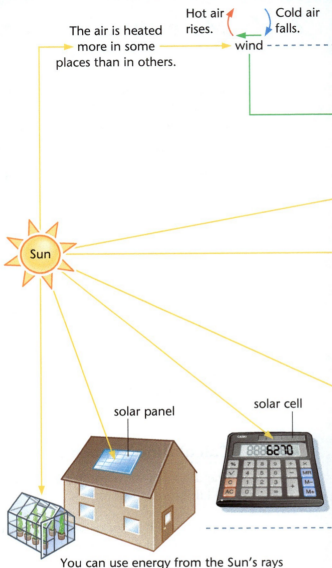

Hot air rises. Cold air falls.

The air is heated more in some places than in others. → wind

Sun

solar panel

solar cell

You can use energy from the Sun's rays to make things warmer, or to make electricity.

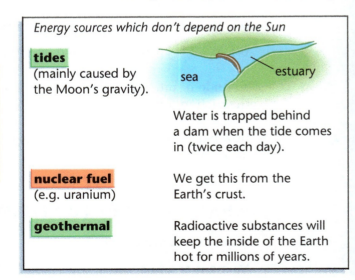

Energy sources which don't depend on the Sun

tides
(mainly caused by the Moon's gravity).

sea   estuary

Water is trapped behind a dam when the tide comes in (twice each day).

nuclear fuel
(e.g. uranium)

We get this from the Earth's crust.

geothermal

Radioactive substances will keep the inside of the Earth hot for millions of years.

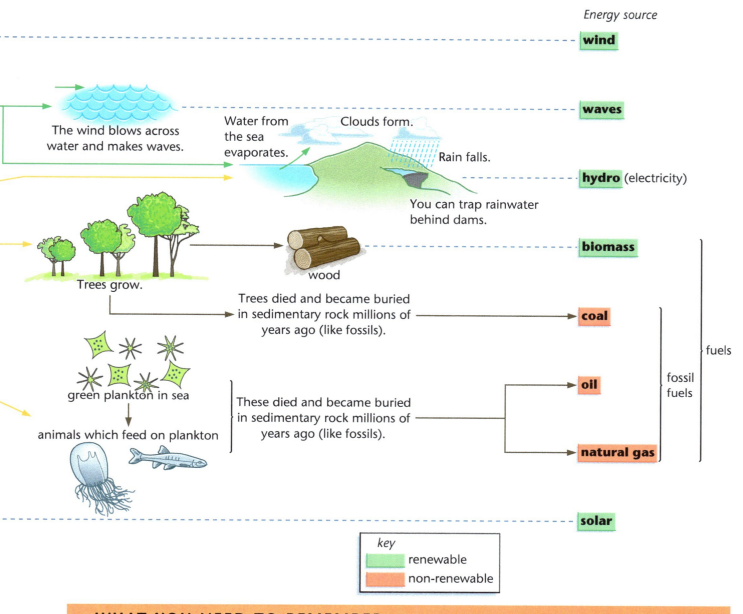

Energy source

wind

waves

The wind blows across water and makes waves.

Water from the sea evaporates.

Clouds form.

Rain falls.

hydro (electricity)

You can trap rainwater behind dams.

wood

biomass

Trees grow.

Trees died and became buried in sedimentary rock millions of years ago (like fossils).

coal

green plankton in sea

animals which feed on plankton

These died and became buried in sedimentary rock millions of years ago (like fossils).

oil

natural gas

fossil fuels

fuels

solar

key
renewable
non-renewable

WHAT YOU NEED TO REMEMBER (Copy and complete using the **key words**)

Energy sources

Energy sources that depend on energy that has come from the Sun are:
w_____, w_____, h_____(electricity), b_____,
c_____, o_____, n_____ _____ and s_____.

Energy sources that do not depend on energy that has come from the Sun are:
t_____, g_____ and n_____ _____.

An energy source that is being replaced all the time is a _____ energy source.

You should know which energy sources are renewable and which are non-renewable.

More about energy from the Sun: C+ 3.9

3.2 Using energy sources to generate electricity

The diagrams show seven energy sources that we
use to generate electricity.

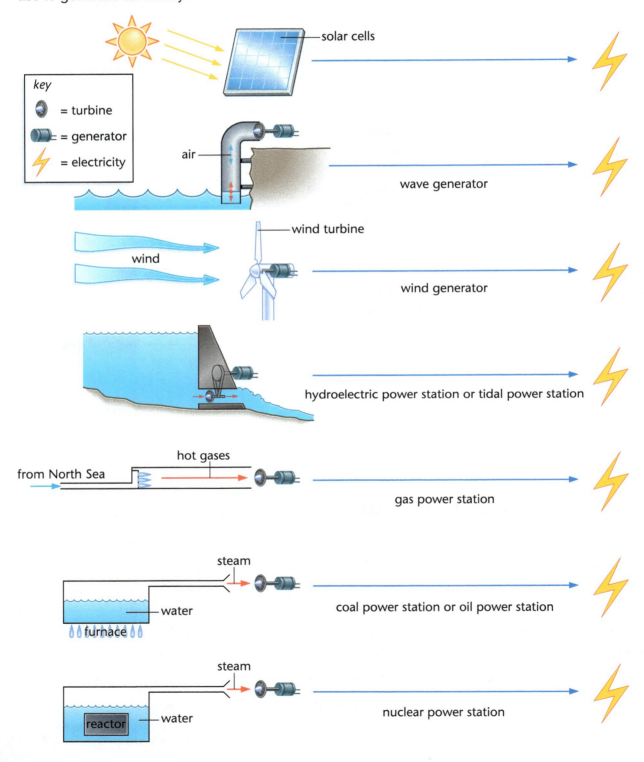

To generate electricity, we usually need a **turbine** and a **generator**. We use an energy source to drive the turbine. The diagrams show the type of energy transferred to and from the generator.

1 Copy and complete the sentences.

When energy is transferred to a turbine, it makes the turbine _____. So the turbine has _____ energy.

The turbine transfers kinetic energy to a _____. This then transfers energy to homes and factories by _____.

Here is an easy way to write down these energy transfers:

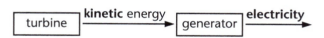

Use the information on the opposite page to answer the following questions.

2 (a) Write down <u>three</u> types of power station that use a turbine driven by steam.

(b) Write down <u>three</u> ways of generating electricity that use turbines driven by air or hot gases (not steam).

3 Which <u>two</u> types of power station use a turbine driven by water?

4 How can you produce electricity without using a turbine or a generator at all?

The turbines rotate. They have kinetic energy. The kinetic energy from the turbines is changed into electricity. This carries energy to houses and factories.

WHAT YOU NEED TO REMEMBER (Copy and complete using the **key words**)

Using energy sources to generate electricity

Most ways of generating electricity use a _____ to drive a _____.

turbine ——— energy → generator ———→

More about energy sources: C+ 3.10, 3.11

3.3 Getting the energy we want from electricity

We transfer energy in lots of ways every day.

When a room is dark, we switch on the light. The light bulb transfers energy to the room.

To boil water, we can switch on a kettle. The kettle transfers energy to the water.

When we want to transfer energy, we often switch on an **electrical** appliance.

The diagrams on the opposite page show what we use some electrical appliances for.

1 Copy and complete the following.

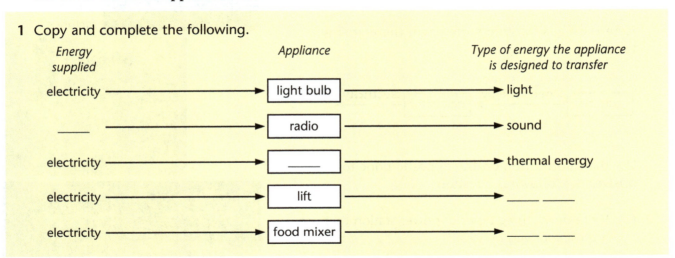

Energy supplied	Appliance	Type of energy the appliance is designed to transfer
electricity	light bulb	light
_____	radio	sound
electricity	_____	thermal energy
electricity	lift	_____ _____
electricity	food mixer	_____ _____

■ We don't only get what we want

Appliances always transfer **all** the energy we supply to them in <u>some</u> way. The problem is that some of the energy is transferred in ways that we don't really want. This energy is **wasted**.

2 Copy and complete the sentences.

A light bulb is designed to transfer _____ energy to its surroundings.

But it also transfers _____ energy to its surroundings. This is not wanted.

3 Make a list of the <u>unwanted</u> energy that is transferred by each of the appliances on the opposite page.

A light bulb makes its surroundings warmer as well as lighter. It transfers thermal energy ∿ *as well as light* — *to its surroundings.*

DO YOU REMEMBER?
from *Core Science 1*

When we lift things higher up, they have more <u>potential</u> energy.

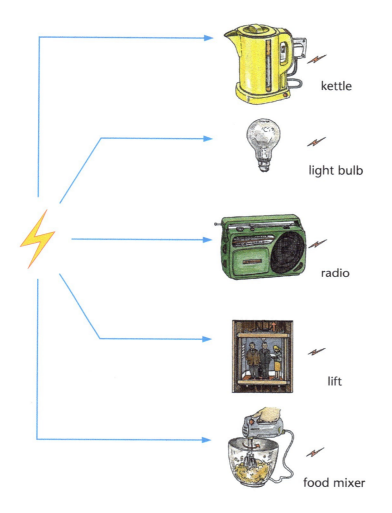

kettle — designed to transfer thermal energy (mainly to water) [but also transfers a little sound]

light bulb — designed to transfer light energy (to surroundings) [but also transfers a lot of thermal energy]

radio — designed to transfer sound energy (to surroundings) [but also transfers thermal energy]

lift — designed to transfer potential energy (to lift) [but also transfers thermal energy and sound]

food mixer — designed to transfer kinetic (movement) energy (to food) [but also transfers thermal energy and sound]

WHAT YOU NEED TO REMEMBER (Copy and complete using the **key words**)

Getting the energy we want from electricity

To transfer energy to our surroundings, we often use _____ appliances.

Electrical appliances transfer _____ the energy we supply to them.

Some of the energy is transferred in ways that we don't want; this energy is _____ .

You should know the energy transfers that everyday electrical appliances are designed to make and the unwanted energy transfers that they also make.

More about energy transfers: C+ 3.12

197

3.4 Static electricity and electric currents

To get an electric <u>current</u>, we need battery or a generator. Batteries were only invented about 200 years ago and generators about 150 years ago. But people have known about <u>static</u> electricity for more than 2000 years.

1 How can you produce static electricity?

These pieces of plastic are charged with static electricity. The charges stay in **one place**. 'Static' means 'not moving'.

■ What's the connection between static electricity and an electric current?

Static electricity and electric currents are both caused by electrical <u>charges</u>.

The diagrams show the differences between static electricity and an electric current.

2 Copy and complete the table.

What happens to the electrical charges	Type of electricity
standing still	_____ electricity
moving	an electric _____

3 Copy and complete the sentence.

Electricity can flow through copper wires because copper is a good _____ of electricity.

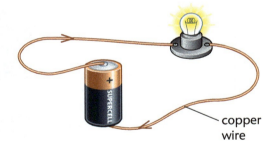
copper wire

An electric current flows round this circuit. Electrical charges **move** through the wires and the filament of the bulb.

Getting an electric current from a static charge

You can make an electric current flow from a charged metal object. To do this, you must connect the charged metal object to the **earth** with an electrical conductor. The diagrams show what happens if you do this with a special lamp.

4 (a) How can you tell that there is an electric current?

(b) How do the electrical charges on the dome make this current?

5 Copy and complete the sentences.

When an object loses its electrical charge, we say that it is _____ .
This happens when the charged object is _____ .

Why do we need batteries and generators?

When you discharge a charged object, you get only a very small current for a very short time. If you want a larger current for a longer time, you need a battery or a generator.

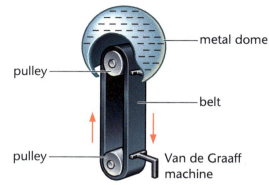

metal dome

pulley

belt

pulley — Van de Graaff machine

When the belt moves round, it makes a very big static charge on the dome. On many machines the dome gets a positive (+) charge. It all depends on what materials the belt and pulleys are made of.

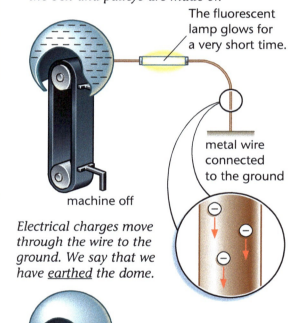

The fluorescent lamp glows for a very short time.

metal wire connected to the ground

machine off

Electrical charges move through the wire to the ground. We say that we have earthed the dome.

The dome has lost its charge. We say that it is discharged.

WHAT YOU NEED TO REMEMBER (Copy and complete using the **key words**)

Static electricity and electric currents

On an object charged with static electricity, the electrical charges stay in _____ _____ .

In an electric current, electrical charges _____ .
The material that an electric current will flow through is called a _____ .

You can discharge a charged conductor by connecting it to the _____ .

More about batteries: C+ 3.13

3.5 Measuring currents in circuits

Some circuits have a light bulb in them. A bulb is brighter when a bigger current flows through it. So the brightness of the bulb tells you about the size of the current flowing through the circuit.

1 The diagram shows the same bulb in two different circuits.

   (a) Which circuit has the bigger current flowing through it?

   (b) How do you know?

   (c) Why do you think there is a bigger current in one circuit than in the other?

■ Using a meter to measure current

If you want to <u>measure</u> the sizes of electric currents, you need to use a meter.

We measure currents in units called <u>amperes</u> (amps or A, for short). The meter we use to measure currents is called an **ammeter**.

The diagrams show the same two circuits as before, but this time with an ammeter.

2 Copy and complete the sentences.

   You measure a current using an _____.

   To measure the current through a bulb you must connect the meter in _____ with the bulb.

   In circuit P, the current is _____ A (amps).
   In circuit Q, the current is _____ A (amps).

3 Draw a circuit diagram for circuit Q with the ammeter in another suitable position.

It doesn't matter which side of the bulb you put the ammeter. Exactly the **same** current flows all the way round the circuit.

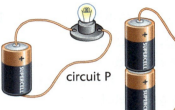

circuit P

circuit Q

These two cells are connected end to end, facing the same way.

You can put an ammeter here ...

... or here.

The same current flows through the bulb and through the ammeter. We say that the ammeter is in **series** with the bulb.

Measuring the current in circuit P.

Measuring the current in circuit Q.

DO YOU REMEMBER?
from *Core Science 1*

A simple way to draw circuits is to use symbols. This is how you can draw circuit Q.

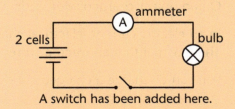

2 cells

ammeter

bulb

A switch has been added here.

Two bulbs connected in series

The diagram shows one way of connecting two bulbs into the same circuit.

circuit R

These two bulbs are connected so that the current flows through one bulb and then through the other. There is **one** circuit for the current to flow round. The bulbs are connected in <u>series</u>.

4 Copy and complete the sentences.

When two bulbs are connected in series, there is only _____ circuit for the current to flow round. You can measure the current through the bulbs by putting an _____ in series at any point in this circuit.

5 Draw a circuit diagram for circuit R with an ammeter in position X.

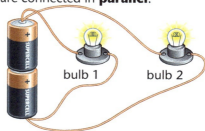

You can measure the current with an ammeter at X (or at Y, or at Z).

Two bulbs connected in parallel

The diagram shows another way of connecting two bulbs into a circuit.

These two bulbs are conected to the same two cells in another way. We say that they are connected in **parallel**.

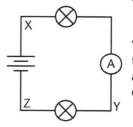

bulb 1   bulb 2

circuit S

6 Copy and complete the sentences.

When two bulbs are connected in parallel, you have two _____ circuits. To measure the current through one of the bulbs, you must put an ammeter in _____ with that bulb.

7 Draw a circuit diagram for circuit S with an ammeter to measure the current through bulb 2.

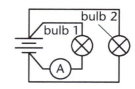

The ammeter has been added in series only with bulb 1. So it only measures the current through bulb 1.

WHAT YOU NEED TO REMEMBER (Copy and complete using the **key words**)

Measuring currents in circuits

To measure electric currents you use an _____.

To measure the current through a bulb, you connect the ammeter in _____ with the bulb.

If you connect two or more bulbs in series, there is still only _____ circuit for the current to flow round. The current through all points in the circuit is exactly the _____.

Two or more bulbs can be connected to a battery so that they are in separate circuits. We then say that they are connected in _____.

More about circuits: C+ 3.14

3.6 Electromagnets

A coil of wire with an electric current flowing through it behaves just like a bar magnet. We call it an **electromagnet**.

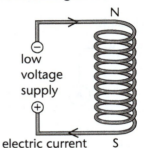

an electromagnet

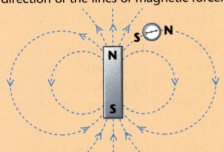

DO YOU REMEMBER?
from *Core Science 1*

A magnetic compass shows you the direction of the lines of magnetic force.

The lines of magnetic force show the magnetic field around the magnet.

A bar magnet has two poles: N = north pole, S = south pole.

1 (a) Copy the diagram of the electromagnet, leaving plenty of space around it.

(b) Now draw the magnetic field around the electromagnet.

■ Making the electromagnet stronger

The diagram shows how you can test the strength of an electromagnet.

You can make an electromagnet stronger in three different ways. The diagrams below show you how.

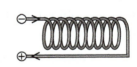

thin thread

steel nut

The stronger the magnet is, the further it pulls the steel nut.

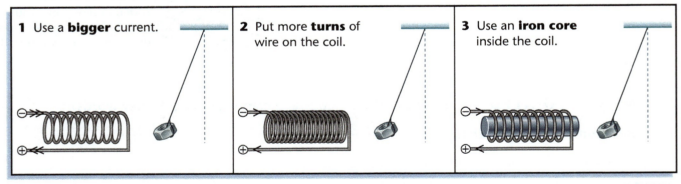

1 Use a **bigger** current.

2 Put more **turns** of wire on the coil.

3 Use an **iron core** inside the coil.

2 What are the <u>three</u> ways of making an electromagnet stronger?

3 You want to make a <u>very</u> strong electromagnet. What should you do?

a very strong electromagnet

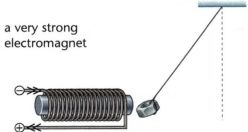

■ How does a magnet attract iron and steel?

When you put a piece of iron or steel close to a magnet, it is attracted. The diagrams show why this happens.

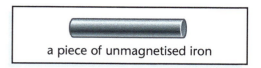

a piece of unmagnetised iron

4 Copy and complete the sentences.

When you put a piece of unmagnetised iron into a magnetic field, it becomes a _____.

The south pole of the magnetised iron is next to the _____ pole of the magnet. So the magnet and the piece of iron _____ each other.

5 Draw a diagram to show what happens when you put a piece of unmagnetised iron close to the <u>south</u> pole of a magnet.

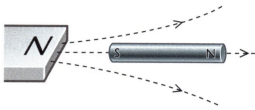

In a magnetic field, the piece of iron becomes a **magnet**.

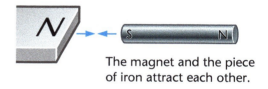

The magnet and the piece of iron attract each other.

■ Why an iron core makes an electromagnet stronger

A coil with a current flowing through it becomes a **magnet**. The magnetic field of the coil then magnetises the iron core.

6 Copy and complete the sentences.

An iron core makes an electromagnet _____. This is because the _____ field of the coil makes the core into a magnet. The magnetic field of the coil and the magnetic field of the _____ _____ then add together.

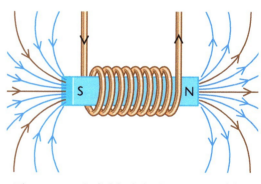

The magnetic field of the iron core adds itself to the magnetic field of the coil.

WHAT YOU NEED TO REMEMBER (Copy and complete using the **key words**)

Electromagnets

A coil with a current flowing through it becomes an _____.
You can make this stronger by using a _____ current, by putting more _____ of wire on the coil or by using an _____ _____ inside the coil.

When you put some unmagnetised iron into a magnetic field, it becomes a _____.

You should also know what is in the 'Do you remember?' box.

3.7 Using electromagnets

A bar magnet stays magnetised all the time. We say that it is a **permanent** magnet.

An electromagnet is only magnetic when electricity flows through the coil. This makes electromagnets a lot more useful. You can **switch** them on and off.

1 Why is a permanent magnet not as useful as an electromagnet on a scrapyard crane?

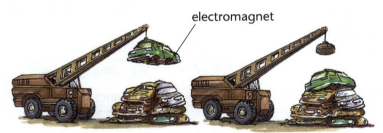

electromagnet

The crane uses an electromagnet to lift scrap cars.

To drop the car, the crane driver switches off the current.

■ A reed relay

Electromagnets can be used to make relays. A relay is a special kind of switch. It uses one current to switch on another current.

With a relay you can use a small current to switch on a larger current. You can also use a safe low voltage circuit to switch on a dangerous high voltage circuit.

The diagrams show how one sort of relay works.

2 Copy and complete the sentences.

When a small current flows through the coil, the steel strips become _____. So the steel strips _____ each other. When they touch, a _____ can then flow though the relay.

When the current through the coil is switched off, the coil is no longer a _____. So the steel strips _____ apart. The current through the relay is switched _____.

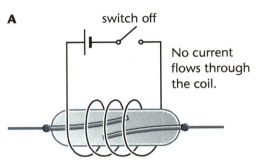

A switch off

No current flows through the coil.

The springy steel strips are apart.

No current flows through the relay.

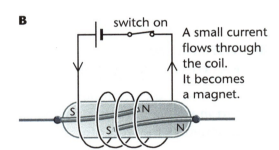

B switch on

A small current flows through the coil. It becomes a magnet.

The magnetic field of the coil magnetises both of the steel strips.

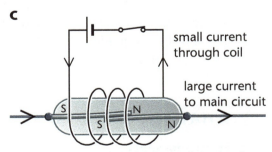

C

small current through coil

large current to main circuit

The steel strips attract and touch each other. A large current flows through the relay.

D

When you switch off the current to the coil, it stops being a magnet. So the steel strips spring apart, like they are in diagram A.

An electric bell

An electric bell uses an electromagnet to make it work. The electromagnet keeps switching itself on and off to make the bell ring.

The diagrams show how the bell works.

3 **(a)** Explain why iron is used in the core of the electromagnet.

(b) Explain why the iron core of the electromagnet is bent into a U-shape.

4 On a copy of the flow-chart, put the following sentences in the correct boxes to explain how the bell works.

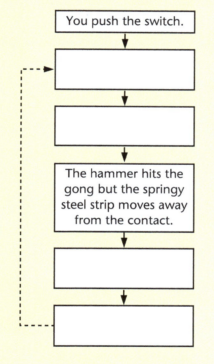

You push the switch.

The circuit to the electromagnet is broken.

A current flows through the coil of the electromagnet.

The springy steel bends back and touches the contact again.

The iron bar is attracted to the electromagnet.

The hammer hits the gong but the springy steel strip moves away from the contact.

DO YOU REMEMBER?
from *Core Science 1*

The magnetic effect of a magnet is strongest near to its north and south poles (ends).

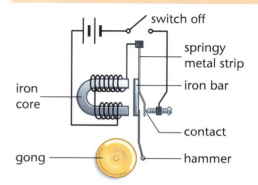

switch off
springy metal strip
iron core
iron bar
contact
gong
hammer

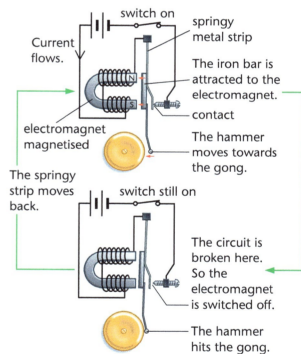

switch on
Current flows.
springy metal strip
The iron bar is attracted to the electromagnet.
electromagnet magnetised
contact
The hammer moves towards the gong.
The springy strip moves back.
switch still on
The circuit is broken here. So the electromagnet is switched off.
The hammer hits the gong.

WHAT YOU NEED TO REMEMBER (Copy and complete using the **key words**)

Using electromagnets

A magnet that stays magnetised all the time is called a _____ magnet.

An electromagnet is more useful than a permanent magnet because you can _____ it on and off.

You may be given information about things which use electromagnets. You should then be able to explain how they work just like you did on these pages.

More about relays: C+ 3.15

3.8 What happens to all the energy we transfer?

Every day we transfer energy in lots of different ways. For example, we burn petrol in car engines to make cars move.

But most of the energy from the burning petrol isn't transferred to the car as movement energy at all. It just makes the surroundings warmer.

The diagram shows the energy transferred to and from a car engine.

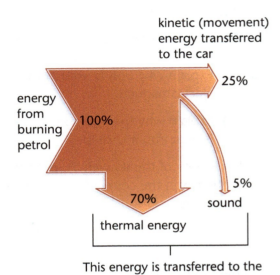

kinetic (movement) energy transferred to the car

energy from burning petrol 100%

25%

5% sound

70%

thermal energy

This energy is transferred to the surroundings. So it is **wasted**.

1 Copy and complete the table.

Where energy from burning petrol is transferred	%
to the surroundings as thermal energy	
to the surroundings as sound	
to the car as kinetic (movement) energy	
Total	_____

70% + 25% + 5% = 100%
So all the energy is transferred somewhere.
Energy is never **lost**. But some is transferred in ways that are not useful to us.

■ What happens to the energy transferred to the car?

When a car is moving at a steady speed, even the energy usefully transferred to it from the engine doesn't make it move any faster. All it does is stop the car from slowing down.

Energy is transferred from the car to the surroundings by friction forces.

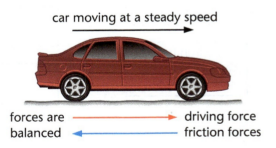

car moving at a steady speed

forces are balanced

driving force
friction forces

2 (a) What force must be overcome to stop the car from slowing down?

   (b) What happens to the energy transferred by the engine to a car when the car travels at a steady speed?

Friction forces transfer kinetic energy from the car to the surroundings as thermal energy and sound. As sounds fade away, this energy too makes the surroundings just a little bit warmer.

Energy transfers in a car engine.

In the end, all the energy from burning petrol in a car engine ends up making the surroundings a little bit **warmer**.

■ Energy that isn't much use

The energy transferred by a car engine doesn't get used up. It all ends up in the surroundings. But it isn't much use to us any more because it's so spread out.

The diagrams show some <u>very</u> hot things. We can transfer energy from them in useful ways because the thermal energy <u>isn't</u> spread out.

3 Write down <u>three</u> useful ways that very hot things can transfer energy.

Each time we transfer energy, it is harder to transfer it again in any useful way.

4 Look at the diagrams.

(a) The thermal energy in a kettle of boiling water is less useful for energy transfers than the electricity that was used to make the water hot in the first place. Explain why.

(b) Why is the thermal energy in a kettle of boiling water even less useful if you pour it into a bathful of cold water?

A hot filament produces light.

A hot flame can cook things.

Hot gases can turn a turbine.

What you can do with very hot things.

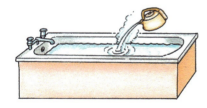

We can use electricity to transfer energy to the surroundings in many different ways.

Boiling water is useful for making tea. But it is difficult to transfer the energy again to light a room or make a TV set work.

■ Energy and energy sources

Energy never gets used up, but each time it is transferred it gets more **spread** out. This makes it less useful.

Energy <u>sources</u> such as fossil fuels <u>can</u> get used up. We say that these energy sources are <u>non-renewable</u>.

If you pour a kettleful of boiling water into a bathful of cold water, it only warms it up a tiny bit. All the energy is still there, but it is spread out and not much use for anything.

WHAT YOU NEED TO REMEMBER (Copy and complete using the **key words**)

What happens to all the energy we transfer?

When you transfer energy, none is ever _____ but some is always _____ .

All the energy that we transfer eventually ends up making the surroundings a tiny bit _____ . This energy isn't very useful because it is very _____ out.

More about storing energy: C+ 3.16

3.9 Energy from the Sun

We measure energy in units called <u>joules</u>.
500 J means 500 joules.

A lot of energy from the Sun reaches the Earth every second of every day.

> **1** Look at the bar-chart. Then copy and complete the table.
>
> | | Energy from the Sun in London (per square metre per second) |
> |---|---|
> | sunny day | _____ J |
> | cloudy day | _____ J |

■ Transferring the energy from sunlight

The diagrams show three different ways energy from sunlight can be transferred to do something useful.

> **2 (a)** Which method transfers most of the Sun's energy in a useful way?
>
> **(b)** Which method transfers least?

In bright sunshine, a 5 m² solar panel can supply all the thermal energy a house needs.

> **3** The solar panel can't supply all the thermal energy the house needs all of the time. Why not?

After the energy from sunlight has been transferred, it is often stored until it is needed.

> **4** How is the energy stored:
>
> **(a)** after being transferred to plants?
>
> **(b)** after being transferred to a solar panel?
>
> **(c)** after being transferred to solar cells?

Energy reaching one square metre of London from the Sun in one second at mid-day.

Energy (J) — bar chart showing 1000 for sunny, approx 200 for cloudy.

Plants transfer about 1% of the energy from sunlight. As plants grow, this energy is stored in the materials the plants are made of. We say that the energy is stored in <u>biomass</u>.

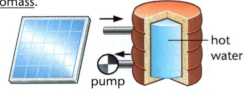

Solar panels transfer about 70% of the energy from sunlight to water by making it hot. The hot water is stored until it is needed.

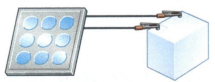

Solar cells transfer about 10% of the energy from sunlight as electricity to the re-chargeable battery. The battery stores chemical energy until it is needed.

WHAT YOU NEED TO REMEMBER

Energy from the Sun

You will need to use Core ideas in different ways like you have on this page.

3.10 Comparing energy sources

The table compares some energy sources that we use to generate electricity.

Energy source	Building and running costs (except for fuel)	Fuel costs	Pollution problems	Overall cost of each Unit of electricity
nuclear fuel	high	low	Few problems provided there are no accidents. Dangerous wastes need to be stored for a long time.	average
fossil fuel	quite low	high	Burning pollutes the air with carbon dioxide, nitrogen oxides and (for coal and oil) sulphur dioxide.	lower than average
wind	high	zero	On tops of hills so can be seen for miles around. Noisy if near homes.	slightly higher than average
solar	very high	zero	None, but can be used on a large scale only in very sunny areas.	much higher than average
tides	high	zero	Destroys habitats of birds and other things that live in river estuaries.	slightly lower than average

1 Write down the energy sources in order, starting with the cheapest and finishing with the most expensive:

(a) for the building and running costs;

(b) for the fuel costs;

(c) for the overall cost of each Unit of electricity.

2 What problems of pollution are caused by burning fossil fuels?

3 Nuclear power stations do not usually cause much pollution. But some people want to ban them because they believe they are a danger to the environment. What makes people believe this?

4 Renewable energy sources don't pollute air or water. But they can still harm the environment. Describe how two of the renewable energy sources affect the environment.

WHAT YOU NEED TO REMEMBER

Comparing energy sources

You will need to use Core ideas in different ways like you have on this page.

3.11 Renewable energy sources in action

This topic was written using a word processor powered by renewable energy sources. The photograph shows how the electricity is generated.

This writer's electricity is produced by the wind generator and the arrays of solar cells on the roof.

1 Copy and complete the table.

Energy source	Device that produces electricity

■ Electricity when it's wanted

Solar cells don't produce electricity at night or in dull weather. Also it isn't always windy. But there is still electricity in the cottage. The diagram shows why.

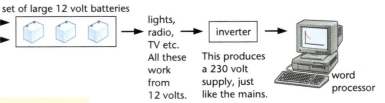

set of large 12 volt batteries

lights, radio, TV etc. All these work from 12 volts.

inverter

This produces a 230 volt supply, just like the mains.

word processor

2 Why is there still electricity even when none is being generated?

3 Copy and complete the sentences.

Most of the appliances in the cottage work from the 12 volt _____.

But the word processor works from an _____.
This provides a 230 volt supply just like the _____.

REMEMBER

Fossil fuels like coal and oil were formed from living things which died millions of years ago. They are <u>non-renewable</u>. Once they are used up, they cannot be replaced.

■ Keeping the cottage warm

The wind generator and solar cells don't produce enough electricity to heat the cottage or for cooking. To do this, peat is burned in a stove.

The photograph shows how peat is formed.

4 Peat is both a <u>renewable</u> fuel and a <u>fossil</u> fuel. Explain why.

Layers of dead moss from previous years.

It takes a few hundred years for the dead moss to turn to peat.

Pieces of peat are cut with a special spade. They are dried and then burned.

WHAT YOU NEED TO REMEMBER

Renewable energy sources in action

You will need to use Core ideas in different ways like you have on this page.

3.12 More about energy transfers

Some devices transfer energy mainly in the way that we want them to. We say that they are <u>efficient</u>.

An electric kettle, for example, is very efficient. Nearly all of the energy we supply to the kettle is transferred to the water inside it.

The efficiency of an appliance is the percentage of energy it transfers in the way that we want it to.

A light bulb that transferred all the electrical energy to its surroundings as light would be 100% efficient. Real light bulbs are a lot less efficient than this.

The diagrams show how efficient some electrical appliances are.

1 Copy the table below. Then complete the <u>first</u> <u>two</u> columns, putting the appliances in order. Start with the most efficient appliance and end with the least efficient.

Appliance	Efficiency (%)	Wasted energy (%)

■ Making it all add up

Energy is never lost. <u>All</u> of the energy supplied to an electrical appliance is transferred in one way or another.

For example, the light bulb transfers 5% of the energy supplied to it as light and the other 95% as thermal energy:

5% + 95% = 100%.

We say that energy is <u>conserved</u>.

2 Complete the <u>third</u> column of your table.

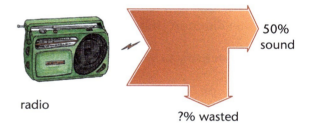

kettle — 98% to hot water — 2% wasted

light bulb — 5% light — 95% wasted

radio — 50% sound — ?% wasted

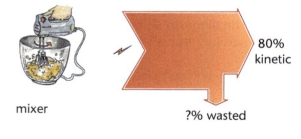

mixer — 80% kinetic — ?% wasted

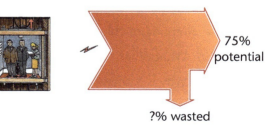

lift — 75% potential — ?% wasted

WHAT YOU NEED TO REMEMBER

More about energy transfers

You will need to use Core ideas in different ways like you have on this page.

3.13 Cells and batteries

A useful but expensive way to get an electric current is from a battery.

The diagram shows the first kind of battery to be invented.

1 (a) When was the battery first invented?

(b) What did Volta use to make this battery?

2 How many cells are there in the battery shown in the diagram?

You can make a cell with <u>any</u> two different metals and a solution that will conduct electricity.

A cell works because one of the metals is more reactive than the other.

The diagram shows how reactive some metals are.

3 Which metal in Volta's cell is the more reactive?

■ Another type of cell

The diagram shows the cheapest type of cell that you can buy in a shop.

4 Copy and complete the following.

The cell is made from:

■ a reactive metal called _____ ;

■ a less reactive element called _____ ;

■ ammonium chloride made into a _____ .

5 (a) What other substance is in the cell?

(b) Why is it there?

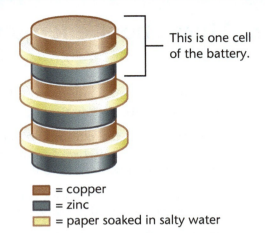

This is one cell of the battery.

■ = copper
■ = zinc
▢ = paper soaked in salty water

Alessandro Volta (1745–1827) made the first battery in about 1800.

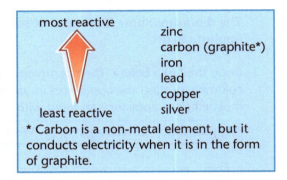

most reactive

zinc
carbon (graphite*)
iron
lead
copper
silver

least reactive

* Carbon is a non-metal element, but it conducts electricity when it is in the form of graphite.

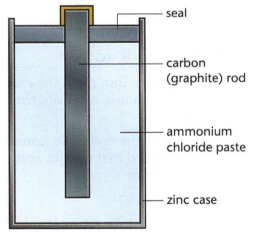

seal

carbon (graphite) rod

ammonium chloride paste

zinc case

The cell also has manganese dioxide around the carbon rod. This stops bubbles of gas from building up around the rod. The bubbles would stop the cell from working.

WHAT YOU NEED TO REMEMBER

Cells and batteries

You will need to use Core ideas in different ways like you have on this page.

3.14 More about circuits

A two-way circuit

The diagrams show a circuit that is often used for a light on stairs. You can switch the light on or off from the top of the stairs or from the bottom. It doesn't matter where you last switched the light on or off.

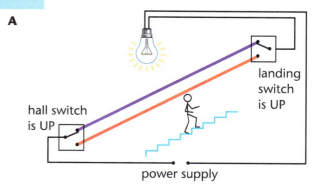

A

hall switch is UP

landing switch is UP

power supply

1 Copy and complete the sentences.

On diagram A, both switches are in the _____ position. So a current can flow along the _____ wire. The light is _____.

If one of the switches is put to the DOWN position, the circuit is _____.
This makes the light go _____.

2 Draw a diagram to show what happens if both switches are DOWN.

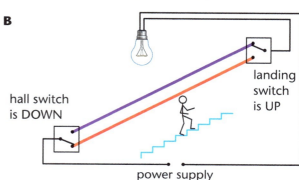

B

hall switch is DOWN

landing switch is UP

power supply

Currents in a parallel circuit

The diagram shows two <u>different</u> light bulbs connected in parallel. The ammeters show the currents in different parts of the circuit.

3 Copy and complete the table.

Part of circuit	Current
red	
green	
blue	

4 (a) Add together the currents in the green and blue parts of the circuit.

(b) What do you notice about your answer?

In a parallel circuit, the current from the supply is the total of the currents in the separate branches of the circuit.

WHAT YOU NEED TO REMEMBER

More about circuits

You will need to use Core ideas in different ways like you have on this page.

3.15 Switching on a car starter motor

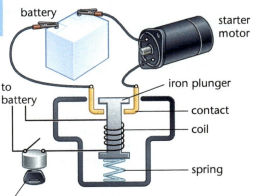

battery

starter motor

to battery

iron plunger

contact

coil

spring

Unless you turn the ignition key, the switch is off.

To start a car, all the driver has to do is turn the ignition key. Under the bonnet, a large electric motor turns the heavy engine to make it start. The motor needs a very big electric current to turn the engine. This current is too big to go through the ignition switch. So a relay must be used.

The diagrams show what happens when the driver turns the ignition key.

1 Write down the following sentences in the correct order to describe what happens. The first one is in the right place.

The driver turns the ignition key.

- A large current flows to the starter motor.
- The top of the plunger connects the two contacts.
- A small current flows through the coil.
- The iron plunger is pulled down.

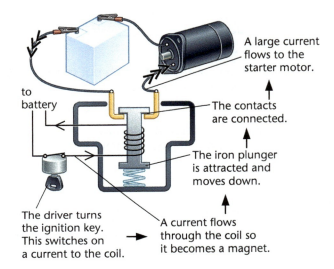

A large current flows to the starter motor.

to battery

The contacts are connected.

The iron plunger is attracted and moves down.

The driver turns the ignition key. This switches on a current to the coil.

A current flows through the coil so it becomes a magnet.

When the driver stops turning the ignition key, the starter motor stops.

2 Copy and complete the sentences.

When the driver stops turning the ignition key, the coil stops being a _____ .
The iron plunger is pushed back up by the _____ .
So the current to the starter motor is switched _____ .

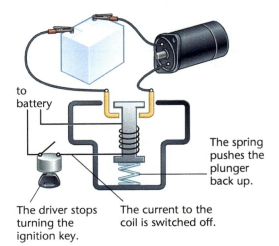

to battery

The spring pushes the plunger back up.

The driver stops turning the ignition key.

The current to the coil is switched off.

WHAT YOU NEED TO REMEMBER

Switching on a car starter motor

You will need to use Core ideas in different ways like you have on this page.

214

3.16 Storing energy for when it's needed

■ Energy for starting a car

A car starter motor needs a very big current. The starter might be used many times every day. This is enough to make even a very big battery go flat very quickly.

The photograph shows why a car battery doesn't go flat.

> 1 Copy and complete the energy transfer diagrams.
>
>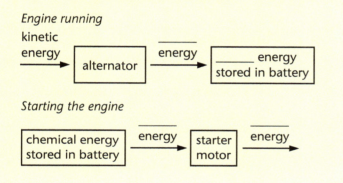
>
> *Engine running*
> kinetic energy → alternator → _____ energy → _____ energy stored in battery
>
> *Starting the engine*
> chemical energy stored in battery → _____ energy → starter motor → _____ energy →

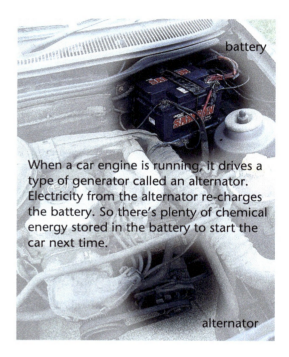

battery

When a car engine is running, it drives a type of generator called an alternator. Electricity from the alternator re-charges the battery. So there's plenty of chemical energy stored in the battery to start the car next time.

alternator

■ Buses with special brakes

Most buses are slowed down using brakes. The brakes get hot and transfer thermal energy to the surroundings. So the kinetic energy the bus had when it was moving is wasted.

The diagrams show how a new type of bus avoids wasting energy when it slows down.

> 2 Copy and complete the sentences.
>
> When the bus slows down, its kinetic energy is transferred to a _____.
>
> To start the bus moving, this _____ energy is transferred back again to the bus.

Inside the bus, there is a large heavy wheel called a *flywheel.*

The bus slows down by transferring energy to the flywheel. This makes it spin very fast.

The rotating flywheel stores kinetic energy. Energy from the flywheel can then be transferred back to the bus to start it moving again.

WHAT YOU NEED TO REMEMBER

Storing energy for when it's needed

You will need to use Core ideas in different ways like you have on this page.

Biology

1 LIVING THINGS

Cells

Living things are made up of **cells**.

Some living things have only one cell; they are **unicellular**. Living things with many cells are **multicellular**.

Both animal and plant cells have a **nucleus**, **cytoplasm** and **cell membrane**.

Only plant cells have a **cell wall** and **vacuole**, and some plant cells have **chloroplasts**.

Working together

We call groups of similar cells a **tissue**. Different tissues are grouped together into **organs**.

Cells, tissues and organs are all suited to the **job** they do.

Life processes

Living things can **sense**, **move**, **respire**, **grow**, **reproduce**, **excrete**, and they need **nutrition**.

Non-living things cannot **grow** or **reproduce**.

Cycles of life

The sexual reproductive systems of plants and animals make special sex cells or **gametes**.

Gametes join together in a process we call **fertilisation**.

The start of pregnancy

The **sperm** and egg (ovum) join in an **oviduct**. We call this **fertilisation**.

The fertilised egg divides as it travels down the oviduct to the uterus. The ball of cells sinks into the lining of the **uterus**. We call this **implantation**.

If an egg is not fertilised, the lining of the uterus breaks down and causes the bleeding called a monthly **period**.

New plants

There are three steps to make a new plant.

1   Pollen is transferred from an **anther** of one flower to the **stigma** of another flower of the same type. We call this **pollination**.

2   A pollen **tube** grows down through the style. The male sex cell uses this to reach the female sex cell.

3   The two sex cells join together. The female sex cell and the male sex cell join to make one cell. We call this **fertilisation**.

Classification

Scientists usually sort living things into five main groups: **plants**, **animals**, **fungi**, **bacteria** and **protoctists**. This is called **classification**.

It is sometimes useful to group microscopic living things as **microbes**.

There are four main groups of plants: **flowering plants**, **conifers**, **ferns** and **mosses**.

Groups of animals

You need to be able to classify animals into their main groups, just as you have done in the questions on this spread.

Variation

Members of a species **vary**. Some of the differences between them are passed on from their parents. We say that these differences are **inherited**.

The **environment** also causes differences. These differences are not passed on.

A **mixture** of inheritance and environment causes other differences.

Specialised cells   C+

You will need to be able to recognise specialised animal and plant cells like those above, and explain how each cell does its job.

Organ systems C+

Groups of similar cells are called **tissues**. These join together to form **organs**.

Organs work together as **organ systems**. They enable life processes to take place.

Pregnancy and birth C+

When an embryo embeds itself in the uterus lining, a special organ called the **placenta** forms. Nutrients and **oxygen** pass from the mother to the fetus. Waste from the **fetus** passes into the mother's blood.

After about 38 weeks, the uterus muscles **contract** to push the baby out. The placenta is no longer needed so it is also pushed out.

The menstrual cycle C+

The menstrual cycle is a way of making sure that the lining of the **uterus** is ready for the implantation of an embryo each time an **ovary** releases an ovum (egg). The menstrual cycle is controlled by **hormones**.

Changing classifications C+

Living things have not always been **classified** in the same way.
Scientists have gathered new information using scientific instruments like the **microscope**. They have also had new ideas like the theory of **evolution**.

Champion leeks C+

We can **choose** the plants and animals which best suit our needs. We can **breed** from them so they pass on their useful characteristics. We call this **selective breeding**.

2 KEEPING FIT AND HEALTHY

Illness and health

You need to look after your body.

Some **microbes**, such as viruses, fungi and bacteria, can make you ill.

Lack of just one mineral or **vitamin** in your diet can cause a disease. Too much fat, salt or **sugar** can harm you.

Some illnesses are passed on from parents to their children; we say that they are **inherited**.

Some chemicals can damage your body

Drugs that can help your body if you use them properly are called **medicines**

Smoking, alcohol, solvents and other drugs **damage** your body.

Healthy eating

You need to eat a variety of food to stay **healthy**. The important things in your diet are **carbohydrates**, **fats**, **proteins**, **fibre**, **vitamins**, **minerals** and water.

Digesting your food

Large food molecules are broken down by **enzymes** in digestive juices. We call this **digestion**.

Digestive juices are made in your salivary **glands**, stomach lining, **pancreas** and small intestine lining. Small, **soluble** molecules are absorbed into your blood in your small **intestine**.

Using your food

Molecules of glucose from digested food travel in your **blood** to all the **cells** in your body. Cells break down the **glucose** to release **energy**. We say they **respire**. They need **oxygen** to do this.

Your food also supplies cells with the **materials** they need to make new cells and to repair or replace damaged ones.

What happens when you exercise?

These are the things that must happen so your muscle cells can release energy when you exercise:

- You **breathe** air in and out of your lungs.

- In your lungs, oxygen goes into the blood and carbon dioxide goes out. We call this gas **exchange**.

- Your blood **transports** glucose and oxygen to your muscle cells.

- Cells break down glucose to release energy. This is **respiration**.

All these things go on more quickly when you **exercise**.

Biology

Keeping fit

Your **heart** pumps blood around your body.

Blood carries **oxygen** and **glucose** to cells and takes away **carbon dioxide** and other waste.

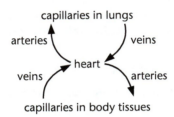

You need to be able to label a diagram of your circulation.

Take care when you exercise

Your bones **protect** and **support** parts of your body.

The **joints** between bones let you move. Muscles cause movement when they **contract**. Muscles are in **pairs**. When one muscle of a pair contracts, the other **relaxes**.

Self-defence   C+

Some of your white blood cells make **antibodies** to destroy microbes, others **digest** microbes. Your white blood cells make new kinds of antibodies when you are infected by, or immunised against, a new disease. **Antibiotics** are drugs which kill **bacteria** in your body.

Smoking and health   C+

Coughing damages the **air sacs** in your lungs. Nicotine paralyses the **cilia** which normally help to keep dirt and microbes out of your **lungs**. These things mean your lungs do not work as well if you smoke.

Vitamin tablets   C+

To stay healthy you need **vitamins** and **minerals**. Some people who don't eat a **balanced** diet take vitamin tablets. Too much vitamin A or D can **poison** you.

More about enzymes   C+

Enzymes are **catalysts**. They **speed up** chemical reactions.

Different enzymes speed up **different** reactions.

Carbohydrases digest **carbohydrates**. Proteases digest **proteins**. Lipases digest **fats**.

The **rate** at which an enzyme works depends on certain conditions, for example **temperature**.

Born athletes   C+

The word equation for the respiration of glucose is:
glucose + **oxygen** → carbon dioxide + **water** + **energy**

How to get a good exchange rate   C+

Organs where **exchanges** take place have a good blood supply and a large **surface area**. Examples are your **lungs** and **small intestine**.

Capillaries in action   C+

Substances pass between the blood and the tissues through capillary walls. They **diffuse** in and out easily because capillary walls are only **one cell** thick.

Different athletes for different events   C+

You need to know examples of variation due to inheritance and variation due to environment.

3 SURVIVAL

Daily and seasonal change

The **temperature** and the amount of **light** vary according to the time of day and the **season** of the year. Plants and animals are **adapted** to survive these changes.

Photosynthesis: a scientific detective story

Green plants make their own **food** using the energy from **light**. This process is called **photosynthesis**.

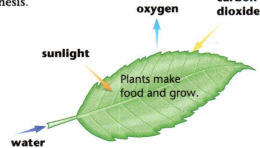

Growing tomato plants without soil

A plant has roots to **anchor** it in soil and for taking in **water** and **minerals**.

The main minerals a plant needs are **nitrates**, phosphates and potassium. A small amount of magnesium is important for making **chlorophyll**. A plant needs chlorophyll for **photosynthesis**.

Feed the world

Only green plants can make food.

We get our food from **plants**, or from **animals** which ate plants.

Our food gives us the **energy** and **materials** we need to move, grow and keep **warm**.

Food in Biosphere 2

Food chains show how food made by **plants** passes from one living thing to another. In a habitat, most plants and animals belong to more than one food **chain**, so we combine food chains to form a food **web**.

Can great crested newts survive?

A habitat must provide the right **conditions** for an animal or plant to **survive**.

Animals and plants are adapted to their habitats, so changes may affect them. Some changes are **natural**, but **humans** cause others.

The American crayfish invasion

Animals compete for **food** and **space**. This affects the sizes of populations.

Predation also affects **population** size. A big population of **predators** decreases the population of **prey**.

Stay-at-homes and migrants   C+

Some animals change with the **seasons**. Others **migrate** to places where conditions are suitable.

More discoveries about photosynthesis C+

The word equation for photosynthesis is:

$$\textbf{carbon dioxide} + \text{water} \xrightarrow[\substack{\text{trapped by } \textbf{chlorophyll} \\ \text{in chloroplasts}}]{\text{energy from } \textbf{sunlight}} \text{glucose} + \textbf{oxygen}$$

Growing enough food   C+

The amount of water and minerals a crop receives affects its **yield**. When we add fertilisers to soil, we add **minerals**. Some **fertilisers** are artificial, others are **natural**.

Plants and animals respire   C+

The breakdown of food to release energy is called **respiration**. Respiration which uses **oxygen** is called aerobic respiration.
glucose + oxygen → **carbon dioxide** + water + energy

Problems of Biosphere 2   C+

We can show the **number** of plants and animals at each level in a food chain as a **pyramid** of numbers.

Disappearing species   C+

If a habitat is **destroyed** or changes too much, the plants and animals **move out** or die. That it why it is important to preserve habitats and not to **pollute** the environment.

Survival   C+

Animals and plants vary. Some variation is **inherited**. Animals and plants which inherit characteristics most **suited** to their environments are more likely than others to survive, **breed** and pass on their **genes**.

A problem with pesticides   C+

We use pesticides to kill **pests**. Pesticides are poisonous or **toxic**.

Pesticides build up in food chains. So animals which are near the top of a food chain contain a higher **concentration** of pesticides than those nearer the bottom of a chain.

Chemistry

1 MATTER

Using everyday materials

We make things from **materials**.

We use different materials to do different **jobs**. This is because they have different **properties**.

Metals and non-metals

Most of the elements are **metals**.

All metals are good conductors of heat and **electricity**, but most non-metals do not **conduct** heat or electricity.

Elements which are gases at room temperature are all **non-metals**.

Solids, liquids and gases

A solid has its own shape and **volume**.

A liquid has its own volume but not its own **shape**.

A gas does not have either its own shape or its own volume. It spreads out to fill all the **space** it can.

A gas can be **squashed**.

Liquids and gases can **flow**.

Making models of matter

Solids have their own **shape** because the particles cannot move around. Liquids and gases flow because their particles can **move** around each other.

You cannot squash liquids and solids easily because there is no space between their **particles**. You can squash a gas because there is **space** between the particles.

Getting warmer, getting colder

When we heat solids, liquids or gases, they normally **expand**.

When solids, liquids and gases cool down, they normally **contract**.

If we stop a gas expanding when it gets hot, we get an increase in **pressure**.

Mixtures

You can mix things together in different amounts. We say that they can be mixed in different **proportions**.

When you dissolve a solid in a liquid, the **particles** of the solid and the liquid get mixed together.

Air is a **mixture** of gases.

Making pure white sugar

We get sugar from plants such as sugar cane. The sugar is **mixed** up with many other things. To get pure white sugar, we need to **separate** it from these other things. We can do this because sugar **dissolves** in water.

We can make more sugar dissolve by using **more** water, or **hotter** water.

Separating mixtures

Most substances in the world around us are parts of **mixtures**.

A substance that is not mixed up with other substances is called a **pure** substance.

To get a pure substance, we need to **separate** it from other substances. We can do this because different substances have different **properties**.

What is density?   C+

A piece of steel weighs more than the same **volume** of water. So we say that steel is **denser** than water.

The density of a material is its **mass** divided by its volume.

Density of gases   C+

When you **squeeze** a gas, the particles move **closer** together. This increases the **density** of the gas.

What makes a solid melt?   C+

When you heat up a solid, you make its particles vibrate **faster**.

The particles start to move around if they **vibrate** strongly enough. The solid has changed into a **liquid**. It has **melted**.

Why do liquids evaporate?   C+

When a liquid changes into a gas, we say that it **evaporates**.

A liquid evaporates as faster moving particles **escape**.

Heating speeds up evaporation because more particles have enough **energy** to escape.

Melting, boiling and temperature   C+

When a solid is melting or a liquid is boiling, its **temperature** doesn't change.

The energy transferred to a melting solid makes the particles **break away** from their fixed positions.

The energy transferred to a boiling liquid makes its particles **escape**.

How does a gas fill its container?   C+

The particles of a gas move about with rapid, **random** motion. So a gas spreads out into all the space it can. We say that the gas **diffuses**.

How can you change gas pressure?   C+

You can increase the pressure of a gas:

- by squeezing it into a smaller **space**;
- by increasing its **temperature**, which makes the particles hit the sides of the container **harder**.

Both squeezing and heating the gas make its particles hit the sides of the container more **often**.

Why do solids expand when they are heated?   C+

The particles in a solid are held in position by strong **forces** of attraction. The particles can't move about but they can **vibrate**.

When a solid is heated, the vibrating particles bang into each other and take up more space, so the solid **expands**.

2 CHEMICAL REACTIONS

Two sorts of change

We call changes that make new substances **chemical** changes. Changes that do not make new substances are **physical** changes.

Two examples of physical change are changes of **state**, and separating **mixtures**.

Physical changes are usually easier to **reverse** than chemical changes.

Chemical changes are produced by chemical **reactions**.

Chemical reactions

Another name for burning is combustion. When things burn they react with **oxygen**. So we also call burning an **oxidation** reaction.

In a thermal decomposition reaction, you split up a substance by **heating** it.

In electrolysis, you split up a substance by passing an **electric current** through it.

Elements and atoms

We call simple substances **elements**.

Elements are made up of very small particles called **atoms**.

All the atoms in one element are the **same** kind.

Atoms of different elements are **different**.

Compounds

Substances made from atoms of different elements joined together are called **compounds**.

A substance made from different atoms <u>not</u> joined together is called a **mixture**.

Compounds have different **properties** from the elements they are made from.

Elements reacting with oxygen

When we burn elements in oxygen, we get compounds called **oxides**.

Some non-metallic elements make oxides that dissolve in water to make **acids**.

Some metals make oxides that dissolve in water to make **alkalis**.

Metals reacting with acids

Most metals react with dilute **acids**. The reactions produce a gas called **hydrogen**. They also produce compounds called **salts**.

We can write down the reaction between zinc and hydrochloric acid like this:

zinc + dilute hydrochloric acid → zinc **chloride** + hydrogen

Chemistry

Displacement reactions

Some metals are more **reactive** than others.

A reactive metal will push a less reactive metal out of a **solution** of one of its compounds. We call this type of chemical change a **displacement** reaction.

A list of metals in order of their reactivities is called a **reactivity series**.

Carrying out tests

When we want to find out what a substance is, we carry out chemical **tests**. Most tests are **chemical** changes.

You need to know what each of these tests tells you.

Different kinds of mixtures   C+

We can have a **mixture** of elements, or of **compounds**. We can also **mix** elements and compounds together.

More about compounds and mixtures C+

In a mixture, elements can be mixed together in different **ratios**.

But in a compound, the atoms of the different elements are always joined together in the **same** ratio. We say that compounds have a fixed **composition**.

Simple chemical formulas   C+

You should be able to use the formula of a compound to tell you what elements are in the compound and the ratio of their atoms.

More complicated chemical formulas C+

You need to be able to work out which elements are in the compound (and what numbers of atoms they have) just as you have for the compounds on this page.

Energy changes in chemical reactions C+

When the atoms of two elements join together, the reaction usually gives out **energy**.

Reactions which **split** up compounds take energy in.

More about the reactivity series   C+

We sometimes include **hydrogen** in the series even though it is not a metal.

Physical change and mass   C+

In a physical change you still have the same substances made from the same **particles**. So in a physical change there is no change in **mass**.

Chemical change and mass   C+

In chemical reactions, there is no change in **mass**. This is because there are still the same **atoms**. They are just joined together in **different** ways.

3 EARTH SCIENCE

Different kinds of rocks

When molten rock cools down **igneous** rocks are formed.

Sedimentary rocks form at the bottom of lakes and seas. They are made up of sediment that builds up in **layers**.

Heat and pressure can change rocks. We call the new rocks **metamorphic** rocks.

Heating up the rock cycle

We live on the Earth's **crust**.

As we go deeper into the Earths crust, it gets very **hot**.

Between the crust and the core, the Earth consists of molten rock called **magma**.

Rocks slowly move around all the time. We call this the **rock cycle**. The energy for this movement comes from **radioactive** substances and from the **weather**.

Getting metals out of rocks

A metal found in the ground as itself is said to be **native**.

Rocks that contain metals or metal compounds are called **ores**.

When we use a chemical reaction to get a metal out of its ore, we call this **smelting**.

We smelt iron in a **blast furnace**.

More reactive metals are smelted using **electricity**.

Corroding metals

Rusting is a special case of **corrosion**. Rusting takes place when iron or steel is in contact with both air and **water**.

Most methods of slowing down rusting use a **barrier**. One of the best barriers is **zinc**.

The less reactive a metal is, the less likely it is to **corrode**.

Acids and alkalis

Sulphur dioxide from volcanoes and nitrogen oxides from lightning are **acidic** gases.

The opposites of acids are **alkalis**.

Chemists tell the difference between acids and alkalis by using **indicators**. These are often natural **dyes**. In acids and alkalis, they change **colour**.

Acids in the soil

We use universal indicator to measure **pH**. A pH of 7 means that the solution is **neutral**.

When the pH is less than 7, we have an **acid**. When the pH is more than 7, we have an **alkali**.

When an alkali neutralises an acid, we get a **salt** and **water** only.

When a carbonate neutralises an acid, we get a salt, water and **carbon dioxide**.

Weathering rocks

Rocks being broken down into smaller pieces is called **erosion**. This is caused by the Sun, the **wind**, water and **ice**. Because erosion is caused by the weather, we call it **weathering**.

Chemical reactions can also attack rocks; we call this **chemical** weathering.

Looking after the environment   C+

Fossil fuels contain carbon and **hydrogen**. When fossil fuels such as petrol burn, they release carbon dioxide and **water**.

The useful thing that we get from fossil fuels is **energy**.

The motor car also produces small amounts of carbon monoxide and **nitrogen oxides**.

More about the rock cycle   C+

When plates in the Earth's crust collide, rocks are slowly pushed up to form **mountains**.

The rocks at the top of the new mountain can be igneous, metamorphic or **sedimentary**. These rocks are then broken down by **weathering** and **erosion**. They are carried down the mountainside; this is called **transportation**. At the bottom of the mountain they form a sediment; this is called **deposition**. Later new rock is formed as the sediment gets covered up; this is called **burial**.

Smelting metals   C+

The more **reactive** the metal, the more **energy** is needed to extract it.

We smelt metals in the middle of the reactivity series, like iron, with **carbon**. But for metals higher in the reactivity series, like aluminium, we use **electricity**.

More about salts   C+

Hydrochloric acid makes salts called **chlorides**. Sulphuric acid makes salts called **sulphates**. Nitric acid makes salts called **nitrates**.

Why are ice and water so strange?   C+

When water freezes, it **expands**. This means that the molecules in ice are **further away** from each other than the molecules in water. This is why ice is less **dense** than water.

Why do some rocks dissolve?   C+

Carbon dioxide dissolves in water to make a very weak **acid**. This reacts with calcium carbonate rocks to make a soluble substance called **calcium bicarbonate**. So the rock slowly **dissolves**.

Carbon dioxide and the greenhouse effect   C+

One of the greenhouse gases is **carbon dioxide**.

The amount of carbon dioxide in the air increases because we burn **fossil fuels**.

An increase in the greenhouse effect will raise the Earth's average **temperature**.

Waste and pollution   C+

Waste is a problem because it can never just **disappear**.

To prevent pollution, we must change waste into **harmless** substances.

Physics

1 LIGHT AND SOUND

The Sun and the Earth's satellites

The Sun gives out its own **light**.

Light travels in **straight** lines.

The side of the Earth that faces away from the Sun is in **darkness**. This is because it is in the Earth's **shadow**.

The Moon **orbits** the Earth. We say that it is a **satellite** of the Earth.

We can see the Moon and other satellites because light from the Sun is **reflected** from them.

The solar system and the stars

You can see stars because they give out their own light, just like the **Sun**.

You can see planets because they **reflect** the Sun's light.

Planets seem to move through the **constellations** of stars.

The constellations seem to move across the sky because the Earth **spins**.

Driving at night

White or pale surfaces **reflect** light better than black or dark surfaces.

A piece of white paper reflects light in all directions; it **scatters** the light.

The diagram shows how a mirror reflects a beam of light.

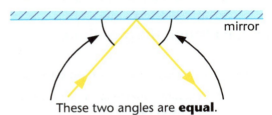

mirror

These two angles are **equal**.

Colour

White light is a **mixture** of many different colours.

We can split white light into a **spectrum** using a glass or plastic prism. We say that the prism **disperses** the white light.

An object looks coloured because it **reflects** only some of the colours in white light. The other colours from the white light are **absorbed**.

A coloured filter only lets some colours pass through; it **absorbs** other colours.

What prisms do to light

When light passes from one substance into another it is **refracted**.

normal— air / glass or plastic — This beam of light is refracted away from the **normal**.

glass or plastic / air —normal — This beam of light is refracted **towards** the normal.

Light at the red end of the spectrum is refracted **less** than light at the violet end of the spectrum.

'Bent' rulers and 'shallow' water

Water always looks **shallower** than it really is. A ruler that dips below water looks **bent**. These things happen because light is **refracted** away from the normal when it passes from water into **air**.

A rock band on the Moon

All sounds are caused by **vibrations**. These can travel through solids, liquids or gases but not through empty **space**. Another word for empty space is a **vacuum**.

Sound travels a lot **slower** than light does.

Sound can be **reflected**, especially from hard surfaces.

Loud sounds are made by vibrations which have a large **amplitude**. Loud sounds can **damage** your ears.

Two different stringed instruments

If a string vibrates faster, we say that it has a higher **frequency**.

Vibrations with a high frequency produce sounds with a high **pitch**.

You also need to know what is in the 'Do you remember?' box.

C+ 1.9–1.16

You will need to use Core ideas in different ways like you have on these pages.

2 FORCES

Things that can attract or repel

A magnet has a **north** pole and a **south** pole.
Like poles **repel**.
Unlike poles **attract**.

Electric charges can be **positive** (+) or **negative** (−).
Like charges repel.
Unlike charges attract.

You also need to know what is in the 'Do you remember?' box.

Gravity – a force that attracts

Any two objects attract each other with a force called **gravity**. This force is very weak unless one (or both) of the objects has a large **mass**.

The force of gravity that acts on an object is what we call its **weight**.

Gravity keeps a planet or a satellite moving around its **orbit**. The force of gravity keeps changing the **direction** in which planets and satellites move.

Looking at orbits

The further away from the Sun a planet is, the longer is its **orbit** time.

Artificial satellites need to be above the atmosphere so they aren't slowed down by **friction** with the air.

Satellites that are used to watch the Earth are put into quite **low** orbits.

You need to know the order of the planets in the solar system.

Getting things moving

An object will not start to move unless an **unbalanced** force acts on it.

To make an object move you need a force which is bigger than any **friction** force that is also acting.

The friction force when an object moves through air is called **air resistance**. When an object moves faster this air resistance becomes **larger**.

To reduce the friction force in air or water you need a **streamlined** shape.

Slowing down

Friction forces always act in the **opposite** direction to movement. So friction forces slow things down unless they are **balanced** by a driving force.

We can use friction forces to slow things down:
- a person falls more slowly using a parachute because of greater air **resistance**;
- brakes use the friction between surfaces which **slide** across each other.

Looking at speed

You can work out speeds like this:
speed = **distance** ÷ **time taken**

If the speed changes, the answer you get is the **average** speed.

On a distance:time graph, a steep slope means a **higher** speed.

Pressure

To reduce the pressure a force produces, you can spread it over a large **area**.

Making a force act on a small area produces a large **pressure**.

You can work out a pressure like this:
pressure = **force** ÷ **area**

Forces that make things turn

The point about which something turns is called a **pivot**. The turning effect of a force is called its **moment**.

To get a bigger moment:
- you can use a **bigger** force;
- you can apply a force **further away** from the pivot.

For an object to turn there must be an **unbalanced** moment acting on it.

An object <u>doesn't</u> turn if the clockwise and anti-clockwise moments are **balanced**.

C+ 2.9–2.15

You will need to use Core ideas in different ways like you have on these pages.

More about moments   C+

Moment of a force = **size** of force × **distance** of force from the pivot

Physics

3 ENERGY AND ELECTRICITY

Energy sources

Energy sources that depend on energy that has come from the Sun are:
wind, **waves**, **hydro** (electricity), **biomass**, **coal**, **oil**, **natural gas** and **solar**.

Energy sources that do not depend on energy that has come from the Sun are:
tides, **geothermal** and **nuclear fuel**.

An energy source that is being replaced all the time is a **renewable** energy source.

You should know which energy sources are renewable and which are non-renewable.

Using energy sources to generate electricity

Most ways of generating electricity use a **turbine** to drive a **generator**.

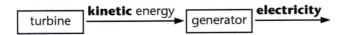

Getting the energy we want from electricity

To transfer energy to our surroundings, we often use **electrical** appliances.

Electrical appliances transfer **all** the energy we supply to them.

Some of the energy is transferred in ways that we don't want; this energy is **wasted**.

You should know the energy transfers that everyday electrical appliances are designed to make and the unwanted energy transfers that they also make.

Static electricity and electric currents

On an object charged with static electricity, the electrical charges stay in **one place**.

In an electric current, electrical charges **move**. The material that an electric current will flow through is called a **conductor**.

You can discharge a charged conductor by connecting it to the **earth**.

Measuring currents in circuits

To measure electric currents you use an **ammeter**.

To measure the current through a bulb, you connect the ammeter in **series** with the bulb.

If you connect two or more bulbs in series, there is still only **one** circuit for the current to flow round. The current through all points in the circuit is exactly the **same**.

Two or more bulbs can be connected to a battery so that they are in separate circuits. We then say that they are connected in **parallel**.

Electromagnets

A coil with a current flowing through it becomes an **electromagnet**. You can make this stronger by using a **bigger** current, by putting more **turns** of wire on the coil or by using an **iron core** inside the coil.

When you put some unmagnetised iron into a magnetic field, it becomes a **magnet**.

You should also know what is in the 'Do you remember?' box.

Using electromagnets

A magnet that stays magnetised all the time is called a **permanent** magnet.

An electromagnet is more useful than a permanent magnet because you can **switch** it on and off.

You may be given information about things which use electromagnets. You should then be able to explain how they work just like you did on these pages.

What happens to all the energy we transfer?

When you transfer energy none is ever **lost** but some is always **wasted**.

All the energy that we transfer eventually ends up making the surroundings a tiny bit **warmer**. This energy isn't very useful because it is very **spread** out.

C+ 3.9–3.16

You will need to use Core ideas in different ways like you have on these pages.

Glossary/index

A few words that occur very often such as <u>force</u>, <u>energy</u>, <u>animal</u>, <u>plant</u>, <u>electricity</u>, <u>chemical</u> and <u>reaction</u> are not included. Some of these words are part of the headings of the nine topics in the book. Words in italics appear elsewhere in the glossary.

A

absorb, absorption: 1. when something 'soaks up' light rather than *reflecting* it or letting it pass through   **150, 163**

2. when *cells* or blood take in dissolved food or *oxygen*   **32–35, 47**

acids: solutions that react with many *metals* to produce a *salt* and *hydrogen*, and that react with *alkalis* to produce a *salt* and *water*   **104, 106–107, 128–131**

adapted, adaptation: when plants or animals have *features* which make them suitable for where they live   **51, 60–62, 69**

aerobic respiration: using *oxygen* to break down food to release energy   **67**

afterbirth: the *placenta* and membranes pushed out of the *uterus* after a baby is born   **22**

air: a *mixture of gases*, mainly *nitrogen* and *oxygen*, that surrounds us   **83, 86**

air resistance: the *friction* force on something moving through *air*; also called <u>drag</u>   **175–176**

air sacs: small sacs at the ends of the air tubes in the *lungs*   **43, 47**

alcohol: a chemical which can be used as a *drug*   **28–29**

alkalis: the opposite of *acids*; they react with acids to produce *salts*   **104, 128–131**

amino acids: carbon compounds which *proteins* are built from   **33, 45**

ammeter: a meter that is used to measure electric *currents* in *amperes*   **200–201**

ampere (amp, A): the unit of electric *current*   **200–201**

amplitude: the size of the *vibrations* that produce a sound; a large amplitude produces a *loud* sound   **157**

anaemia: *disorder* of the blood caused by lack of iron in the *diet*   **27**

anther: part of a flower which makes the *pollen*   **8, 12**

antibiotics: *drugs* used to kill *bacteria* in the body   **29, 42**

antibodies: chemicals made by white blood cells to destroy *bacteria* and other *microbes*   **42**

anti-clockwise: opposite of *clockwise*

anus: opening at the end of the *digestive system*   **7, 33**

arteries: blood vessels which carry blood away from the *heart*   **38–39**

arthropods: *invertebrate* animals with an outer skeleton and jointed legs   **16**

atom: the smallest *particle* of an *element*   **101–103, 113**

attract, attraction: things pulling towards each other   **168–171**

B

bacteria: *microbes* made of *cells* without a true *nucleus*; one is called a bacterium   **7, 14, 26–27, 29, 42, 65**

balanced forces: forces that are the same size but act in opposite directions   **174, 176, 182–183**

battery: made from two or more electrical *cells* joined together   **212**

bell: a device that uses an *electromagnet* to make it ring   **205**

Glossary/index

biceps: the muscle that *contracts* to bend your arm 41

bile: a greenish-yellow *digestive juice* made in the liver 32

bladder: a stretchy bag which stores *urine* 9, 21

blast furnace: used for *smelting* iron *ore* 125

boiling point: the temperature that a *liquid* boils at 92

brakes: these use *friction* to slow down bicycles and motor vehicles 177

breathe, breathing: taking air in and out of the lungs 36–37, 46, 61

breed: *reproduce* or make new young plants and animals 24

burning: when substances react with *oxygen* and release thermal energy; also called <u>combustion</u> 98

C

cancer: a *disorder* in which *cells grow* out of control 26, 28, 43

capillary: narrow blood vessel with walls only one *cell* thick 38–39, 47–48

carbohydrase: *enzyme* that breaks down *carbohydrates* 45

carbohydrates: carbon compounds used by living things as food e.g. *starch* and sugars 30, 45

carbon: a solid *non-metal element* 75, 105, 138

carbonates: *compounds* that react with *acids* to produce *carbon dioxide* 131

carbon dioxide: 1. a *gas* whose *molecules* are made from *carbon atoms* and *hydrogen atoms* 98, 131, 141–142

2. a gas in the air used by plants in *photosynthesis* and made in *respiration* 6–7, 18, 22, 28, 35–38, 46–48, 52–54, 59, 65, 67

3. test for carbon dioxide 99, 110

carbon monoxide: a poisonous gas 28, 43

catalyst: a substance which speeds up a chemical reaction and which can be used over and over again 45

cell: 1. building block of plants and animals 2–8, 15, 20, 26, 32, 34–38, 48

2. contains chemicals that produce an electric **current** when it is connected to a complete *circuit* 200–201, 212

cell membrane: outer layer of the living part of a *cell* 2

cell wall: outer supporting layer of a plant *cell* made of cellulose 2, 65

characteristics: the special *features* of any plant or animal 70

charges: these produce an electric *current* when they are moving and *static electricity* when they are standing still 169, 198–199

chemical change: a change that produces new substances 96–99, 119

chlorine: 1. a *non-metal element*; it is a poisonous, greeny-yellow *gas* 99, 111

2. test for chlorine 99, 111

chlorophyll: the green substance in *chloroplasts* which traps light energy 55, 65

chloroplasts: the parts of plant *cells* which contain *chlorophyll* 2, 15, 20, 55, 65

chromatography: a way of separating different *dissolved solids*, for example dyes 86

cilia: tiny hairs that move back and forth, found on the surface of some cells 20

circuit diagram: an electric circuit drawn using circuit *symbols* 200

circulate, circulation: when blood flows through the *heart* and blood vessels **24, 38–39**

classify, classification: sorting things into groups **14–15, 24**

clockwise: the direction that the hands of a clock move round **182–183, 191**

combustion: another word for *burning* **98**

comet: a lump of rock and ice that moves in a very elliptical *orbit* around the *Sun* **186**

compass: see *magnetic compass*

compete, competition: when several plants or animals are all trying to get the same things **62–63**

compound: a substance made from the *atoms* of two, or more, different *elements* joined together **102–103, 113–114**

conductor: 1. electrical a substance that an electrical *current* easily passes through **74**

2. thermal a substance that thermal energy easily passes through **174, 198–199**

conservation: preserving or taking care of living things and their *habitats* **63**

constellation: a group of *stars* that form a pattern **147**

contract, contraction: 1. *solids, liquids* and *gases* do this when they cool **80–81**

2. in the case of a muscle, become shorter and fatter **22, 41**

corrosion: what happens to metals when they react with chemicals such as *water, oxygen* or *acids* in the air **126–127**

current: electric *charges* flowing around a complete *circuit* **198–201**

cytoplasm: the contents of a *cell* excluding the *nucleus*; the place where most chemical reactions happen **2, 15, 20**

D

decomposition: splitting up a *compound* into simpler substances **99**

dense: a dense substance has a lot of *mass* in a small volume **88–89**

density: the *mass* of a certain volume, e.g. $1\,cm^3$, of a substance **88–89**

diaphragm: a sheet of muscle which separates your chest from your lower body **21**

diet: all the food that you eat **26, 30–31, 44**

diffuse, diffusion: 1. the spreading of liquids and gases from where the concentration is high to where it is low **48**

2. the spreading out of a *gas* because its *particles* are moving about **93**

digest, digestion: breakdown of large insoluble food *molecules* into small, *soluble molecules* which can be *absorbed* **32–35, 42**

digestive juice: juice made by a digestive gland that helps to *digest* food **32–33**

digestive system: all the *organs* which are used to *digest* food **33–34, 42**

disease, disorder: when some part of a plant or animal isn't working properly **26**

disperse: splitting white light into different colours by *refracting* it through a *prism* **150**

displace, displacement: when a more *reactive element* pushes a less reactive element out of one of its *compounds* **108–109**

dissolve: when the *particles* of a *solid* completely *mix* with the particles of a *liquid* to make a clear solution **83, 85, 97, 141**

distance–time graph: graph which plots the distance something travels against the time it takes to travel; the slope of the graph represents *speed* **179**

Glossary/index

distil, distillation: *evaporating* a *liquid* and then *condensing* it again to get a pure liquid   85, 87

drag: see *air resistance*

drug: a substance which can change the way your body works   29, 42

E

eclipse: when the *Moon* is in the Earth's *shadow*, or the Earth in the Moon's shadow   160

ecosystem: a community of animals and plants interacting with each other and with the physical environment   58

efficiency: the fraction, or percentage, of the energy supplied that is transferred in the way that we want   211

egg cells, eggs: female *sex cells*; also called *ova*   8–11, 20–21, 23

egg tube: the tube that carries an *egg cell* from an *ovary* to the *uterus* (*womb*); also called an *oviduct*   9

electromagnet: a *magnet* made by passing an electric *current* through a coil of wire; it usually has an iron core   202–205, 211, 214

element: a substance that can't be split up into anything simpler   74, 100–101

embryo: 1. a baby in the *womb* (*uterus*) before all its *organs* have started to grow   11, 20, 23

2. the tiny plant inside a seed   19

enzymes: *protein* substances made in *cells* which speed up chemical reactions and are not used up   32, 34–35, 45

epithelium: tissue that forms a skin around an *organ* or organism   4

evaporate, evaporation: when a *liquid* changes into a *gas*   91

evolution: changing of a plant or animal *species* over a long period of time   24

excrete, excretion: getting rid of the *waste* made in body *cells*   7, 21, 35

expand, expansion: when things get bigger, usually because they are hotter   80–81, 95

extinct, extinction: no longer existing   63, 69

F

faeces: undigested *waste* which passes out through the *anus*   7, 33

fat: part of our food which we use for energy   30, 32–33, 45, 50

fatty acids: one of the building blocks of *fats*   33, 45

features: another word for *characteristics*   49

fertilise, fertilisation: when a male *sex cell* joins with a female *sex cell* to start a new plant or animal   8, 11, 13, 20

fertilised egg: *cell* formed when a male and a female *sex cell* (*gamete*) join   10

fertiliser: you add this to soil to provide the *minerals* that plants need to *grow*   25, 55, 66

fetus: a baby in the *womb* (*uterus*) whose *organs* are all growing   11, 22

fibre: indigestible cellulose in our food (roughage)   30, 33

filament: the *stalk* of a *stamen* in a flower   8

filter: 1. a thin piece of glass or plastic that only some colours of light can pass through   84, 87

2. separating a *liquid* from an <u>un</u>*dissolved solid* by passing it through small holes, usually in paper; the solid doesn't pass through the holes and is left behind   150

food chain: diagram showing what animals eat 58–59, 68, 71

food web: diagram showing what eats what in a *habitat* 59, 63

formula: uses *symbols* to tell you how many *atoms* of each *element* are joined together to form a *compound* (or *molecule* of the *element*) 114–115

fossil fuels: fuels that were formed from the remains of animals or plants that died millions of years ago; they are burned to release thermal energy 134–135, 193–195, 209

fossils: remains of plants and animals from a long time ago 24

frequency: the number of *vibrations* in a second; this gives a sound its particular *pitch*; units are *hertz* 158–159, 167

friction: a force that acts in the opposite direction to something that moves or is trying to move; friction can be between *solid* surfaces or when things move in *gases* or *liquids* 174–177, 187–188

fuels: see *fossil fuels* and *nuclear fuels*

fungi: plants which do not make their own food but break down dead bodies of plants and animals and other *waste*; one is called a fungus 15, 26–27

G

gametes: another name for *sex cells* 8

gases: substances that spread out (*diffuse*) to fill all the space they can; they can be squeezed into a smaller volume 77–79, 81, 88–89, 91, 93

gas exchange: taking useful gases into a body or *cell* and getting rid of *waste* gases 28, 37, 47

generator: produces electricity when it is supplied with *kinetic* energy 194–195

genes, genetic material: these control the *characteristics* of plants and animals; they are passed on by parents 20, 70

geothermal energy: energy stored in hot rocks in the Earth's crust 122, 192

gills: *organs* for *gas exchange* in some animals that live in water 24, 61

glucose: a **carbohydrate** that is a small, *soluble molecule* (a sugar) 6, 33–38, 45–46, 48, 67

glycerol: one of the building blocks of *fats* 33, 45

gravity: force of *attraction* between two objects because of their *mass* 170–171, 185

greenhouse effect: *gases*, such as *carbon dioxide*, in the air that make the Earth warmer than it would otherwise be 142

grow, growth: to become bigger and more complicated 6–7, 56

gullet: the tube that goes from the mouth to the *stomach*; another name for the *oesophagus* 32–33

H

habitat: the place where a plant or animal lives 59–61, 69

heart: an *organ* which pumps blood 24, 27–29, 36, 38–39, 43

hertz (Hz): the number of *vibrations* each second; the unit of *frequency* 159, 167

hibernate: go into a deep sleep through the winter 50, 60

hormones: chemicals secreted in small amounts which coordinate the *growth* and activities of living things 23

hydrogen: 1. a *non-metal element*; it is a gas that burns to make *water* 107, 109–110, 117

2. test for hydrogen 107, 110

I

igneous: rocks that are formed when molten *magma* from inside the Earth cools down 111, 129–131

Glossary/index

immune: able to resist an infectious *disease* because you have had the disease or because you have been immunised against it   **42**

implantation: the settling of an *embryo* in the lining of the *uterus*   **11**

indicator: a substance that can change colour and tell you if a solution is an *acid* or an *alkali*   **120–122**

inherit, inheritance: passing on in the *genes* from parents to offspring   **18–19, 25–26, 46, 49, 70**

interbreed: breed with each other   **17**

invertebrates: animals without backbones   **16**

iron: a chemical element that is a *mineral nutrient* for living things   **27**

J

joints: places where bones meet   **39–41**

joule (J): the unit of energy   **56, 200**

K

kidneys: *organs* which remove *urea* from your blood and excrete it in *urine*   **7, 21, 44**

kilojoule (kJ): 1000 *joules*   **56–57**

kinetic energy: the energy that an object has because it is moving   **195**

kwashiorkor: an illness caused by lack of *protein* in the *diet*   **31**

L

large intestine: wide part of intestine between *small intestine* and *anus*   **32–33**

life processes: what living things can do (*move, respire, sense, grow, repoduce, excrete* and *feed*)   **6, 56**

ligament: fibres which hold bones together at *joints*   **40**

limewater: a clear solution that *carbon dioxide* makes cloudy   **99, 110**

lines of magnetic force: these tell you which way a *magnetic compass* will point in a *magnetic field*   **184**

lipase: *enzyme* which *digests fat*   **45**

liquid: substances that have a fixed volume but take the shape of their container   **76–77, 81, 90–91**

litmus: an *indicator* that is red in *acids* and blue in *alkalis*   **104–105**

liver: large *organ* in the lower part of your body, just under your *diaphragm*   **21, 28–29, 31, 44, 48**

loud: a loud sound is produced by *vibrations* with a large *amplitude*   **157**

lungs: *organs* for *gas exchange* between the blood and the air   **7, 24**

M

magma: molten rock beneath the Earth's crust   **122**

magnetic compass: a magnet that is free to *pivot*; it comes to rest with one end (*pole*) pointing north and the other pole pointing south   **168, 184**

magnetic field: area around a magnet where it *attracts* or *repels*   **184, 202–203**

mass: the amount of stuff in an object; it is measured in grams (g) or kilograms (kg)   **118–119, 170**

melt: changing a *solid* into a *liquid* by heating it   **90, 92**

menstrual cycle: the monthly cycle in the human female *reproductive system*   **23**

metals: substances that *conduct* electricity; they are usually shiny and often hard   74–75, 104, 106–109, 117, 124–127, 138

metamorphic: rocks that are made when other rocks are changed (but not melted) by heat and *pressure*   120–122

microbes: microscopic living things; also called micro-organisms   14–15, 24, 26, 42–43, 59

migrate: what animals do when they move to other places with the *seasons*   50, 64

minerals: simple chemicals living things need in small amounts to stay healthy   18, 27, 30, 44, 54–55, 59, 66

mirror: a surface that *reflects* each narrow beam (ray) of light in one direction   149, 162

mixture: different substances that are mixed but not joined together   82–87, 102, 112–113

molecule: the smallest part of a chemical *compound*   32–35, 83, 113

moment: the turning effect of a force   182–183, 191

monthly period: see *period*

Moon: the natural *satellite* of the Earth   145

multicellular: living things made of many *cells*   3

muscle tissue: *tissue* that can *contract* or shorten to move parts of the body   4

N

native metals: these are found in the Earth's crust as the *metals* themselves rather than as *compounds*   124

nectary: part of a flower which produces nectar to attract insects   8

negative: one of the two types of electrical *charge*; the other type is called *positive*   169, 198–199

nervous system: *organ system* which coordinates the activities of the body

neutral: what we call a solution that is neither *acid* nor *alkali*   129

neutralisation: a reaction between an *acid* and an *alkali* that produced a *neutral* solution of a *salt* (plus more *water*)   130–131

newton (N): the unit of force   170

nicotine: a *drug* in tobacco to which people can become addicted   43

nitrogen: the main *gas* in *air*; it is fairly unreactive but will react with the *oxygen* in the air at high temperatures   83

nitrogen oxides: *acid*ic gases produced when *nitrogen* reacts with *oxygen* at high temperatures   128, 133, 135

nocturnal: animals that feed at night   50

non-metals: what we call elements that aren't metals   74–75, 104

non-renewable: energy sources, such as *fossil fuels*, that are not replaced and will eventually be used up   192–195, 209

normal: a line drawn at right angles (90°) to a boundary   152

nuclear fuel: a fuel, such as uranium, that is used in nuclear power stations   192, 194, 209

nucleus: the part of a *cell* which controls what happens in the *cell*   2, 8, 13, 15, 20, 65

nutrients: foods needed by animals, or *minerals* needed by plants   59

nutrition: obtaining the materials needed for energy and for making new *cells*   7

O

oesophagus: another word for *gullet*   32

orbit: the path of a *satellite* as it moves round a *planet*, or of a *planet* (or *comet*) as it moves round the *Sun*   145–146, 161, 171–173, 186

ores: *compounds* of *metal* and *non-metal* elements that are found in the Earth's crust   124–125

Glossary/index

pollen tube: the tube which grows from a *pollen* grain through the *stigma* and *style* to the *ovary* **12–13**

pollinate, pollination: transfer of *pollen* from the *anther* to the *stigma* of a flower of the same *species* **12**

pollute: contaminate the *environment* with undesirable materials or energy **69**

pollution: harmful chemicals that humans allow into the *air*, soil or *water* around them (the environment) **134–135, 143**

population: all the plants or animals of one *species* which live in a particular place **63**

positive: one of the two types of electrical *charge*; the other type is called *negative* **169, 198–199**

predator: an animal which eats other animals **63, 70**

pressure: how much force there is on a certain area **81, 89, 94, 180–181, 190**

prey: an animal which is eaten by another animal **63**

prism: a triangular block of clear glass or plastic **150, 152–153, 164**

properties: what a material is like, for example whether it *conducts* electricity or whether it *burns* **72–73, 87, 103**

protease: *enzyme* which digests *proteins* **45**

protein: the part of your food which you need for *growth* and repair **30–33, 45**

pyramid of numbers: pyramid-shaped diagram showing the decrease in the number of organisms as you go up a *food chain* **68**

R

RDA: Recommended Daily Allowance (of *vitamins* and *minerals*) **44**

reactivity series: a list of *metals* in order of how quickly they react with *oxygen, water* or *acids* **106–109, 117, 124–125, 138**

recycle: to use materials over and over again **59**

reflect, reflection: light, or sound, bouncing off whatever it strikes **145, 147–150, 156, 162, 164**

refract, refraction: light bending when it passes from one transparent substance into another **152–156, 165**

relax: in the case of a muscle, become longer and thinner; the opposite of *contract* **41**

relay: a switch that works using an *electromagnet* **204**

renewable: an energy source that is constantly being replaced and won't get used up **193–195, 208–210**

repel: when things push each other away **168–169**

reproduce, reproduction: producing living things like themselves **6–7, 21**

respire, respiration: the breakdown of food to release energy in living *cells* **6, 34–37, 46, 67**

rock cycle: the way that the material rocks are made from is constantly moved around and changed **122, 136–137**

root hairs: plant roots absorb water and *minerals* mainly through these **20**

rusting: the *corrosion* of iron (or steel) as it joins with *oxygen* in damp *air* to form iron *oxide* **126–127**

S

saliva: *digestive juice* made by *salivary glands* **32–33**

salivary glands: glands in the mouth which produce *saliva* **32–33**

salt: a *compound* produced when an *acid* reacts with a *metal* or with an *alkali* **107, 131, 139**

satellite: an object that *orbits* a *planet*; it may be natural like the *Moon* or artificial like a weather or communications satellite **145, 171, 173**

Glossary/index

scurvy: a *disorder* caused by lack of *vitamin* C in the *diet*   **31**

seasons: the different parts of each year (spring, summer, autumn, winter)   **50–51, 64**

sedimentary: rocks made from small bits which settle in layers on the bottoms of lakes or seas **120–122, 136–137**

seeds: contain the *embryo* flowering plants and their food stores; new plants grow from them **14, 24–25, 51**

selective breeding: breeding only from the plants or animals which have the *characteristics* that we want   **25**

sense, sensitive: we say this about living things when they can detect changes in their surroundings and react to them   **6**

sepals: parts which cover and protect a flower in bud   **8, 12**

series: a way of connecting two or more bulbs etc. to a *cell* or power supply so that a *current* flows through each of them in turn   **200–201**

sex cells: *cells* which join to form new plants or animals   **8–9, 12–13, 21**

shadow: the dark area formed behind an object when light can't pass through it   **144, 160**

sickle cell anaemia: an *inherited disorder* of the red blood cells   **26**

small intestine: narrow part of intestine between *stomach* and *large intestine*; *digestion* finishes and *absorption* takes place here   **32–34, 47**

smelting: the process of getting a *metal* from its *ore* **125, 138**

solar cells: these produce electricity when energy is transferred to them by light   **192, 209–210**

solar energy: the energy that reaches Earth by the Sun's rays   **208**

solar system: the *Sun* and all of the *planets* that *orbit* the Sun   **146–147, 171–172**

solid: substances that stay a definite shape **76–78, 80, 90, 95**

soluble: able to dissolve   **32**

solvent: a chemical in which other substances will dissolve; some solvents are *drugs*   **29**

species: we say that plants or animals which can *interbreed* (breed with each other) belong to the same species   **18–19, 62, 69**

spectrum: the coloured bands produced by splitting up (*dispersing*) white light, for example by *refraction* through a *prism*   **150–153, 163**

speed: the distance an object moves in a certain time   **161, 166, 178–179, 189**

sperm: male *sex cell* or *gamete*   **8–10, 20–21**

spores: tiny reproductive cell made in asexual reproduction in some plants e.g. mosses, ferns and fungi   **14–15, 24**

stamens: male parts of a flower made up of an *anther* and a *filament*   **12**

star: distant 'suns' that give out their own light **146–147**

starch: a *carbohydrate* with large insoluble *molecules*   **30, 32–35, 45**

states of matter: *solids*, *liquids* and *gases* are the three states of matter   **76–79, 90–91, 96**

static electricity: unbalanced *positive* or *negative* electric *charges* that are standing still on an object   **198–199**

stigma: for a flower to be *pollinated*, *pollen* must land on this part   **8, 12–13, 21**

stomach: an *organ* in the *digestive system*   **20, 32–33**

streamlined: a shape that has very little *friction* or *drag* when it moves through a *gas* or a *liquid*   **175**

style: the part between the *stigma* and the *ovary* of a flower   **8, 12–13, 21**

Sun: the *star* at the centre of the *solar system*   **144–147**

sweat: liquid made in sweat glands which evaporates to cool you   **7, 36**

symbols: 1. a shorthand way of writing *elements*, e.g. H for *hydrogen* and Mg for magnesium   **100–101, 114–115**

2. a simple way of showing bulbs, *cells* etc. in a *circuit diagram*   **200**

T

tendon: connective *tissue* at the ends of muscles that joins muscles to bones   **4, 41**

terminal velocity: the highest *speed* that an object reaches when it moves through a *gas* or a *liquid*   **188**

testes: where *sperm* (male *sex cells*) are made in animals; one is called a testis   **9**

tides: the twice daily rise and fall of the level of the sea; a *renewable* energy source   **192–194, 209**

tissue: a group of similar *cells* that do the same job   **4, 21, 48**

tissue fluid: liquid between all the *cells* of your body that materials can *diffuse* through in solution   **48**

toxic: poisonous   **71**

triceps: muscle which *contracts* to straighten your arm   **41**

tumour: a growth, sometimes a *cancer*   **26**

turbine: a device for transferring the *kinetic energy* of a moving *gas* or *liquid* to a drive shaft (e.g. of a *generator*)   **194–195**

U

umbilical cord: a tube containing the blood vessels between the *fetus* and the *placenta*   **22**

unicellular: organisms made of only one *cell*   **3**

urea: poisonous *waste* made when the liver breaks down *amino acids*   **21–22, 48**

urethra: tube in which *urine* leaves your *bladder*   **9**

urine: liquid containing water, salts and *urea excreted* by the *kidneys*   **7, 21**

uterus: where a baby develops before birth; also called the *womb*   **9–11, 21–23**

V

vacuole: space filled with cell sap in the *cytoplasm* of a plant *cell*   **2**

vacuum: another name for empty space   **156**

vagina: opening of human female reproductive system   **9–10, 21**

vary: differ   **18, 25, 70**

veins: blood vessels which carry blood towards the *heart*   **38–39**

vertebrates: animals with skeletons made of bone inside their bodies   **16–17**

vibrations: to-and-fro movements; these can produce sounds and are also the only way that the *particles* in a *solid* can move   **90, 95, 156–159, 167**

villi: tiny finger-like bumps in the lining of the *small intestine* that increase its surface area for *absorption*; one is called a villus   **47**

virus: a *microbe* which can only live inside another *cell*   **26–27, 42**

Glossary/index

vitamins: substances in food which we need in small amounts to stay healthy   27, 30–31, 44

W

waste: unwanted material or energy   35–37, 39, 48, 58–59

water: 1. a *compound* formed when *hydrogen* reacts with *oxygen*   131, 140

2. test for water   111

waves: a *renewable* energy source produced by the *wind* blowing over the sea   192–195

weathering: the ways that the weather, and chemicals in *air* or *water*, break up or wear away rocks   122, 132–133, 136–137

weight: the force of *gravity* (usually the Earth's) on an object because of its *mass*   170

wind: moving *air*; a *renewable* energy source   192–194, 209–210

womb: another word for *uterus*   9–10

X

xylem: a *tissue* that carries water and *minerals* from the roots to other parts of a plant   5

Y

yield: how much food a plant crop or farm animal can produce   66

For EU product safety concerns, contact us at Calle de José Abascal, 56–1°,
28003 Madrid, Spain or eugpsr@cambridge.org.

www.ingramcontent.com/pod-product-compliance
Ingram Content Group UK Ltd.
Pitfield, Milton Keynes, MK11 3LW, UK
UKHW052143150625
459711UK00016B/161